THE FIFTH-CENTURY INVASIONS
SOUTH OF THE THAMES

Silver-gilt buckle and plate, with double-sided plate from Misèry, Somme (*Musée Danicourt, Péronne*).
Scale: 3/2.

The Fifth-Century Invasions South of the Thames

by

VERA I. EVISON

Reader in the Archaeology
of the Anglo-Saxon Period
at Birkbeck College,
University of London

UNIVERSITY OF LONDON
THE ATHLONE PRESS
1965

Published by
THE ATHLONE PRESS
UNIVERSITY OF LONDON
at 2 Gower Street, London WC1
Distributed by Constable & Co Ltd
12 Orange Street, London WC2

Canada
Oxford University Press
Toronto

U.S.A.
Oxford University Press Inc
New York

Printed in Great Britain by
WESTERN PRINTING SERVICES LTD
BRISTOL

Acknowledgments

I should like to express my grateful thanks to the authorities of the following museums who have allowed me free access to material in their keeping: Abingdon Museum; Aylesbury Museum; the British Museum; the Museum of Archaeology and Ethnology, Cambridge; Royal Museum, Canterbury; Dartford Museum; Hull Museum; Carisbrooke Castle, Isle of Wight; Barbican House Museum, Lewes; Maidstone Museum; Borough Museum, Newbury; Ashmolean Museum, Oxford; Musée Danicourt, Péronne; Rochester Museum; Musée départemental des antiquités de la Seine-maritime, Rouen; Salisbury, South Wilts. and Blackmore Museum; Musée de la Princerie, Verdun; Winchester Museum; Worcester Museum; Worthing Museum.

The following museums and institutions have provided photographs: Oudheidkundig Bodemonderzoek in Nederland, Amersfoort; Landschaftsmuseum des Niederrheins, Krefeld-Linn; Museum van Oudheiden, Leiden; Landesmuseum, Linz; Metropolitan Museum of Art, New York; Landesmuseum für Kunst u. Kulturgeschichte, Oldenburg; the Louvre, Paris; Musée des antiquités nationales, St. Germain-en-Laye. Expenses for photography and drawings have been met by Birkbeck College.

I am also greatly indebted to Dr D. B. Harden for consultations on glass, Mr H. Hodges of the Institute of Archaeology for the cleaning of some of the objects and advice on technical matters, Mrs E. M. Fry-Stone for most of the drawings, Mrs Conlan, Institute of Archaeology, for enlarging my photographs, Mr J. Musty and Miss J. Cook for the loan of drawings (Figs. 20 and 11, *m* respectively), Messrs Kodak Ltd for radiograph prints (Pls. 5, *b, d*; 6, *c, d, e*) and the Society of Antiquaries of London for the loan of blocks (Pls. 5, *b, e, f*; 6, *a, d*; 11, *a*; 14, *a, b*).

I am grateful to Messrs Eyre and Spottiswoode and Rutgers University Press for permission to reprint excerpts from Professor Dorothy Whitelock's edition of *The Anglo-Saxon Chronicle*.

V. I. E.

Contents

I

Current Theories about the Invasion

HISTORICAL records of the invasion of Britain by Germanic tribes from the continent after the withdrawal of Roman troops are very scanty indeed; moreover, they are suspect in many particulars and capable of different interpretations by individual historians.[1] In attempts to reconcile information gleaned from various sources, only one of which is anywhere near contemporary, the up-to-date scholar has included the evidence of archaeology in his deliberations. This has not been entirely successful for a number of reasons. While Anglo-Saxon archaeological studies are still in their youth, new sites are continually being excavated, with the result that there is a mass of new information unpublished and undigested. The next move is clearly up to the archaeologists. Theories put forward in the past must be shelved for the time being, and all the archaeological material now available will have to be carefully sifted and assessed objectively on purely archaeological grounds. Not until this work is completed is a comparison with the historical records likely to prove of value. This is a course easy to visualize, but one that, at the present pioneering stage of Anglo-Saxon archaeological research, is, in its entirety, impracticable. Most of the finds which made their way to museums before the dawn of twentieth-century organized archaeology, and a large percentage of material excavated only recently, or even decades ago, are still not published. Until detailed reports are accessible a final evaluation cannot be made, but in the meantime, some efforts in the right direction will not come amiss. Thousands of objects in various collections throughout the country are open to inspection, and the large body of information already available in print rewards diligent search, for much material has been either largely ignored or misinterpreted up to now. Therefore as an interim measure one may put forward a working thesis in respect of a limited field, i.e. the invasion of the southern part of England, mainly south of the Thames, by drawing on the material already known, and by basing the dating on defined points in Roman and continental archaeology.

It has always been recognized that, from the archaeological point of view, Kent, at any rate, is different from the rest of pagan Anglo-Saxon England, and much of

---

[1] The sources are summarized: Collingwood and Myres 1937, pp. 326–30.

this difference has rightly been assigned to its proximity to the continent, and the trade between the two shores which would naturally ensue. The map of sites in England (Map 1)[1] where cremation was practised shows a distribution throughout most of the English settlements, with the exception of the area south of the Thames. This indicates a basic difference, for the method of disposal of the dead is a reflection of important distinguishing factors regarding religious beliefs and tribal entities. This map is already outdated, for, since it was compiled, new cemeteries have been excavated where cremation is present as well as inhumation, e.g. at Alton in Hampshire. Moreover, one may suspect that in excavations of earlier days the presence of cremations in a cemetery may well have been missed, for the pots were often buried only a few inches from the surface and modern ploughing has smashed up the urns to minute fragments. Many of the cemeteries found in the nineteenth century were left to the mercies of labourers, who tended to keep only unbroken pots. Some of the complete pots extant may have been emptied of their burnt bone fragments by the workmen who found them before they sold them to the local antiquary. It was not realized that cremations were often deposited in a hole in the ground, either without a container or in something perishable like a cloth or leather bag. These burials, of course, are usually only detected by the trained archaeologist. Nevertheless, faulty information caused by earlier lack of scientific methods was indiscriminately widespread, and would not affect any one area more than another, so that, in spite of the inherent shortcomings of a distribution map, the overall picture of scanty cremation to the south of the Thames, compared with a much higher proportion to the north, still holds good. It should be noted that the generally accepted view that Kent stands alone in this respect is not correct, for it shares a slight sprinkling of cremations with the rest of the counties south of the Thames. Inhumations also occur amongst the cremations north of the Thames, but on the whole the difference in the method of disposal of the dead in the two areas is fairly clear-cut, and the implications of this must be considered. Full data on which to base investigations are not to hand, for only rough figures regarding inhumation versus cremation have been produced; statistics have not been abstracted of inhumations or cremations according to date of deposition, so that the numbers are not known even for such wide periods of time as the fifth, sixth or seventh century. The reason for this is that even where the grave goods have been published, they are not always clearly datable. The position regarding cremations is even more difficult, for the dating of the pottery containers has not yet reached the point where the margin of error is often less than a hundred years. The forthcoming publication of some large cremation cemeteries may go some way towards amending this sad position.

To find out what is the considered opinion of leading archaeologists in the field

[1] Map 1 is taken from Leeds 1954, fig. B.

regarding the earliest invasions, one can do no better than to turn first of all to the posthumous paper on 'The Growth of Wessex'[1] by the leading English figure in this sphere, E. T. Leeds. In this article, he reaffirmed his theory of the earliest arrival of the Saxons on the shores of East Anglia, and their advance *en masse* down the Icknield Way as far as the area of the upper Thames. This theory is substantially supported by the presence on this route of some of the earliest post-invasion objects in the country, including continental brooch types which must have come in on the dress of the Saxon women, i.e. the 'Luton' type of brooch (Stützarmfibel)[2] found at Luton and Kempston, Beds., the equal-armed brooch at Kempston, Beds., Abingdon, Berks., Sutton Courtenay, Oxon., Little Wilbraham and Haslingfield, Cambs., a tutulus brooch at Abingdon, and various early cruciform brooches. Reinforcement of this theory is further given by other items which may be assigned to a similarly early date such as the *Buckelurne* with foot,[3] the distribution of which has been plotted by Dr J. N. L. Myres, so that not only can we see where these particular invaders settled in this country, but also we may see that they came from the area between the Elbe and Weser occupied by the Saxons. We might note in passing, however, that the upper Thames area was not the only objective of these folk, for cruciform brooches of the fifth century are found also in Kent, although the area is devoid of any later developments of this brooch type. 'Anglo-Frisian' pottery, too, occurs in eastern England from Kent to Yorkshire.[4]

Leeds further expressed the opinion that the cremation dots on the map in the southern Midlands represent the southern limit of early cemeteries.[5] His dating of Harnham Hill to the last half of the sixth century will be discussed below. He contemplated the idea of invasion by Saxons from northern France northwards through Hampshire, but rejected it because 'No trace of late fifth- or even early sixth-century Saxon archaeological evidence is known from south Hampshire' and admitted only 'a band of adventurers, apparently mixed Juto-Saxons advancing from the south coast'.

In his contribution to *Dark Age Britain, Studies presented to E. T. Leeds* (1956), 'The Jutes of Kent', Professor C. F. C. Hawkes supported Leeds' theory by restating it as follows:[6] 'In our funerary archaeology, therefore, the initial period of the Kentish settlement was rightly called by Leeds in 1936 the Jutish phase, since for the first two generations what graves we know are those only of the leading minority, Jutes or Juto-Frisians. But in the third generation, by about 520–525, the main body of the

---

[1] Leeds 1954.

[2] Werner 1958, Abb. 4–7.

[3] J. N. L. Myres, *Ant. Journ.* XXXIV (1954), 201; *Ant. Journ.* XXXVII, 224–5.

[4] J. N. L. Myres, 'Some English parallels to the Anglo-Saxon pottery of Holland and Belgium in the migration period', *L'Antiquité classique*, XVII (1948).

[5] Leeds concedes an early date to the chieftain buried at Lowbury Hill, Berks., but this is untenable in view of the seventh-century hanging bowl and sugar-loaf shield boss buried there; V. Evison, 'Sugar-loaf shield bosses', *Ant. Journ.* XLIII (1963), pp. 46–7, figs. 26 c–h, 27 and 28 a–f.

[6] p. 109.

people had achieved a steady enough prosperity to do as their continental Frankish kindred were now doing, and inhume their dead with grave-goods.'

G. J. Copley in *The Conquest of Wessex in the sixth century* (1954) agreed with Leeds that early settlement of the upper Thames valley was predominantly effected by an advance south-westwards along the Icknield Way, but noticed that some of the fifth-century objects found in these areas, such as Stage I cruciform brooches, saucer brooches with spiral design or foliated cross, etc., are also to be found in Kent, and at Croydon and Mitcham in Surrey. From this he concludes that the Thames itself was also used as an invasion route. For the invasion from the south he followed the items of the Anglo-Saxon Chronicle, commenting 'Nor is there any real conflict between the story of the annals, and that which may be deduced from the burial grounds of Hampshire and Wiltshire. The absence of typically Saxon material of early sixth-century date from the region through which the Gewissae passed cannot in itself be regarded as decisive for the rejection of the annals.'[1]

Aspects of the subject have been touched upon by Professor J. Werner, who has pointed out the presence of early Frankish swords at Petersfinger, Wilts., and Abingdon, Berks.[2] These two swords have since been mentioned by S. Hawkes, who has suggested Frankish settlement at Lyminge, Kent, about A.D. 500.[3]

As these examples show, those who have approached the problem have taken as a working basis the series of dates and events as presented by the Anglo-Saxon Chronicle and compared with these the results of an examination of what archaeological and place-name material was available. Unfortunately, neither of these sources was in a reliable state. For the most part scholars have been aware of the pitfalls set before them by the early records of the Anglo-Saxon Chronicle, but they have had to rely entirely on their own discretion in accepting or rejecting dates or facts, and because of the traditional reverence accorded to this unique written record, they have naturally been reluctant to reject anything even remotely capable of reconciliation with other sources. To add to their difficulties, when working with the results of another discipline, i.e. place-name and archaeological evidence, historians have perforce more or less to accept the facts as presented to them.

Use has often been made of place-name evidence to plot the distribution of the earliest Germanic settlements in this country, the principal evidence resting on names ending in -*ingas*, e.g. Reading (Rēādingas = the followers or men of Rēāda) and -*inga* formations such as Hastingleigh (Hæstingalēāh = 'the clearing of the Haestingas'). Not all place-names with these formations are early, however, as recent investigations have emphasized, and it is necessary for each name to be thoroughly studied before any valid conclusion may be reached concerning its date. Until this is done, place-names can form no reliable basis for the establishment of the history of

[1] p. 159.   [2] Werner 1953a and 1956.   [3] Hawkes and Dunning, 1963.

the settlement.[1] The most recent map showing the distribution of certain early place-name elements (-ing and -ingham) published by Wainwright is stated to be based on the names listed in E. Ekwall, *English Place-Names in -ing* (Lund, 1923) and can therefore be interpreted, for the time being, as a guide of only the most general nature, to be compared with statements regarding distribution made by Professor A. H. Smith.[2] In connection with the disparity between the distribution of pagan burials and archaic place-names in the Trent valley, he makes the salutary remark: 'The discrepancy may be accounted for by our inability to distinguish other types of archaic place-names which might have had a greater frequency in these districts.' In any event, we must not look to place-names to provide material datable within very narrow limits, i.e. it will not be possible to be certain that a place-name must have been formed within any particular fifty-year span.

As to the historian's own material, there is little which can be accepted without question. Unfortunately, Britain was on the outskirts of the Roman Empire, and so, at this crucial point when Rome itself was being attacked, it merited little more than a hasty glance from the Mediterranean historians of the period. Most information is to be culled from writers in this island. Amongst these was the British priest Gildas, a nearly contemporary author, whose main object was invective against the sins of his people. There are some historical facts which may be gathered from his *De conquestu et excidio Britanniae*, but his terms are so vague, and his blunders so patent, that much rearrangement and pruning is necessary.[3] The main facts extractable are that three appeals by the Britons to the Romans for help against the barbarian invasions were followed by a period of prosperity, then a pestilence; Saxon federates were then invited by a British king (Vortigern) and turned upon the Britons, over-running the land from sea to sea. Led by a Roman, Ambrosius Aurelianus, the Britons won a victory at *Mons Badonicus*, an event datable to between A.D. 490 and 516[4] and noted by Gildas as coincident with the date of his own birth. There was no more trouble from the Saxons after this battle up to the time when Gildas was writing forty-four years later, towards the middle of the sixth century.

Bede found little data worthy of recording in his period. When referring to the arrival of the Saxons, he regarded it as either occurring about 446–7 or in the reign of Marcian and Valentinian, i.e. A.D. 450–455. In mentioning the people who came to join the foederati in Kent, he gave important information about their continental origins and areas of settlement in this country. He said that the invaders who came

---

[1] C. I. Ståhle, *Studier över de svenska ortnamnen på -inge* (Lund, 1946). A. H. Smith, 'Place-names and the Anglo-Saxon settlement', *Proc. Brit. Acad.* XLII (1956), pp. 67–88. F. T. Wainwright, *Archaeology and Place-names and History* (1962), pp. 65–70.

[2] A. H. Smith, *op. cit.*, pp. 83–4.
[3] E.g. J. N. L. Myres, 'The Adventus Saxonum' in *Aspects of Archaeology, Essays presented to O.G.S. Crawford* (1951), pp. 221–42.
[4] Collingwood and Myres 1937, pp. 460–1.

to Kent to join the federates already there by invitation were Angles, Saxons and Jutes.

'From the Jutes are descended the Cantuarii and the Victuarii, that is, the people which holds the Isle of Wight and that which to this day is called the *Jutarum natio* in the province of the West Saxons set opposite the Isle of Wight. From the Saxons, that is from that region which is now called that of the Old Saxons, came the East Saxons, South Saxons, and West Saxons. Moreover from the Angles, that is from that country which is called Angulus, and from that time to this is believed to remain uninhabited between the provinces of the Jutes and the Saxons, are sprung the East Angles, Middle Angles, Mercians, the whole stock of the Northumbrians . . . and the other Anglian peoples.'[1]

This explanation of Bede's is far more clear-cut than the evidence of archaeology will allow, for it is certain that the tribes were inextricably mixed already on the continental seaboard before they even embarked for England. The passage is considered by Myres to be a later interpolation made by Bede as an afterthought in his own work, for it breaks up the sense sequence, and Myres is not inclined to give much weight to it.[2] We must remember, however, that if this passage is really to be abandoned, with it will go the only literary evidence of the presence of Jutes in the invasion, and although other sources[3] confirm their presence in these districts in later times, they may not have taken part in the first onslaught.[4]

It is therefore the early entries of the Anglo-Saxon Chronicle, comparatively detailed as they are, which must be mostly resorted to in the quest for historical fact, but the accuracy of these entries has been attacked more than once. One criticism is that the events are laid end to end;[5] beginning with the invasion of Kent in 449, they occur at regular intervals until the invasion of Kent is completed, only the accession of Aesc in 488 overlapping with the entries of the invasion of Sussex which begin in A.D. 477. These entries regarding Sussex only amount to three, then the invasion of Wessex begins in A.D. 495 and goes on till it is finished.[6] It looks as though a compiler working centuries later had on the one hand three sets of records of events, possibly verbal, and on the other blank pages prepared with the numbers of the years in a column on the left-hand side. What choice had he but to place his entries in order at regular intervals to fill up the available space? The folio of the Parker MS. of the Chronicle dealing with Cerdic, Cynric and Port reproduced by

[1] *Ibid.*, p. 336.

[2] *Ibid.*, pp. 336–7.

[3] *Ibid.*, p. 364.

[4] By the ninth century the Anglo-Saxon translator of Bede's *Ecclesiastical History* omitted the reference to Jutes on the mainland in the passage quoted above, and also in Chapter IV. 16. These two instances have been pointed out by Professor D. Whitelock, 'The Old English Bede', *Proc. Brit. Acad.* 1962, p. 66, who considers that the translator was modernizing his text. A reference to Stoneham in the land of the Jutes earlier in Chapter IV. 16 was presumably retained as it does not imply the contemporary presence of Jutes.

[5] See Appendix, p. 88.

[6] C. E. Stevens, 'Gildas Sapiens', *E.H.R.* LVI, 369.

Hodgkin,[1] shows a page filled in this pleasant pattern method. Stenton was not satis-fied with these records:[2] 'The curious fact that the entries relating to the English conquest tend to be spaced out at intervals of four or eight years suggests that they were derived from notes inserted retrospectively into chronological tables devised for the finding of Easter, for in these tables the margin was divided into isolated spaces by recurrent indications of leap year. The influence of the Easter-table is very evident in the earliest Frankish annals, which were imitated from English models, and it is highly probable that the English traditions of Hengest and Cerdic were first com-mitted to writing within this incongruous framework.' The dates given after 449 he decides are not authoritative, and as to the invasion of Wessex, he suggests that a record of thirteen years has been duplicated and that the battles against Natanleod and at Cerdices leaga recorded at 508 and 527 were one and the same. Like many another before him, however, he stubs his toes on the battle of Bedcanford recorded as taking place in A.D. 571, for this would mean that 'An annal which implies that the downs above Luton were British in 571 means that four generations after the traditional date of Hengest's landing, the Britons were still holding ground within forty miles of London.'[3] Nevertheless he feels that such an important event must be correctly recorded, and explains it as a recovery of territory rather than a first con-quest.

Myres begins by stating his attitude towards the dating in the early part of the Chronicle: 'For the crucial period of the early settlement from 449 to 538 there were apparently in Bede's considered judgement no datable events to be recorded at all. In estimating the place which the precisely dated annals in the Chronicle should take in our story, it is wise to bear in mind the salutary scepticism of Bede.'[4] Neverthe-less, his interpretation of the historical, archaeological and place-name evidence allows him to adhere closely to the traditional dating, and as to the direction of invasion: '. . . so far from the West Saxon communities of the upper Thames being derived from the south, they were themselves in all probability the source from which late in the sixth and early in the seventh century much of this region obtained its Saxon population.'[5] Hodgkin, on the contrary, tends to regard the Chronicle story of an invasion from the south in 495 as more or less correct, in spite of lack of archaeo-logical support: 'While we accept the main tradition of the Chronicle, we reject many of its details.'[6] Followed by Myres, he regarded the settlements in the Isle of Wight and on the mainland opposite as secondary Jutish colonizations from Kent.[7]

In spite of their divergences in opinion historians are at least firmly united on one

---

[1] R. H. Hodgkin, *A History of the Anglo-Saxons* (1952), I, pl. 25.

[2] Stenton 1943, pp. 15–16.

[3] *Ibid.*, p. 27.

[4] Collingwood and Myres 1937, p. 328.

[5] *Ibid.*, p. 405.

[6] Hodgkin, *op. cit.*, p. 133.

[7] *Ibid.*, I, 100–1; Collingwood and Myres 1937, pp. 364–5.

point: they all agree that the dates accorded to the events in the Chronicle are highly suspect. As they have before them no evidence which would justify juggling with these dates, they find it necessary to quote them in connection even with events where such a coupling is grotesquely incongruous, e.g. the battle of Bedford in 571. This attitude of dissatisfaction with existing data implies a readiness to consider sympathetically any kind of well-testified evidence which would make possible a sensible substitution of other dates for these irksome ones. Now, the relevant archaeological facts have not so far been presented in a balanced or even a palatable form, and such a gigantic task as the definitive publication of all the material of the period which has already been excavated in every part of the country is one which is not likely to be accomplished in this century. Selection is the only rational procedure and, accordingly, an attempt will be made here to examine the problem only as it applies to the region south of the Thames, for this area in the fifth century was archaeologically homogeneous and also archaeologically distinct from the rest of the invaded parts of England.

In the study of the pagan Anglo-Saxon period of archaeology, the collection of data over wide areas and their synthesis have so far been limited to a very few fields, but such surveys as have been accomplished are invaluable for the purpose of teasing out the presence of fifth-century material in this country. For the rest, it is reasonable to employ, with reservations, such *ad hoc* distributions as it is possible to collect. Many objects are known to have been produced in continental workshops and an examination of their final destinations may indicate whether it is trade relations or the import of personal possessions that has to be reckoned with. As a complement to this, examination of individual graves will sometimes enable us to ascertain whether their occupants died in the fifth century, but this method must necessarily be an exclusive one, first because of the enormous size of the task of examining every grave in the country, and secondly, because a comparatively small percentage of graves happens to contain enough objects of sufficient individuality to be dated with certainty. At best the method will reveal the presence, and perhaps the nationality, of a fifth-century invader, though the date and nationality of his fellows in neighbouring graves may remain concealed. Even this, however, will get us well on our way to establishing the existence of a settled Germanic community in the neighbourhood. As has been seen, it is already widely acknowledged that fifth-century settlers may be identified in the upper Thames area, Kent and Sussex, but they have not been detected in the area between the upper Thames and the Isle of Wight. It is hoped to prove that the identity of the people in some early graves may be established, that the date and course of the initial settlement in Hampshire and the Isle of Wight have been misunderstood, and that a completely different picture of the first invasion may be built up on a firm archaeological basis.

II

Fourth- and Fifth-century Frankish Graves on the Continent

THERE are various considerations which will direct our interest in the Germanic peoples in their homes on the continent immediately before the crossing to England. A rich supply of finds is more likely to supply detailed information than a poor one. For this reason the coastal regions north of the Rhine mouth where the occupants of graves show no particular opulence are not very promising. Moreover, the rite of cremation which was prevalent there ensured that belongings that would have preserved characteristics of their possessors were consumed by fire and so rendered unrecognizable before consignment to the burial urn. The fact itself that cremation was prevalent shows that it is not among these inhabitants that we should look for the people who landed in the south of England practising the custom of burial by inhumation. It would be more profitable to cast our eyes south of the Rhine mouth. Although in the late fourth century the territory of northern Gaul was under the control of the Romans, nevertheless there are traces here of Germanic people. Inhumation was practised, some of the graves provide rich material for study, dating problems are assisted by the presence of coins, and, most important of all, the coast of this area is nearest to the south-eastern coast of Britain, and so the most likely departure point for the crossing. In addition, the archaeological material has received a good deal of study and is at hand in publications.

In some of the large Gallo-Roman cemeteries of the fourth century, a few graves distinguish themselves from most by the different character of the furnishings provided, as well as by their richness, and by the direction in which the corpse was aligned. During the course of the fourth century, the beginning of the influence of Christianity is to be seen in the orientation of the graves with the head to the west and the feet to the east, together with an increase in the practice of refraining from providing the deceased with his worldly possessions. Here a few richly furnished graves are sharply at variance with the hundreds of others in the vicinity, and the occupant is provided with objects never to be found in Gallo-Roman graves but which are of usual occurrence in Germanic graves. For women, this means all the paraphernalia of their dress fastenings, brooches, and other trinkets, and for men it means their war gear, weapons and bronze belt equipment.

Most of these cemeteries of northern Gaul were excavated in the nineteenth century and recorded with varying degrees of competence. As much of the grave furniture has now been lost through the dispersal of private collections and the effect of two wars, there are now extant, for the most part, only the descriptions and drawings made in the last century, and from these it is possible to reassemble a few grave groups. The Germanic character of these graves was recognized by one of the excavators, Pilloy, who considered them to belong to Frankish *laeti* settled within the Roman frontiers, i.e. captured Germans who were allowed their freedom in return for military duty. The theory has been held by some[1] that there was a hiatus between the Gallo-Roman cemeteries of the fourth century and the Merovingian cemeteries which became so large and numerous in the sixth century, so that there was no continuity at all in the culture of the inhabitants. This point was taken up by Professor Werner in 1950,[2] who examined these few outstanding well-furnished graves in fourth-century Gallo-Roman cemeteries and stated the opinion that they show the origin of the numerous Merovingian cemeteries of the sixth and seventh centuries as the practices begun there were continued without a break. This theory was criticized by de Laet, Dhondt and Nenquin,[3] but some of the objections made by them have been met by subsequent discoveries and publication. The characteristics of the graves were noted by Professor Werner as follows: a few rich graves occurred amongst many others which were poorly furnished; men and women had vessels of glass, pottery and bronze, gold finger-rings, a silver spoon and a gold or silver coin, usually in the mouth for ferry-fare to Charon. In addition, men were provided with weapons, sword, shield-boss, spear, axe, arrows and bronze belt mounts, and the women had toilet boxes, hair-pins and sometimes as many as three pairs of brooches. These are usually silver and are in the form of bow brooches, and disc brooches which project in a conical shape (tutulus brooches).

The question of the compass point to which the graves are orientated is an important one, for it is a manifestation of the beliefs of the people. Certain minor deviations from the direct compass points may be observed, but amongst inhumations of the period there are three main directions, W–E, S–N and N–S. W–E is the direction favoured by the Christians, and when it occurs in northern Gaul in the second half of the fourth century, especially in connection with unfurnished graves, it is obvious that this is the reason. Christianity is also the reason for the adoption of W–E orientation which took place gradually throughout the Merovingian period. The direction

[1] E. Brenner, 'Der Stand der Sachsen Forschung', *Bericht der Römisch- Germanischen Kommission*, 7, 1912 (1915).

[2] Werner 1950.

[3] De Laet, Dhondt and Nenquin 1952.

S–N was usual for Gallo-Roman graves in northern Gaul in the fourth century before the change to W–E, and it became usual in north-west Germany and the lower Rhine. N–S is the direction usual in Scandinavia, the right bank of the Rhine, south-west Germany and the Danube before the adoption of Christianity altered the orientation. The N–S orientation is important here for it is the one adopted by some of the graves to come under review in the Namur region, i.e. at Haillot and Furfooz, although others in this area have the usual direction of S–N.

Among the graves belonging to the period A.D. 350–425 may be numbered Abbeville and Monceau-le-Neuf, first published by Pilloy in his now rather inaccessible volumes, *Études sur d'anciens lieux de sépultures dans l'Aisne* (1886–1912), vols. I and III. The few reconstructable grave-groups have been republished for ease of reference by H. Roosens, 'Quelques mobiliers funéraires de la fin de l'époque romaine dans le nord de la France', *Dissertationes Archaeologicae Gandenses* VII (1962), 7–42. The second volume by Pilloy was mostly occupied by the cemeteries at Vermand. He considered the finds from these cemeteries under classes of objects and published a number of plates; T. Eck, in *Les deux cimetières Gallo-Romains de Vermand et de St. Quentin* (1891), gave a list of the contents of each grave, and reproduced Pilloy's plates. As a result, the composition of individual grave-groups is not clear, but the two most important grave-groups are famous, and are shown here as far as reconstructable.

The grave of the military officer at Vermand excavated on 13 November 1885 was described by Pilloy and by Eck.[1] A stone coffin was surrounded by a ditch and covered by a tumulus. Eck gives dimensions of the coffin which was five centimetres wider at the head than the foot, and says specifically that the head was at the north and the foot to the south. One corner of the coffin was broken open, the contents were disturbed, and two days afterwards one of the workmen disappeared, so that Eck was disposed to think the robbery was a recent one. Nevertheless, much remained (Pl. 1, Fig. 1, *a–f*). Outside the coffin was the conical umbo of a shield, its iron base covered in a silver-gilt sheet, with imitation chalcedony studs on the flange. The grip is in iron, covered with silver, the middle of the grip with up-curved edges, and the ends extended beyond the edge of the boss. Each end of the grip is fastened to the shield by three rivets where a pair of diminishing spiral shapes give the impression of birds' heads. Fragments of gold foil and purple leather testified to the magnificent appearance of the rest of the shield, and the diameter of 80 cm indicated by the circle of carbonized wood shows it to have been very large. There was a francisca type of axe and ten spearheads, a large spearhead with silver inlay, the socket wound round with bronze bands and a projecting lion's head at the junction of blade and socket. A silver-gilt cylindrical mount ornamented with scrolls, and a silver-gilt plaque

<hr />

[1] Pilloy, II, 38–52; *Bulletin archéologique* (1887), 213; Eck 1891, pp. 22–3. See also W. H. Forsyth, 'The Vermand Treasure', *The Metropolitan Museum of Art Bulletin* 9 (1951), 236.

also lavishly ornamented, were thought to have been fixed to the spearshaft, as well as a rectangular plaque. Inside the coffin were three buckles with animal head decoration, a strap-end and remains of a sword, and an oval silver plate. Eck reports that he himself found at the bottom of the excavation a rectangular flat plate of stone with incised squares—possibly a playing table.[1] Also he suspected that a solidus of Arcadius (383–408) found at this time came from this tomb. Neighbouring graves contained coins of the late fourth century up to Honorius.

Near by was a woman's grave, richly furnished (Fig. 1, *g–m*);[2] it contained a gold solidus of Valentinian I (364–75) placed in the mouth as a Charon's obol, a gold ring and a necklace of large, spindle-shaped gold beads; three pairs of brooches adorned the chest. There were also two silver-gilt repoussé disc brooches, one decorated with a lion's head, and the other with a star, and the latter was enclosed in a silver collar 3 mm tall.

The military leader's grave contained the residue of a particularly splendid accoutrement, but other military graves of a more common nature occurred at Vermand, e.g. 284, head to north, feet south, containing: iron strike-a-light, knife with bone handle, spearhead, axe, bone comb, bronze bowl, two attachment plates, bronze buckle with animal heads on the loop, strap-end, disc attachments, chape and various other bronze plates and studs.[3]

Also belonging to the latter part of the fourth century is the grave of the Roman army officer at Misèry (Figs. 2, 3, Frontispiece)[4] who had a shield boss covered with a silver-gilt sheet like that at Vermand, a human figure and the letters MAR being stamped on the rim. The animal-ornamented belt buckle and plates must have come from the same workshop as some at Vermand (cf. Fig. 26), the spear has the same pronounced central rib as the one owned by the military leader at Vermand, and the sword pommel is a type found at Richborough. There was also a knife with an inlaid blade. Two more cemeteries of the same period which have been fully published are Vert-la-Gravelle (Marne)[5] and Furfooz (Belgium).[6]

At Belleray on the Meuse near Verdun, a cemetery was discovered in 1872 which contained both Roman and Merovingian objects. A list of those that passed into the possession of Verdun museum was published by F. Liénard,[7] together with some drawings. Grave-groups are not mentioned, but under items 6, 7 and 8 he groups sets of objects; item 6 is a buckle with fixed plate and diamond-shaped strap-end (Pl. 3, *e, f*), item 7 three mounts for a purse (Pl. 2, *a, b* and *d*), item 8 three similar mounts for a purse (Pl. 3, *a, b* and *d*), all in tinned bronze. Confirmation of this

[1] Eck 1891, pp. 129–30.

[2] This grave has been quoted frequently, but the contents have been incompletely stated; see p. 101–2.

[3] Eck 1891, pp. 84–5 and 252–8; pl. XI, 5; pl. XII, 7, 9–11; pl. XVII, 1–20; pl. XVIII, 11.

[4] Rigollot 1850, pp. 216–20, pl. X, 5–8, pl. XI.

[5] Lantier 1948.

[6] Nenquin 1953.

[7] Liénard 1881–5, II, 121–3, pl. XXXI, 1–9.

grouping is evident from the objects themselves; the tubular plates and rosette pendants are well-known parts of belt equipment worn in the Roman army at the turn of the fourth and fifth centuries. Bronzes with curved bifurcations terminating in animal or birds' heads are rare in this type of association,[1] but their cohesion with the group is assured by the identity of form of the upper parts of Pl. 3, *a* and *b*. Further relationships may be observed. The ring-and-dot motif is extremely common, but it is arranged in an unusual way on the plate attachment (Pl. 3, *d*) where it is placed within each triangle in a row, and also on the apex of each triangle. The same arrangement is used on the plate of the buckle (Pl. 3, *e*) so that identity of grave-group for the five objects, figured by Liénard (nos. 4–8) is possible, and identity of workshop origin certain.[2]

All these objects are still preserved at Verdun museum, together with others from the same workshop. Two other pendants (Pls. 2, *f* and 3, *c*) are ornamented with the zigzag plus ring-and-dot motif of the buckle, as well as the tubular attachment (Pl. 3, *d*) which was grouped by Liénard with his figs. 5 and 6 (Pl. 3, *a*, *b*), and there is also a second tubular attachment decorated in this way. The other tubular attachment with double ring stamps and dot clusters is likewise one of a pair. A similar motif of double ring-and-dot stamp with dot clusters occurs on the birds' head pendant (Pl. 2, *d* and *b*).[3] Liénard's fig. 2 grouped with these is probably Pl. 2, *a*, although his figure does not show the long bronze strap at the back; this has the double ring stamp also found on another pendant (Pl. 2, *c*). It is very likely that the belt equipment of two soldiers only is represented by these thirteen pieces as grouped on Pls. 2 and 3. The tubular and rosette attachments were in use in the Roman army of the late fourth century, but extended into the fifth, and the later date for the manufacture of the group is confirmed by the buckle with fixed plate.

The men and women buried in these graves were therefore living during the last decades of Roman rule, and they were distinguished from their Gallo-Roman neighbours in many ways. It is true that both classes enjoyed the use of the goods manufactured in the Roman workshops of northern Gaul, i.e. pottery, glass, and bronze vessels, but the men wore bronze chip-carved belt equipment of a type found all along the Roman frontier of the Rhine and Danube, and which must have represented part of the equipment of the Germanic Roman soldier. The men were also distinguished from their fellows by the fact that they carried heavy weapons and the women wore bow and tutulus brooches in pairs. Moreover, their graves were orientated from north

---

[1] This is an extension of the motif of horses' heads curving away from each other on strap-ends (Forssander 1937, Abb. 25, 1) and griffins' heads in the same arrangement on buckle plates (Forssander 1937, Abb. 19, 1, 2a, Abb. 22); cf. Tournai, Werner 1958, Taf. 76, 5.

[2] The grouping as stated by Breuer and Roosens 1957, p. 323, is not in accordance with the information given by Liénard.

[3] Liénard's drawing of the pendant, his fig. 3, does not show the dot clusters, and other decorative details are incorrect.

to south instead of west to east. Their Germanic nationality is not doubted, and their presence in Gaul at this time is explained by written records which note the settlement in the third century of various Germanic peoples with military duties as *laeti* in a number of places, some of which are in areas where these cemeteries occur.[1] Among these people Franks are mentioned most often. Confirmation of the dating is forthcoming from other sources besides grave goods, such as the hoard of coins, issued between A.D. 402 and 406, found with an animal-decorated chip-carved buckle at Chécy (Loiret).[2] In 1962 a hoard of coins and metal objects found in a jug at Wiesbaden-Kastel[3] added first-rate dated material to this group. Out of 686 coins, the latest were of Constantine III (407–411). The objects, mostly silver, represent the equipment of a soldier of high rank, and include one brooch, finger-rings, arm-ring, strap-end and sword scabbard mounts.

A number of cemeteries went out of use at the beginning of the fifth century, presumably because of the disturbances following the invasions across the Rhine of A.D. 407; these cemeteries included Furfooz, Vert-la-Gravelle and Vermand. Various cemeteries in Belgium found in the last century were not systematically excavated with the result that, although grave-groups are not distinguishable, it may be seen that types of objects do not end at this period. These cemeteries show a continuity in the development of objects until the furniture of a normal Merovingian cemetery is reached, e.g. Samson went on from the late fourth century to the late sixth century, and Spontin continued till the mid-fifth century.[4] Belleray also bridges the Roman and Merovingian periods. In this they mirror the unbroken continuity visible in the cemeteries of Rhenen in Holland on the lower Rhine,[5] and Krefeld-Gellep in the Rhineland[6] which are large cemeteries excavated and recorded by modern methods, although not yet fully published.

Recent publications have added considerably to the evidence linking this civilization with the later Merovingians. The first half of the fifth century is covered by the well-furnished warrior's grave at Vieuxville[7] near Liège, which is dated by two coins, one of Constantine III (407–411), and one of Jovinus (411–413); a woman's grave at Fécamp[8] (Seine-Maritime) belongs to the beginning of the century, and graves at Krefeld-Gellep ranging from c. A.D. 400–450 have been selected for early publication by R. Pirling.[9] Others from between the Scheldt and Weser, i.e. Tournai, Helle, Mainz and Kostheim, as well as Vieuxville, have been examined by Werner.[10] The

---

[1] E.g. Verlinden 1954, p. 5.
[2] Gricourt 1958.
[3] H. Schoppa, 'Ein spätrömischer Schatzfund aus Wiesbaden-Kastel', *Fundberichte aus Hessen*, 2 (1962), 158–67.
[4] Breuer and Roosens 1957.
[5] Glazema and Ypey 1956.

[6] Steeger 1937a, Steeger 1937b, Pirling 1959, Pirling 1960a.
[7] Breuer and Roosens 1957, pp. 343–59.
[8] Werner 1962.
[9] Pirling 1959.
[10] Werner 1958.

furniture of these graves is very similar and Werner concludes that the graves at Vieuxville and Tournai belonged to Franks of the early fifth century. At Mainz and Kostheim the nationality is not so certain, for as well as Franks there were Burgundians, Alamanni and other tribes in the area. The burial at Helle in Oldenburg he takes as Saxon because of its geographical situation, but this does not seem to be the most important factor. Everything distinctive in the grave is of Frankish origin (pattern-welded sword, angon, boss, buckle, diamond-shaped strap-end, attachment plate and glass bowl) except for a Saxon hand-made pot. Werner points out that an angon and boss (common in Frankish graves) have not so far been found in early Saxon burials. The grave was an inhumation N–S with two other inhumations, but also four cremations. A small community of mixed origin is therefore indicated, and it would seem the probability is very strong that the occupant of grave 1 was a Frank.

The contents of the seventeen graves at Haillot[1] in the vicinity of Namur show that it did not come into use until the cemetery at Furfooz had ceased to exist, and its span of time may be limited to c. A.D. 425–500 (Figs. 4–7). New additions to the grave goods as found at Furfooz are a straight-backed knife instead of the late Roman curved blades, different kinds of glasses, including those with moulded Christian motifs, garnet jewellery and buckles with animal heads and fixed plates.

While brooches were important possessions of Germanic women and their lavish ornamentation reflected the wealth of the owner, the sword was to the Germanic man something more than the weapon on which his life depended; its reputation as a blade and the splendour of its ornament were status symbols of the time. These were buried with their owners so that it has been possible to distinguish a number which were kept in scabbards ornamented in such a similar fashion that they must have been made in the same workshop. The find spot of some, i.e. Éprave, Samson, shows this must have been in the Namur area, and the accompanying finds with others such as in Krefeld-Gellep grave 43 (Pl. 4, *a*, *b*) and Oberlörick grave 5 give the date of manufacture as the second half of the fifth century.[2] The same type of scabbard has also turned up in England at Abingdon, Berks., and Petersfinger, Wilts., as will be noticed later.[3]

The most definite dating point, however, the most informative material, and the most dazzling of the finds were provided by the tomb of Childeric (died 482) king of the Franks, which was found by accident in 1693.[4] Because of the time and conditions of finding, and because of a theft in the nineteenth century, not much of the original treasure now remains, but these few objects, together with written records

[1] Breuer and Roosens 1957.

[2] Böhner 1951, Werner 1953a and 1956.

[3] See p. 38.

[4] J. J. Chiflet, *Anastasis Childerici I* (1655); J. B. D. Cochet, *Le Tombeau de Childéric I* (1859); Böhner 1948, Böhner 1950; H. Arbman, 'Les epées du tombeau de Childeric', *Meddelanden från Lunds Universitets Historiska Museum; Årsberattelse, Kungl. Humanistiska Vetenskapssamfundet i Lund*, 1947–8, pp. 97–137.

and drawings, testify to the richest Germanic royal tomb in Europe, on a par with
the ship burial in this country at Sutton Hoo. The identity of the person buried was
established by a signet ring bearing a portrait of a man with long hair (a custom of
Frankish kings) and the inscription CHILDIRICI REGIS (Pl. 4, *d*). The weapons provided
were a francisca or throwing axe, spear, sword and seax. On the hilt and scabbard of
the sword and seax was lavished excellent workmanship in gold and garnet cell-
work, a technique also to be found on accompanying buttons, buckles, purse mount
(Fig. 8) and on three hundred cicadas, presumably sewn to a garment such as a cloak.
A crystal ball, gold bracelet and cross-bow brooch and a hundred gold coins and two
hundred silver coins were also amongst the treasure.

With the grave of Childeric I, we have finally come to a burial which comprises all
the essential characteristics of a normal Merovingian burial, although, because of its
royal nature, the ensemble is on an abnormally grand scale. The products of Gallo-
Roman workshops were evident already at Vermand, and although pots, glasses
and bronze vessels were not recorded with Childeric, probably because they were
destroyed in the over-enthusiastic disorderly rush of the finders, there are nevertheless elements in the developed cross-bow fibula, the finger-rings, the buckles and the
fish-scale attachment plate[1] and sword with strap slides and ornithomorphic chape[2]
which show close connections with the Krefeld-Oberlörick group. Germanic elements
are embodied in the presence and form of the weapons. The third element now added
is that of the splendid use of garnet cloisonné work, particularly on the sword with
golden grip, of which the type has its origin in south Russia. Influences of this last
kind must have come in the train of Attila in the middle of the century.

During the course of the fifth century, therefore, the graves of Franks may be distinguished in northern Gaul, and the tribe had begun its career in this territory as
laeti, or freed captives, for there are traces of Franks here in historical sources of the
third century and in archaeological sources of the fourth century. The Franks buried
in these graves had held high rank amongst their own people, and the military service
obligatory on *laeti* gave them opportunities for reasserting their former status—con-
sequently the furniture in the graves often includes equipment fitting for a noble.
The Franks of the fifth century, however, were free men, helping the Roman army
to defend the territory of their own free will, but for wages. During the whole of this
century, too, the manufacture of glass and metalwork continued in the Meuse area,
without suffering any serious disruption as a result of invasions.

Here, then, on the continent, is a rich series of archaeological finds relating to a
limited period and place, to the period when Germanic tribes were crossing the sea to
England, and to the area of northern Gaul, particularly by the Meuse. Richness of

[1] J. J. Chiflet *op. cit.*, pp. 182, 96, 236 and 226
centre, respectively.

[2] Böhner 1950; this was previously thought to be a
strap-end.

finds and certainty of dating are not yet available on this scale for any other area at this turbulent period. Since Germanic invaders continued their practice of inhumation with grave goods after settlement in England, the contents of graves here may be compared with graves on the continent, and consistent similarities would indicate either personal immigration or trading connections.

Unfortunately very few graves of the end of Roman rule in this country are known, graves which would correspond to the *laeti* graves at Vermand, Misèry, etc., but many of the objects of the late fourth century manufactured on the Meuse, such as bronze belt equipment and glass vessels, are to be found on Roman settlement sites and also in cemeteries of the early Anglo-Saxon period. Where they occur in grave groups where the accompanying goods are of the same date, the owner might be one of the Germanic members of the Roman army in Britain; where the accompanying goods are of slightly later date, the owner is probably an early settler. Only the evidence of a completely excavated cemetery to show continuance from earlier Roman graves or development into Saxon graves would make the identity clear, and that evidence is not so far available. The grave at Dorchester[1] is one of the very few known from this period, and this, with its near-by graves of women with Saxon brooches, was no doubt deposited about A.D. 400, but possibly as late as 415 after the Roman troops had gone. Burials of the immediate post-invasion period are more plentiful, however, and it is these which we must now examine.

[1] Kirk and Leeds 1952–3.

C

III

Distribution of Frankish Fifth-century Objects in England

Metal-inlaid work

IT HAS already been demonstrated[1] that in northern Gaul during the fifth century A.D. production was continued of the various kinds of glass, bronze and iron goods which had been manufactured there during the last years of Roman rule, and that the export of these goods also continued to take place. Information on one class of goods produced there is unusually plentiful as it has been the subject of close study both on the continent and in England.[2] This is the group of iron objects such as buckles, spears, etc. inlaid with another type of metal, silver, brass, or copper, for decorative purposes. Less often, bronze objects were inlaid with silver. The craft was practised on the continent and in Scandinavia during the Roman period, but appeared to be on the wane on the continent by the end of the fourth century, while it continued in Scandinavia. On the continent and in England the end of the fifth century saw a certain amount of revival, but products were few in number until the seventh century, when a series of enormous and magnificent buckles were produced by the Franks and Burgundians.[3]

As the work was generally carried out on iron, the ornament is usually completely covered with rust when excavated; it can only be traced by the use of radiographs, and the facilities of a laboratory are necessary for the cleaning and preservation. There is always the possibility, therefore, that surveys or distribution maps may present a false picture because of undetected specimens, but the subject has now been under consideration for some years, and the likelihood of the picture being altered radically by new discoveries has become much less.

Buckles with oval or kidney-shaped loops and rectangular plates placed with the long side adjacent to the loop, are decorated with transverse wire or strip inlay on

---

[1] Bjørn 1929.
[2] Salin 1943, pp. 131 ff.; Holmqvist 1951; Dasnoy 1954; Evison 1955; Salin 1957, III, pp. 166 ff.; Evison 1958; Pirling 1960b; Garscha 1962.

[3] Salin and France-Lanord 1943, pls. XXVII–XXXVI, etc.

the loops, and inlaid concentric circles on the plate (Map 2, list, p. 90). A date in the fifth century is ensured for these by their close connection with late Roman bronze buckles with incised circles on the plate.[1] Related to these are a number of inlaid loops without plates. A second group also have inlaid loops, but the plates are covered with a rectangular sheet of bronze or silver bearing a repoussé design. As the design is often of Christian inspiration, e.g. peacocks and vase (Broadstairs, Fig. 9, *d*), Daniel in the lions' den (Bifrons), and as practically identical buckles are found in northern Gaul (Map 3), their production must be assigned to the workshops which also produced repoussé bronze sheeting in Christian designs for wooden vessels and buckets in the second half of the fifth century in northern Gaul.[2] The bust of Daniel in the lions' den (Pl. 5, *a*) shows considerable resemblance in style to the bust of Childeric on his signet ring (Pl. 4, *d*) and both men are represented wearing the long hair of the Frankish kings.

As all these types have their parallels in northern Gaul, the English examples may be regarded as imports, but there are other types which have not yet been found abroad, and which may be regarded as developments on English soil. Amongst these are loops with sheet metal inlay, plates with circles inlaid with bone or glass, plates with more elaborate inlay (Pl. 6, *d, e*) and buckles with elaborate inlay carried out with advanced finesse (e.g. Pl. 6, *a, c*).[3] Inlay of this level of accomplishment has not so far been detected outside England at this period,[4] and the only attempts at complicated incrusted patterns abroad are the buckle from Fère-Champenoise,[5] and the plate in the Sammlung Diergardt.[6]

---

[1] Roosens 1962, pl. I, 4; Eck 1891, pl. xv, 9, 15; pl. xvi, 11; pl. xvii, 4a.

[2] Map 8. Chenet 1935.

[3] The quatrefoil motif on this buckle plate appeared on the Misèry buckle plate (Frontispiece) where it was executed in niello.

[4] A photograph of the St. Prex buckle seems to show that it is inlaid with cabochon stones. Further discoveries of continental examples of inlaid buckles have been made possible by the use of radiographs (Garscha 1962). Three of these are said to have metal sheet inlay on the loops. They do not appear to be closely similar to the English examples, and sheet inlay is not obvious on the published photographs and radiographs. Taf. 44, 6 and 8 (buckle loops from Kleinhüningen grave 229 and Basel 'Gotterbarmweg' grave 17) show the same effect as Taf. 44, 2, i.e. dark strips on a lighter background which indicates inlay of bronze, silver or copper strips on the rusty iron of lesser density. Conclusions as to this type of work, however, must be backed by actual examination of the object, plus inspection of the original radiograph against a strong light, and finally, if possible, examination of the object when cleaned. A great deal of detail is lost in printing a radiograph, and even more in its publication. Dr. Garscha has been misled by the published prints regarding the shape of the buckle loops from Kempston, Croydon and Chessell Down (Evison 1958, pls. III, b and f, IV, c), when he describes them as round oval and long oval; they are all kidney-shaped, the protrusion of the tongue obscuring the outline of pl. III, b, and as the Croydon and Kingston loops are rusted firmly at an angle to the plate, the radiographs show the plate full-face, but the loop at an angle. There is also no indication that the buckle from Chessell Down, pl. III, b, has sheet inlay on the loop, or that the metal used is silver, as described by Dr. Garscha. Details of this nature are not apparent until the object is cleaned.

[5] Salin 1957, III, fig. 73 bis.

[6] Holmqvist 1951, Abb. 25, 2.

Amongst various imported items there is inlaid work on spearheads (circles and stars on the blade and girth bands on the socket),[1] and two axes from Howletts are inlaid—a francisca[2] and a hammer-axe.[3] As to purse mounts, border strips occur on one from High Down,[4] and on one, recently radiographed, from Alfriston, grave 91 (Fig. 23, *b*). Another recently X-rayed, and probably from grave B at Alfriston, bears a more elaborate cable design (Pl. 6, *e*).

The evidence of associated objects places the bulk of the inlaid metal work in the second half of the fifth century; the craft was almost non-existent in England during the sixth century, and this suggests that the few survivals into that century may have been in the nature of heirlooms. A few spearheads, some inlaid bronze objects, etc. of that date were probably Frankish imports.[5] In the seventh century, the garnet-decorated buckle plate from Kingston, Kent,[6] seems to herald the re-establishment of the technique in England.

The distribution map of inlaid iron buckles and purse mounts in England (Map 2) shows them both north and south of the Weald, in fact more or less surrounding it, with a few outliers north of the Thames. It is to be noted that the Isle of Wight, usually said to be settled at a later date and secondarily by migrants from Kent, has its quota too. The distribution of the same type of buckles on the continent is shown in Map 3. This shows the repoussé rectangular plates occurring in the Seine and Meuse valleys in the periphery of the find spots of most of the bronze-bound wooden vessels in the same technique (Map 8). Concentration of the other objects is in the valleys of the Seine, Meuse and Rhine, with outliers in Thuringia and on the Danube. A separate production centre for buckles with oval inlaid loops and oval or semicircular plates is indicated on the Upper Rhine. Scandinavia is not taken into account as, apart from a few inlaid buckle loops, there are no other comparable buckles.

Intimately concerned with this class of object by reason of the technique of inlaid metal and the form of one well-known buckle, is the Quoit Brooch Style of animal decoration. No less than ten of the objects bearing this style are of bronze inlaid with silver, and, conversely, all the examples of bronze objects inlaid with silver of this period are in the Quoit Brooch Style.[7] As may be seen from Map 4 the distribution of these two is very similar, many of the sites appearing on both maps.

---

[1] Inlaid spearheads, axe-heads, etc. are omitted from the distribution maps as it is not yet possible to date them securely. Early cloisonné work with large cells, which often has inlaid strips on the edges (Holmqvist 1951 Abb. 17, 4 and 6), is also omitted.

[2] See pp. 50, 60.

[3] Evison 1955, p. 37, No. 10.

[4] *Ibid.*, pl. VI, f.

[5] *Ibid.*, fig. 4, pl. IX, c.

[6] *Ibid.*, pl. XI, a.

[7] See below, Chapter 5.

Glass

Dr. Harden, in his survey of Anglo-Saxon glasses,[1] has published four maps showing their distribution divided as to late Roman survivals, and fifth, sixth, and seventh century glasses. Of the first category, there are two kinds, the first being Roman shapes which did not continue into the fifth century, i.e. they had been made some time before being buried, and were either brought over by the immigrants, or were looted here. The second kind are 'border line glasses whose general shape continued', and as Dr. Harden says, 'these presumably indicate a cemetery of actual settlers'. He points out that a number of cemeteries in this category also come into the next category containing fifth-century glasses, but not into the later categories. There was apparently no appreciable amount of trading traffic between them and continental glass-producing centres after this, and the glasses of the sixth and seventh centuries, probably mostly of foreign make and from the same factories as the earlier glasses, are to be found differently distributed in England; even where the area is still in Kent, the actual cemetery site is not the same. Dr. Harden pointed out that the late Roman glasses came from High Down and Alfriston in Sussex, Bifrons, Faversham, Westbere, Eastry, Howletts and Milton-next-Sittingbourne in Kent, Chessell Down, Isle of Wight, East Shefford, Berks., Mitcham, Surrey, Newport Pagnell, Bucks., and Holme Pierrepont, Notts., and a number of these sites also figure in the fifth-century list. Some early glasses appear in the Isle of Wight, but no later ones. The distribution of Roman glasses therefore is confined to the area south of the Thames, with the exception of Great Chesterford, Essex, Newport Pagnell and Holme Pierrepont, of which the last two may not have been found in Saxon contexts (Map 5).[2] The find spots of the fifth century, too, cluster to the north and south of the Weald, with some in the upper Thames basin, and a few to the north of the Thames, especially in the vicinity of the Icknield Way (Map 6). As to the position of production centres, the distribution of mould-blown glass vessels, some with Christian motifs, of the type found at Westbere, Kent,[3] and Selmeston, Sussex,[4] has been mapped by Werner,[5] and shows concentration in the Namur region and in northern France.

Another class of object which cannot be later than early to middle fifth century is the glass armlet (Map 7). The large D-sectioned type occurs in late Roman contexts, e.g. Richborough in a ditch of third to fourth century A.D.[6] Four have been found in Anglo-Saxon cemeteries: Chessell Down, Isle of Wight (Fig. 9, *a*);[7] Malling Hill,

---

[1] Harden 1956.

[2] Harden 1956, p. 136 and note 15.

[3] *Ant. Journ.* XXVI (1946), pp. 17–18, pl. III, 29, fig. 2.

[4] This, however, has a sharp, unfinished rim and may be slightly earlier.

[5] Breuer and Roosens 1957, p. 338, fig. 28.

[6] Bushe-Fox 1932, III, pp. 44–5, No. 914, Ditch Section 21.

[7] Carisbrooke Castle Museum, Isle of Wight, No. 53.5.

Sussex;[1] Milton Regis (Fig. 9, *b, c*)[2] and Chatham Lines (grave XVII) in Kent (Fig. 15, *b*).[3] A silver-gilt bracelet which must be intimately connected with the glass bracelets from Milton Regis, as it is identical in shape with diagonal fluting, was found at Ribchester in Kent.[4] Many of the glass bracelets on the continent of comparable date were found in the Meuse valley, so indicating the probable source of supply.[5] In England, the associated finds are not known except at Chatham Lines (Fig. 15), and here they fully support an early date.[6]

Bronze-bound wooden containers

A group of bronze-bound wooden buckets found in northern Gaul were evidently produced there, and because of their associations may be placed mostly in the latter half of the fifth century to early sixth.[7] The repoussé bronze bands are decorated with distinctive arc and dot motifs, and buckets or fragments of buckets which are very similar have been found in England (Map 8). It is particularly interesting that one of them is the famous bucket from Bidford-on-Avon which is also adorned with the appliqué animals allied to the Quoit Brooch Style. Any doubt about whether the animals are contemporary with the rest of the decoration is dispelled by the ornamentation on the bodies of the animals themselves, which is partly carried out in the same arcs and dots. The arcaded band type of bucket occurs at Faversham and Howletts in Kent; Fetcham in Surrey; Chessell Down, Isle of Wight; Brockbridge near Droxford, Hants; and Petersfinger, Wilts. Only two were found with associated objects: Howletts grave 23 was said to contain two square-headed brooches, a bird brooch and two beads, and Petersfinger grave LX contained a shield, spear, knife and buckle. Both graves are likely to be early sixth century, but the Bidford bucket and some of the others must be earlier. Buckets from Abingdon, graves 7 and 61, with simple lines of repoussé dots, were considered by Werner to be closely connected with the continental series.[8] There are many more Anglo-Saxon buckets decorated in this way, and they may be fifth-century imports from the continent or Anglo-Saxon copies, but as a detailed study is not yet available, they must be omitted for the present.[9]

The same workshops must have produced the wooden stoups and other vessels with coverings of bronze sheet decorated by Christian scenes in repoussé technique. Already in the late fourth century rectangular wooden boxes covered in this way

---

[1] G. A. Mantell, *A Day's ramble in and about the ancient town of Lewes* (1846), p. 134. This is probably the same cemetery as *Sussex Arch. Coll.* 94, p. 10; *Arch. Journ.* xv, 160; Baldwin Brown 1915, iv, pl. clvi, 8. The bracelet is not traceable in the British Museum.

[2] *Arch. Cant.* lxxiv (1960), pp. 181–2, pl. iii.

[3] Douglas 1793, pl. 14, pp. 58–62.

[4] British Museum, Reg. No. 1949 5–4 1.

[5] Information from G. C. Dunning.

[6] Cf. pp. 34–5.

[7] Leeds 1936, pp. 17–18, figs. 4 and 5; Chenet 1935.

[8] Breuer and Roosens 1957, p. 319.

[9] A study of Anglo-Saxon buckets is in preparation by Miss J. Cook and Miss J. Travers.

were in current production, and towards the end of the Roman period the pagan scenes depicted were superseded by Christian ones, e.g. at Vermand.[1] The mount for a cylindrical wooden vessel with scenes featuring a seated Christ which was found in a grave at Strood, Kent, is allocated to this period,[2] but a later, fifth-century example of Christian figure scenes was found in England at Long Wittenham (Fig. 13, c).[3]

Bow brooches with upturned foot

A rather rare type of brooch may be allowed to make its contribution here. This is a variety of long brooch with a narrow bow describing a wide arc; the tip of the foot turns up, and a ring on the head provides means for securing by a thong or chain. The English varieties were noticed by Leeds,[4] who regarded them as the products of Britons at the time of the invasion, products influenced perhaps by the Anglo-Saxon cruciform brooch. His only reason for this view regarding their origin was that they were decorated with the bull's-eye motif which occurred on disc and annular brooches and which Leeds regarded as British. However, the bull's-eye motif (ring-and-dot) was popular amongst Germanic people, and disc and annular brooches so ornamented were in use by Germanic tribes in the early fifth century.[5] There is no reason, then, to regard the bow brooches as British, and their origin must be reconsidered.

The brooches found at West Stow, Suffolk, Glaston, Rutland and Howletts, Kent (Fig. 10, a, d, f), have been compared by Werner[6] to similar continental products: they are a development of bow brooches of the Roman period and are quite widespread, but the series with curled-up foot are limited to the above examples, plus a splendid specimen with zoomorphic decoration of unknown provenance at the museum of St Germain,[7] and simple ones from Cys-la-Commune (Aisne), and Krefeld-Gellep, grave 792. The Krefeld brooch was associated with a francisca, a pot and silver coin.[8] The brooch has a loop at the head and a wide coil of iron spring. This cemetery also contains in grave 530 iron bow brooches with bronze ribbed foot and spherical foot terminal which are very similar, but although the foot of one comes up

---

[1] Pilloy 1895, II, pl. 13; Eck 1891, pl. XIV.

[2] See p. 34.

[3] B.M. Guide 1923, pp. 68–71, figs. 77 and 78; p. 32 below.

[4] E. T. Leeds, 'A late British brooch from Glaston, Rutland', Ant. Journ. XXVIII, 169–73; 'The brooch from West Stow', Suffolk, Ant. Journ. XXIX, 91; E. T. Leeds and J. L. Barber, 'An Anglian cemetery at Glaston, Rutland', Ant. Journ. XXX, 185–9.

[5] For disc brooches with ring-and-dot decoration, see Pirling 1959 (Krefeld-Gellep, grave 968), p. 231,

Abb. 22, 3, cf. Fig. 24, a. For annular brooches, see pp. 48–9 below.

[6] J. Werner, 'Römische Fibeln des 5. Jahrhunderts von der Gurina im Gailtal und vom Grepault bei Truns (Graubünden)', Der Schlern, 32 (1958), pp. 109–12.

[7] Acta Arch. V, 137, Abb. 30.

[8] Dr. R. Pirling kindly informs me that the coin was lost in the war, but the francisca and pot are types which belong to the period A.D. 450–525.

at an angle, it is not curved.[1] The associations at Cys-la-Commune are not known, but it is important to note that brooches of the same type, except that the foot is straight, occur in the Aisne district, Armentières, for example, and that one of them was found in a grave with a fifth-century glass bowl with Christian moulded decoration.[2]

There is one more example of the brooch type in England, which, curiously, has been omitted from lists. It is the most complete of the series for the iron spring is still preserved on its bar with knob terminals. The ring at the head is immovable and in one piece with the brooch. With a provenance of West Stow, it came to the Museum of Archaeology and Ethnology at Cambridge in 1892 in the Foster Bequest.[3] It cannot be the brooch illustrated by Roach Smith in 1852[4] as being from West Stow and then in the collection of Mr J. Gwilt. As Leeds saw,[5] this drawing tallied with the brooch bought at a sale in 1949 for the Ashmolean Museum, but this brooch was bought with a Frankish shield-on-tongue buckle, and the two pieces affixed to a card inscribed 'Fibula and buckle from a Roman grave, Icklingham, Suffolk' (Fig. 10, *b*, *c*). Icklingham and West Stow are near together and there is a Saxon cemetery in each place. Either there are two brooches from West Stow cemetery, or Roach Smith's information of provenance was wrong, and his brooch and buckle came from Icklingham.

The other English examples have associated objects, but those said to belong to Howletts grave 4 constitute a mixture that is not credible, and it must be remembered that the grave groups in this cemetery are not reliable.[6] Most of the objects said to have been found with the bow brooch are distinctly Frankish, i.e. two radiate brooches, a garnet disc brooch, garnet-set polyhedral ear-ring, garnet-set kidney-shaped plate, the bronze pin and Roman intaglio finger ring being late Roman types. The bow brooch and large finger ring would be more suitable for a male, while the disc and radiate brooches and the ear-ring indicate a female. It is possible that two graves are confused, the earlier male one containing the bow brooch, finger ring and kidney-shaped plate, while the other objects belonged to a sixth-century female grave, but this is conjecture.

The iron associated fragments in the grave group at Glaston were fragile and disintegrated, but the penannular brooch remains, a ring of circular section, but with terminals turned back, flattened and decorated. The decoration is geometric but reminiscent of horses' heads, particularly as to the vertical groove at the end, as if

---

[1] This information I owe to the late Dr. A. Steeger, who showed me the contents of some of the graves in this cemetery in 1953. A. Steeger 1937a, 22, bottom right. Pirling 1959, pp. 215–42, Abb. 11. 16.

[2] J. Werner, *op. cit.*, 1958, Abb. 15; Breuer and Roosens 1957, pl. XIII, 1.

[3] C. Fox, *Archaeology of the Cambridge Region* (1948), pl. XXXV, 4, p. 281.

[4] Smith, 1852, II, p. 167, pl. XLI, B, fig. 3.

[5] *Ant. Journ.* XXIX, 91.

[6] This excavation was not professionally supervised.

between the ears at the back of the head.[1] The type occurs frequently on Romano-British sites,[2] and an almost identical specimen, as well as others similar, was found at Lydney, Glos.[3] Amongst decadent examples, Savory lists one from Whitford Burrows (Glam.).[4] He notes that brooches with terminals like horses' heads come from more eastern sites such as Icklingham, Suffolk,[5] Silchester and York and suggests connections with 'Romano-British' forms such as the Alfriston brooch. This may be possible, but the connection between horses' head terminals and the Glaston type, together with an exact parallel at Lydney, makes it more likely that the Glaston one is Welsh in origin. Savory points out that Leeds' distribution map of penannular brooches[6] shows, in general, concentration in the Saxon areas which bordered on the Celtic lands. A Celtic origin therefore seems indisputable at least for the popularity of the type at this period.[7]

Of the finds associated with the bow brooch type, the Glaston penannular is fifth century but probably Celtic, the West Stow buckle is Frankish of fifth to sixth century, and the Howletts grave-group is unreliable but probably Frankish of the fifth century. Placing these facts beside the information on the fifth-century group of these brooches in France, one comes to the conclusion that Leeds' declaration of a British origin for the type must be abandoned in favour of a Frankish one. The number in England is small, but the distribution, which points partly to the north of the Thames, indicates that the invaders in the Wash, too, had some connection with the Franks (Map 7).

Bronze vessels with triangular lugs, bows and arrows, pottery, shield grips

One of the types of bronze vessel manufactured in the Meuse valley in the fifth and early sixth century is the bowl with concave sides with carination and two perforated triangular lugs on the rim.[8] Three examples have been found in Anglo-Saxon graves, at Long Wittenham, Berks. (Fig. 13, *b*), Sawston near Cambridge, and Ixworth Thorpe, Suffolk.[9] Apart from Long Wittenham, the sites are north of the Thames, and

[1] Cf. the double grooving on the heads on the penannular brooch from Riseley (Fig. 28, *i*).

[2] Kilbride-Jones 1937, figs. 27–9.

[3] R. E. M. Wheeler and T. V. Wheeler, *Excavation of the Prehistoric, Roman and Post-Roman site in Lydney Park, Glos., Reports of the Research Committee of the Soc. of Ant. of London*, No. IX (1932) fig. 14, 38; cf. also one from Porth Dafarch, Holyhead, B.M. Guide 1923, fig. 173.

[4] Savory 1956, p. 51, pl. v, d and fig. 11, 4.

[5] *Idem*, pl. v, c.

[6] Savory 1956, p. 52; Leeds 1945, fig. 28.

[7] But cf. pp. 47–8.

[8] F. H. Thompson, 'Anglo-Saxon Sites in Lincolnshire', *Ant. Journ.* xxxvi (1956), pp. 181–99; Bjørn 1929; G. Ekholm, 'Bronskärlen av Ostlands- och Vestlandstyp', *Det Kongelige Norska Videnskabers Selskabs Skrifter* (1933); H. Norling-Christensen, 'Vestlandskedler og malede glas', *Kuml* (1953), pp. 47–60; G. Ekholm, 'Neues über die Westlandkessel', *Trierer Zeitschrift*, 23, 224–30.

[9] The hoard of bronze vessels which included three of this type at Halkyn mountain, Flintshire, was obviously brought by a sea-borne merchant, and may belong to the pre-invasion period.

suggest import via the Icknield Way, but the number is too low to be significant (Map 7).

One would expect bows and arrows to have been in general use amongst the Anglo-Saxons. They are mentioned in connection with early battles in literature,[1] and figure in the illustrations on the Franks Casket, where a man (Egil) defends himself with bow and arrow. In spite of this, they are hardly to be found at all in pagan Saxon graves. Little or nothing is likely to remain of a bow, but the iron arrow-tips at least should remain in a recognizable state. We may recall that arrows were noticed by Werner as one of the usual classes of object occurring in Frankish men's graves of the fourth century in northern Gaul, and they persisted into later cemeteries, e.g. Haillot. It is therefore relevant to notice here that arrows have been found in English pagan graves only at Chessell Down, Isle of Wight and Buttsole and Chatham Lines in Kent, with traces of bows at Chessell Down and Bifrons (Map 7).[2]

So far there appears to be no imported wheel-turned pottery of the fifth century in pagan graves, with the exception of one bowl from Chessell Down (Fig. 9, *f*).[3] This is light brown-grey ware with girth grooves and bands of rouletting; it is a developed Argonne form, and the shape occurs in Haillot graves (Fig. 4, 1 and 4).[4] On both Argonne ware and the pots in the Haillot graves the rouletting is on the lower half of the vessel; on the Chessell Down bowl it has moved to the upper half, the usual position for rouletting on Merovingian pots (Map 7).

The form of the shield grip in the military leader's grave at Vermand (Pl. 1, *f*) is unusual. At the points where the grip met and was attached to the edges of the hand aperture in the shield, the iron bar divided and curled round in a diminishing spiral. There is a rivet in the middle and one on each spiral, while the middle bar extended further. A shield grip found at High Down (grave unknown) has no middle extensions, but the bifurcation with diminishing spirals and three rivets are similar. Derived types occur at Alfriston, grave 3,[5] and Petersfinger, grave VII,[6] and Droxford, Hants.[7]

---

[1] *Beowulf*, ed. F. Klaeber, ll. 3116–19 refers to battles, ll. 2437–8 to a single slaying, both of which would have occurred about A.D. 500 in Sweden.

[2] Brown 1915, III, pp. 203 and 242, pl. XXXII, 1 and 5; IV, pp. 717 and 747. Hillier, p. 37, figs. 108–11. Arrows were noticed in connection with two graves at Bidford-on-Avon, but neither context is satisfactory: in grave 79 the arrow was found above the grave, and in grave 95 it was the only item of grave furniture and the depth of the grave was only one foot, so that dis-

turbance is likely to have occurred. The arrowhead from Bowcombe Down, burial 20, is included in the map, but this was a disturbed burial.

[3] British Museum Reg. No. 67 7–29 141.

[4] Breuer and Roosens 1957, figs. 4, 4; 7, 1; 8, 3; 12, 1; 14, 4; 16, 6;, 18, 12.

[5] *Sussex Arch. Coll.* LVI (1914), pl. XVII, 7.

[6] Leeds and Shortt 1953, fig. 8, 16.

[7] *P.S.A.* 2nd ser. XIX, p. 129, fig. 6.

Bronze belt mounts, etc.

A type of bronze buckle which has been closely studied in its continental contexts[1] is a continuation of a late Roman type. This has an oval loop with animal heads at the point where it joins a rectangular or trapezoid plate (cf. Belleray, Pl. 3, *e*, and Haillot, Fig. 4, 8). The loop and plate are cast in one and decoration is usually by means of circle-and-dot stamps and beaded borders, but occasionally there is more complicated chip-carved decoration. Similar buckles were made in the fourth century, but on those the plate was always loose and separate from the loop. The buckles with fixed plate were being manufactured from the beginning to the middle of the fifth century, and the distribution map (together with consideration of stylistic features) indicates the Meuse valley as the original source.

Four of these buckles have been found in England, all of them in Anglo-Saxon graves (Map 7).[2] One comes from Sarre, Kent, but its grave associations are not known, and the example in the Royal Museum, Canterbury, has no provenance. Long Wittenham, grave 57, said to be a woman's grave, also contained a pot and a knife (Fig. 12, *a–c*), Alfriston, grave 14 (Fig. 24, *a–e*), a flattened bronze tube of the kind discussed below (pp. 50–1) and a bronze buckle loop, disc brooch, knife, spearhead and fragments of an iron ring and rim.[3] All of these four buckles must have been made in the first half of the century, their Frankish origin is unquestionable, and their importance as evidence of early settlement is paramount.

Occasional mention has been made of objects of Roman origin, made in the fourth century, or even earlier, which have turned up in Anglo-Saxon burials. They do not necessarily have any bearing on the date of the actual deposition, but they do not occur in later contexts with anything like the frequency that applies to the fifth century. The various kinds of bronze attachments to the soldier's belt of the late fourth century, such as zoomorphic buckles, strap-ends, and disc attachments found on late Roman sites in Britain, also occur in Saxon graves. The main zoomorphic characteristics consist of confronted dolphins with separating sphere (Fig. 9, *e*), and horses' heads back to back, both of which are motifs derived from fourth-century models current in the Roman army on the continent, and they belong to a large group of chip-carved Romano-Germanic products. Those found in Britain have recently been listed and attributed to the work of Romano-Britons.[4] It may be that they were made in Britain but (even if it is true that there are no examples abroad) they are nevertheless in continental Germanic taste, and presumably made for Germanic members of

---

[1] Breuer and Roosens 1957, pp. 320–3, pls. VI–VIII; Werner 1958, p. 391, Abb. 14.

[2] Three were included in Hawkes and Dunning 1963, figs. 19 bis b, 20 g and h.

[3] *Sussex Arch. Coll.* LVI, p. 32, pls. IV, 6, X, 3 and 4, XI, 8.

[4] Hawkes and Dunning 1963.

the Roman army; the craftsmen could equally well have been Germanic smiths who
came to Britain with the army.[1] The distribution of these objects, when found in
Germanic graves, is confined to the upper Thames, Mitcham, East Kent, Sussex and
the Avon valley, i.e. the area we have been discussing, while their counterparts on
Roman sites, which are more numerous, cluster round the Roman centres of Caer-
went, Cirencester, Leicester, Water Newton, Caistor and Silchester, as well as in
Kent (Map 9).

This represents the only attempt so far made to list late Roman objects in early
Germanic graves. Many other varieties remain to be dealt with, pots,[2] brooches,[3]
etc., and of the latter it is possible to list one type here. The oval or circular brooch
with cabochon stone centre which appears widespread on many late Roman sites in
Britain and on the continent, has been found in Saxon graves in England only at
East Shefford[4] and Long Wittenham (grave 129),[5] Berks., Gilton (grave 87),[6] Kent,
Bensford Bridge, Warwicks[7] and Woodstone, Hunts (Map 9).[8] A number of the finds
from Bensford Bridge are early: a Roman lion mask, a Frankish type of strap-end,
cruciform brooches etc. There is no indication of the sex of the wearers of the brooches
found on Roman sites, but of the Saxon graves, one at East Shefford was a woman's
as there were a pair, Long Wittenham grave 129 also had a second brooch, and the
beads at Gilton mark this grave, too, as female.

Of the objects which were in use in Britain in the late Roman period, the zoomorphic buckles and other belt bronzes are found widespread in Britain in areas presumably being defended by the Roman army. The disc and oval brooches worn by
their womenfolk are found in similar places. After the invasion, however, the Germanic graves in which these same objects appear are almost exclusively in the area
of the Thames and to the south. If their presence in post-invasion graves were the
result of plunder, then their distribution should at least approximate to the earlier
Roman distribution.

Bronze objects of undisputed continental origin have been found in Saxon graves
at Croydon (rosette attachment,[9] diamond-shaped strap-end,[10] buckle with triangular
open plate),[11] where no note is recorded of grave-groups, and a diamond-shaped strap-
end also occurred in a well-furnished woman's burial at Cassington, Oxon.[12] of early,

---

[1] See p. 29.

[2] E.g. from a grave at King's Worthy, in Winchester
Museum.

[3] E.g. a Roman cross-bow brooch at Droxford,
Hants., *P.S.A.* 2nd ser. XIX, p. 128, fig. 5.

[4] *V.C.H. Berks.*, I, 240, fig. 11, three, one with inset
intaglio; British Museum Guide 1923, p. 71.

[5] *Arch.* XXXIX, pl. XI, 1, p. 138; with a knife and
'plain circular bronze fibula 1½ in. diam.'; Baldwin
Brown IV, pl. CII, 4.

[6] Faussett 1856, p. 28, pl. X, 15; found with beads,
bronze toilet implements, knife, nails, iron fragments
and four iron corner pieces to box or coffin.

[7] Akerman 1855, p. 35, pl. XVIII.

[8] *V.C.H. Hunts.*, I, 276, fig. 15.

[9] Hawkes and Dunning 1963, fig. 24, e; cf. Pl. 3, *a*.

[10] *Ibid.*, fig. 23, c; cf. Pl. 3, *f*.

[11] Unpublished, No. 3855, cf. Nenquin 1953, pl.
VIII, D, 11.

[12] Hawkes and Dunning 1963, fig. 23, f.

date (Map 9). Buckles with confronted dolphin heads on the loop and with long rectangular plates occur on late Roman sites in Britain, and a case has been made out for their manufacture in this country. The buckle loops, however, do not form a compact group as each one is different, and of the examples appearing in Anglo-Saxon graves, none has a plate. It has been supposed that these Anglo-Saxon ones are of the same origin as those of Roman Britain, but as the dolphin loop with bar (instead of curling tails) was well known on the continent,[1] it is quite possible that some[2] were brought from there, or are the result of influences from that direction.

The position regarding these post-invasion bronze mounts, is complex but the distribution shows that: (a) continental bronzes are only found at Croydon, Surrey, and Cassington, Oxon., whereas in the Roman period they occurred sporadically north of the Thames. (b) Horse's head buckle loops, presumably made in Roman Britain, lived on at Bifrons and in a woman's grave at Stratford-on-Avon. (c) Dolphin-head loops, whether of British or continental origin, occur only in the Thames valley or to the south of it, except for Broadway, Worcs., and Sleaford, Lincs., whereas in the Roman period both dolphin and horse's head types occurred at Cirencester and other Roman sites north of the Thames. The numbers involved are not large enough to form a reliable basis for conclusions, but one may conjecture that possible reasons for this distribution are: (a) people arriving from the continent brought the belt mounts with them, or (b) Romano-German soldiers and their wives stationed in Britain were withdrawn to the continent, but returned in the southern invasions. Otherwise it is necessary to suppose that the presence of these bronzes in post-invasion graves is due to plundering activities limited, for some unknown reason, to an area in the south, and this is hardly credible.

Discussion

The examination of the distribution of fifth-century objects in England has produced a number of highly informative points. The original production centre of the imports, i.e. inlaid metalwork, glass vessels, glass armlets, bronze-bound buckets, brooch with upturned foot, zoomorphic buckles with fixed plate, late Roman zoomorphic buckles, is securely traced to the Meuse valley or northern Gaul. The area in which they are found in England is almost exclusively limited to the Thames valley and from there to the south coast, including the Isle of Wight. Some late Roman pre-invasion goods occur in post-invasion graves, but also, for the most part, only in this area.

---

[1] Cf. Nenquin 1953, pl. VII, D, 7; W. Haberey, 'Spätantike Gläser aus Gräbern von Mayen', *Bonner Jahrbücher*, 147 (1947), pp. 249–84, Abb. 11, e.

[2] E.g. Ash, Kent; Hawkes and Dunning, fig. 13, o, of which there is a near replica in the Landesmuseum, Bonn.

What, then, is the reason for the arrival in quantity, in the southern part of Britain only, of goods manufactured in northern Gaul? The two areas in question are, it is true, comfortably positioned for easy trading conditions, but it is difficult to believe that the early settlers, in whose graves they were found, were enjoying such tranquil conditions as to be able to indulge in untrammelled commercial activities of this sort. If this were so, however, there would seem to be no reason why the trade should not continue into the sixth century, but the evidence of glass vessels is against this, for later glass is not found on the same sites. Then, in the case of the inlaid metal-work, which, like the glass, constitutes a weighty amount of material, although some pieces are clearly imported as their twins are to be found abroad, there are others which show developments not found elsewhere. This suggests that the knowledge of a technique and of motifs was brought over and underwent further developments in this country which have no parallel in their original continental production centre. Nevertheless, inlaid metalwork fails in England in the sixth century; it continued to be practised among the Franks, but only a few examples of their work were imported to England. The presence of late Roman bronze belt fittings, etc. in invasion graves suggests the not unreasonable conjecture that some of the Germanic members of the Roman army in Britain may have returned to assume somewhat of the authority of Rome in much the same way as the Franks did in Gaul.

There is therefore a strong case for considering whether in the plentiful traces of foreign goods we have evidence not of trade, but of the invaders themselves, and their possessions. With this in mind, we may turn to pursue another line of investigation and examine individual graves of the fifth century in this area in the south of England. The nationality of these people is mixed, and Saxons and Anglo-Frisians are occasionally distinguishable. The localization and dating of the material culture of these tribes is not yet so firmly established as that of the Franks in northern Gaul, and that side of the picture will therefore be left unexplored for the present. As most of the imported goods come from northern Gaul, there is a possibility that the invaders were inhabitants of that area, and were Frankish. If so, there should be close correspondence between some of the grave-groups on both sides of the Channel.

IV

Individual Graves of Franks of the Fifth Century in England

The Thames valley

IN THIS search among individual graves of the fifth century cremations and inhumations with goods obviously brought from Anglian, Saxon or Frisian lands will be passed by, and only inhumations with close affinities to the cultural group described in the previous chapter will be singled out. It must not be forgotten that a mixture of peoples throughout the area is evident from Anglo-Frisian pots and Saxon saucer brooches, etc., but the proportion of influence from each quarter cannot yet be estimated.

Beginning in the region of the upper Thames which was settled early in the fifth century, our attention is immediately attracted by the grave of a warrior of the fifth century at Brighthampton (Fig. 11).[1] Here, in grave 31, a man was buried with his sword in its very distinctive scabbard, the chip-carved spiral decoration on the silver mouth fitting and the animal figures on the chape being conclusive pointers in dating.[2] The S-shaped spirals in relief, clearly related to late Roman chip-carving, occur on scabbard mounts from Evebø, Norway,[3] and Kragehul, Denmark,[4] and in a similar fashion on Nydam mounts.[5] Although the S-spiral motif is here in the position where the Krefeld group swords have the wave motif, the moulding at each side edge is the same. The Brighthampton scabbard mount is, however, most closely connected with the early fifth-century mount found with the hoard of coins at Wiesbaden-Kastel.[6] This mount also was silver-gilt, and in chip-carving, with tongue-shaped moulding along the edges.

U-shaped chapes of this width are usually short, but one of similar length occurred in grave LXXXVII at Riseley, Horton Kirby, Kent.[7] The animals are realistic,

[1] Brown 1915, IV, p. 660; *Arch.* xxxviii, 87.
[2] The animal decoration is discussed below, p. 61.
[3] Behmer 1939, Taf. II, 2a.
[4] *Ibid.*, Taf. xxvi, 6.
[5] *Ibid.*, Taf. xxvii, 4 and 5.
[6] See p. 14.

[7] This chape is now (1963) exhibited on the sword from grave LXXXVI, but it seems it must belong to grave LXXXVII for the report, *Trans. Dartford District Antiquarian Soc.* VIII (1938) says the chape in LXXXVII was 6½ in. long, and was 'the only chape found on the site'.

and are probably derived from the Roman hare and hound motif. The two pairs of birds' heads near the tip of the scabbard recall the birds' heads on either side of the human mask on the cast bronze scabbard-tip fittings of the Krefeld-Gellep type; the small, disc-headed rivets must have fastened a supporting strap or baldric as they did on the Krefeld sword where they are still *in situ*. The pyramid-shaped pommel has already developed separate lugs for the rivets, but still retains the early arrangement of a hole at the top for penetration by the tang. Splendid mounts in silver are rare, and these emphasize the high rank of the occupant of the grave. With the body was also a sword-knot bead, bronze strip, spear, knife, an early type of strap-end and elaborate bronze-mounted bucket. There was also a small cross-pattée mount for the scabbard, an obvious Christian emblem.[1] Everything in this grave points to the Namur metal-working area, probably before the middle of the fifth century.

In grave 93 at Long Wittenham[2] was a boy who had come straight from the vicinity of Namur. Not only did he possess the stoup covered in repoussé bronze depicting Christian scenes, and a bronze cauldron with triangular lugs (Fig. 13, *b, c*, Maps 7, 8), both of which could have come from nowhere else, but even at the early date of the excavation Akerman noticed that his spear was placed with 'point turned downwards', i.e. towards the feet, 'a custom more common among the Franks than here'. The Frankish zoomorphic buckle (Map 7) was found in grave 57 of this cemetery with a knife, but also with a pot decorated by stamps of Saxon origin (Fig. 12, *a–c*).[3] Grave 111 contained the inlaid iron buckle loop, two saucer brooches, beads, needle, coin, bronze ring, knife, two finger rings, bronze fragments and a strap-end of a type also found on late Roman sites (cf. Fig. 27, *k*).[4] There are many other indications of early settlement in this cemetery, such as the late Roman type of brooch with cabochon centre in grave 129 (Map 9).

Moving down the Thames we come to Reading, where grave 13 contained a zoomorphic buckle, early strap-end, Roman coin, finger rings, bronze tube, pedestal pot and iron rings.[5] The strap-end and finger rings suggest Frankish sources, and the zoomorphic details of the buckle have connections with Roman army equipment on the continent. The bronze tube may have Frankish connections, but the pedestal pot has a basically Anglo-Frisian decoration with intrusion of Saxon stamps. The date of the grave is undoubtedly mid-fifth century, although the pot brings a Saxon note to an otherwise Frankish grave.

[1] A similar cross-pattée mount, together with another of shoe shape, was found *in situ* on the scabbard of a sixth-century sword at Bülach, Switzerland, and they were evidently functional in fastening the scabbard to the baldric; Werner 1953 b, Taf. xxxiv, 1 and xxxix, 2.

[2] *Arch.* xxxviii, 345, pls. xvii and xviii, 2; B.M. Guide 1923, pp. 68–9, figs. 77 and 78. The occupant cannot have been a warrior, as suggested by Werner in Breuer and Roosens 1957, p. 318, for the grave was only 3 ft. 6 in. long.

[3] *Arch.* xxxviii, 342, pls. xix, 10 and 2.

[4] *Ibid.*, 347; Holmqvist 1951, Abb. 27.

[5] Evison 1955, p. 28, note 2; Hawkes and Dunning 1963, fig. 14, b.

Further east, and some way south of the Thames, there are two graveyards in Surrey which have much in common with one another. Mitcham has an early grave, no. 229, containing an inlaid buckle[1] with annular brooch, disc brooch, knife, bronze pin, bronze ring and a nail.[2] Grave 38[3] had a zoomorphic buckle,[4] knife and Roman finger ring. Grave 199 contained a Roman glass amphora and grave 200 a glass bowl. From the photograph published by Baldwin Brown,[5] it looks as though there once existed also a typical inlaid iron buckle and plate.

Near by, at Croydon, the contents of each grave were not noted, but there is much evidence of fifth-century settlement and of Frankish material, of which some is undoubtedly fifth century. There are, first of all, late fourth–fifth century objects such as the rosette belt fitting[6] as at Dorchester and Belleray (Pls. 2, *a*, *e*; 3, *a*, *c*), a diamond-shaped strap-end (cf. Belleray, Pl. 3, *f*)[7] and a buckle loop with triangular plate in one piece.[8] Objects decorated with metal inlay or closely associated with the same production centre are the tubular mount with animal decoration (Pl. 13, *a*), the iron buckle,[9] the bronze buckle plate[10] and two strap-ends.[11] In addition, Frankish production centres were responsible for a stemmed glass beaker,[12] a bronze cauldron,[13] three franciscas, an angon and swords.

Kent

It is hardly necessary to examine Kentish cemeteries in detail, for they are well known, a date of settlement in the middle of the fifth century is generally accepted, and in any case it has the blessing of the Anglo-Saxon Chronicle. As we have seen, however, a date before about A.D. 520 has been denied for the Frankish element and this must be challenged. It is sufficient merely to point out that metal-inlaid work is mostly to be found in this county, so indicating the early date of the settlements at Higham, Bifrons and Howletts, and overwhelming support of this contention may be culled from the distribution maps of fifth-century glass, etc.

At Riseley, near Horton Kirby, Kent, an early annular brooch with zoomorphic

[1] Evison 1958, pl. xxvi, a; Bidder and Morris 1959, pp. 75 and 104.

[2] R. E. M. Wheeler, *London and the Saxons* (1935), fig. 14; Bidder and Morris 1959, p. 75, pls. xi, xii and xv.

[3] *Ibid.*, 62, pls. xiii and xiv.

[4] Hawkes and Dunning 1963, fig. 18, f.

[5] Brown 1915, iii, pl. lxxv, 3.

[6] Hawkes and Dunning 1963, fig. 24, e.

[7] *Ibid.*, fig. 23, c.

[8] Cf. Richborough, no. 3855, unpublished; Nenquin 1953, pl. viii, D 11.

[9] Evison 1955, pl. iv, c.

[10] Evison 1958, pl. xxvi, c and d.

[11] One is Fig. 14, *b*. The other, unpublished, is of spatulate shape with circle-and-dot ornament, one rivet at one end and a pair at the other.

[12] *P.S.A.* 15, fig. on p. 333; Harden 1956, fig. 25, I, a 1.

[13] Brown 1915, iv, p. 472, pl. x, cxvii, 3; F. H. Thompson, 'Anglo-Saxon sites in Lincolnshire', *Ant. Journ.* xxxvi, 198.

D

terminals was found in grave XXII (Fig. 28, *i*). Grave LXXXVI, with a shield boss, knife, iron buckle and bronze-mounted wooden cup, also had a sword with large glass bead and a pair of bronze strap-slides ornamented with criss-cross scoring in imitation of the trellis-work inlay on the strap-mounts of Oberlörick type. The chape of the sword in grave LXXXVII was of the long U-shape similar to the Bright-hampton mount. Grave XLII contained the top of a Roman bronze key, a bronze ring, amber beads and a short bronze 'nail cleaner' with ring terminal.[1]

At Strood,[2] at the mouth of the Medway in north Kent, a single Anglo-Saxon grave was discovered next to a Roman cemetery (Fig. 14). A high warrior's rank is indicated by the sword with shield boss, spear and knife; his shield-on-tongue buckle and shoe-shaped rivets are of types which were used by the Franks mainly in the sixth century, but some may be dated to the period A.D. 450–525.[3] The bronze mount in repoussé with Christian scenes must have come from a production centre in northern France at the end of the fourth century, as its figure style is less crude than the later school which produced the Long Wittenham stoup, and is much nearer the figure scenes, both pagan and Christian, which appear on late Roman work.[4] The suspension loop at the side also occurs on buckets as early as the late fourth century.[5] It is reasonable to assume that the grave belonged to a Frankish warrior, but the date of deposition could be anywhere between A.D. 450 and 525, although its position as a single post-invasion burial near a Roman cemetery is in favour of a point nearer the earlier date.

On the east bank of the Medway, at Chatham Lines, tumulus XVII contained some very interesting finds. The grave is said to have been a double one, for two women, but as the goods accompanying the woman in tumulus XVIII are of a later date (amongst other things there was a Frankish radiate brooch of the second half of the sixth century)[6] it must be accidental that it was dug so close and parallel to the first. It was tumulus XVII which contained the glass bracelet (p. 22, Fig. 15), together with some dark blue glass disc beads (common in early graves), an iron ring, two bronze bracelets with rivet fastening, two finger rings and a penannular bronze bracelet. The decoration of one bracelet (Fig. 15, *h*, *h*¹), which has a Roman type of rivet fastening, includes an equal-armed cross, possibly Christian, certainly akin to the cruciform chip-carving on the fragmentary belt plate from Howletts which has part of an animal border (Pl. 13, *b*). The penannular armlet (Fig. 15, *c*) has arced stamp decoration, probable animal heads and flat disc terminals with incised scrolls. This is the same type as one found at Chessell Down (Fig. 13, *a*),[7] of which

---

[1] There is no mention of these finds in the report, but according to records at Dartford museum, these were identified from a photograph.

[2] Smith 1852, II, pp. 158–60, pl. XXVI.

[3] Böhner 1958, II, 181–2.

[4] E.g. a box from Vermand, Chenet 1935, fig. 31.

[5] Nenquin 1953, pl. XII, G, 11.

[6] Werner 1961, Taf. 51, S. 56.

[7] R. Walker, *Phoenicia in Freshwater*, 1892, pp. 10–12, pl. IV.

only an early drawing remains. The drawing is in two parts, and the evidence of the Chatham Lines bracelet makes it quite clear that the second drawing is the full-face view of the disc terminal, for in both bracelets the band of the armlet thrusts as a pointed shape into the centre of the disc. This arrangement is also found on late Roman rosette belt mounts, as at Dorchester. A penannular bracelet from Abbeville has similar characteristics—it swells in the middle and at the ends, and although the ends are squared instead of rounded, they also are overrun by the pointed ends of the band. No other bracelet illustrated by Pilloy shows any of these characteristics, but he says that most of the bracelets have this increased girth in the middle.[1] The arc-and-semicircle stamp of the Chatham Lines bracelet is unusual, but it is the stamp used to decorate the animals on the spear mount of the warrior at Vermand, and it recurs on other pieces in the grave (Pl. 1, *a*, *c*, *d*) and on the buckles from Vermand (Fig. 26, *a*, *b*, *d*). This woman, then, was wearing two riveted bracelets of late Roman type, but one of these has decorative connections with the Quoit Brooch Style of the post-invasion period; the penannular bracelet is a type also found in another Saxon cemetery at Chessell Down, its form and decorative stamps connect it with north French products of about A.D. 400, but the incised spirals on it recall the Quoit Brooch Style.[2] The finger rings and glass bracelet point to the Franks. Her belongings must have been made in the first half of the fifth century, and we must conclude that her death is not likely to have occurred much after A.D. 450.

At Dover,[3] grave 22 (Fig. 12, *d–i*) is not richly furnished, but there is enough to indicate a warrior of the later part of the fifth century who possessed a spear and glass from northern Gaul. The grave was superimposed by another, and had been partly destroyed by a mechanized scraper. Nevertheless, only the blade of the spear-head had been disturbed. There was a sword, bronze ring, knife and Kempston type of glass cone beaker. The iron ferrule of the spear with bronze disc attached remained, and of the spearhead the socket only, furrowed with ribbing and inlaid with one strip of bronze.

From Lyminge, a cemetery lately excavated, and not yet fully published, comes evidence of Franks of the fifth century.[4] Grave 32 has a buckle with kidney-shaped plate set with glass in large cloisons, its early date, already vouched for by dated contexts at Lavoye and Haillot (Fig. 7, 4), being here emphasized by the setting of a Roman intaglio stone in the centre. Cloisonné work of the same period occurs in the rectangular plate of the buckle in grave 36 and the purse mount of grave 27 (cf. Childeric's purse mount, Fig. 8, top middle). There is an inlaid iron buckle in grave

---

[1] Pilloy 1880, i, pl. v, 18, p. 261.
[2] See p. 63.
[3] Excavated by the author, on behalf of the Ministry of Works.

[4] A. Warhurst, 'The Jutish cemetery at Lyminge', *Arch. Cant.* LXIX (1955), pp. 1–40.

29. Other early Frankish signs were two axes, one inlaid spear and a glass bottle and claw beaker, and two graves, 3 and 10, contained Quoit Brooch Style animal ornament.

Sussex

Continuing clockwise round the coast we come to Alfriston in Sussex,[1] which, in common with High Down a little further west, possesses a large quantity of early glass and inlaid metalwork. There were also three franciscas and another axe. Some of the most interesting graves for the present purpose are those containing one of the bronze flattened tubes, but the discussion of these will be more profitably followed in connection with the animal-decorated Croydon piece.[2]

Grave 24, which produced the inlaid buckle loop with repoussé silver plate in vine-scroll design, also contained a hammer-axe, a pierced bronze circular hook and a crescent-shaped eye, and an iron object, probably a knife (Fig. 16, *a–d*). The inlaid buckle of grave 20 had a similar repoussé silver plate, a square bronze mount with a chip-carved pelta pattern, and a bronze tang and a knife not now identifiable (Fig. 16, *h, i*). The inlaid buckle of grave 10 (Pl. 6, *d*) was with a knife and glass and metal fittings. Grave 52 contained an inlaid buckle-loop, a knife, a 'metal instrument' and a horned pedestal urn (Fig. 16, *j–l*). The small francisca in grave 39 was with an iron buckle, knife, and tall, glass cone-beaker (Fig. 16, *e–g*). This and grave 24 were furnished with objects which could only have belonged to a Frankish warrior of the second half of the fifth century, and a more elevated rank of the same type is denoted by grave 26; here a francisca was accompanied by other weapons, a spear and a sword with bronze pommel and scabbard strap-slides;[3] there was also a knife and thin bronze plate (Fig. 17, *a–d*).

The most interesting grave is 17 with the bronze buckle plate and counter-plate inlaid with silver animals and glass discs. An early type of bronze strap-end accompanied this, and a triangular openwork bronze mount (Fig. 17, *e–g*). This mount is cut out of a plate which had borne an incised pattern, and recent examination shows that the pattern is sufficiently preserved to permit the reconstruction of one more specimen of the work of the craftsmen responsible for the Quoit Brooch Style (Fig. 17, *e*). Further, a rusted mass from grave A has recently been X-rayed and cleaned, and proves to contain, besides the bronze tongue and plate of a buckle, a duplicate

---

[1] A. F. Griffith and L. F. Salzmann, 'An Anglo-Saxon cemetery at Alfriston, Sussex', *Sussex Arch. Coll.* LVI (1914), pp. 16–151; A. F. Griffith, 'An Anglo-Saxon cemetery at Alfriston, Sussex', *Sussex Arch. Coll.* LVII (1915), pp. 197–208.

[2] See pp. 50–1.

[3] A pair of iron strap-slides (this pair is not inlaid) is usual on Frankish fifth-century swords, but rare in England. The pommel, a straight-sided pyramid on a rectangular base, is an early form without rivet lugs, and with tang aperture.

triangular mount cut from the same original plate (Fig. 17, *i*). Amongst the contents of grave A were an iron buckle with rectangular plate probably covered by an ornamented bronze sheet, an iron purse mount with birds' head terminals, etc. (Fig. 17, *h–r*).

Apart from the specific graves mentioned above, there are a number of other objects at Alfriston of Frankish origin, i.e. purse mounts, buckles, bronze bowl, glass vessels and perhaps some of the other swords. It is quite a fair-sized cemetery of more than 150 graves, but even so, early Frankish elements are present in an unusually large proportion.

At High Down,[1] grave XIV no doubt contained the remains of a fifth-century Frank, for he owned, apart from the common possessions of spear, knife, bronze pin and rivets, a shallow glass bowl with white threads and an inlaid purse mount. From other graves came such distinctive things as a Frankish angon and Roman objects, e.g. a bronze head and a pot of New Forest ware (grave LXXXII).

The Isle of Wight

Chessell Down, a site on the Isle of Wight reputed to have been settled in a secondary movement from Kent, has, in fact, some of the earliest traces in the country of invaders. The bronze bracelet of late Roman form has already been mentioned, and the island also has its share of inlaid iron buckles and early glass. In addition to extant objects of this type, already noted in studies of inlay and glass, there are some preserved only in the form of a record. A kidney-shaped loop and rectangular iron plate are now lost, but the remaining sketches in a manuscript by the excavator, J. Dennett (grave 12) show that the form of the buckle is the type which is usually inlaid. This was found with four knives, a pair of bronze tweezers, a fragment of lead and of bronze (Pl. 7, *a*).[2] Another grave (13) contained the remains of four knives, two mask button brooches, a flat bronze ring and a buckle with oval loop and oval plate (Pl. 7, *b*), a well-known Frankish type occurring at Haillot,[3] graves 8, 13 (Fig. 6, 7), and 17, and with a coin of Zeno (474–491), at Rochefort, grave 46.[4] From Bowcombe Down comes a Roman enamelled hare brooch, and a Quoit Brooch Style bronze (see p. 63, Fig. 28, *a*).

Hampshire and Wiltshire

Crossing to the mainland and going northwards up the Meon valley, we come upon an Anglo-Saxon cemetery at Droxford in Hampshire, which produced, amongst other

---

[1] *Arch.* LIV, 374–5, pl. XXVII 3.

[2] Dennett MS. No. 1 in Carisbrooke Castle Museum.

[3] Breuer and Roosens 1957, figs. 9, 6; 15, 7; 19, 11.

[4] Dasnoy 1955, pl. III and pp. 21–2.

things, Roman coins and a Roman cross-bow brooch, the inlaid buckle published here (Pl. 6, *c*), and as many as six sword-bearing graves.[1]

Harnham Hill[2] also produced early material, including grave 40, containing a spindle whorl, two button brooches, Frankish finger rings, a Roman brooch, knife, beads, comb and strap-end of Romano-Saxon type.[3] The iron buckle with rectangular plate in grave 54 is a fifth-century shape and, judging from the allusion to ornament on it, was possibly inlaid.[4] Many of the graves were poorly furnished or unfurnished.

Before noticing the contents of the cemetery of Petersfinger, Wilts., we must remind ourselves of some of the continental finds. Frankish warriors interred at Oberlörick (grave 5) and Krefeld-Gellep (grave 43) in Germany and at Samson and Éprave in Belgium all possessed swords with scabbards which must have been made in the same workshop, for the bronze band edge to the mouth was ornamented with the same formal leaf pattern at Oberlörick and Krefeld (a pattern occurring also on some buckles with fixed trapezoid plate), and the scabbard tip was fitted with a bronze mount in the form of a human mask between two birds' heads at Krefeld (Pl. 4, *a*, *b*), Samson and Éprave.[5] Of the continental graves, the groups at Samson and Éprave are not known, but at Oberlörick there were two silver-inlaid strap-slides, an inlaid iron buckle and fragment of a spur, a shield boss, tweezers, and bronze ring. Krefeld-Gellep no. 43 was a very well-furnished tomb with claw-beaker, buckle with fixed trapezoid plate, strap-end, tweezers, etc.[6] and with this evidence and that of the technique of the silver-inlaid strap-slides from the scabbard of the Oberlörick sword which are in trellis design akin to that on the loop of the Bifrons buckle, the manufacture of these swords may safely be placed in the second half of the fifth century. The question which immediately arises is whether the English graves containing this type of sword scabbard may be placed in the same period, and with regard to grave XXI at Petersfinger, where the same scabbard mouth edging appears, the associated objects are in full support: a small spearhead, carinated shield boss with extended grip, purse fragments, knife, tweezers and earscoop, iron disc and remains of an iron-bound bucket, an axe and a buckle loop with cloisonné plate (Figs. 18, 19). Most of these are types which were current into the sixth century, but the axe is not likely to occur after A.D. 525, and similar ones were found in graves XIII and XVII at Haillot (Fig. 6, 8).[7] The buckle has a simple iron loop and tongue, and in the cloisonné arrangement on the rectangular plate two rows of rectangles are placed each side of a square containing a disc garnet set in a white diamond-shaped cell. An

---

[1] Brown 1915, IV, 744, *P.S.A.* XIX, 125–9, fig. 5.

[2] Brown 1915, IV, 619; *Arch.* XXXV, 259 and 475.

[3] *Ibid.*, pl. XI, 8 and 9, pl. XII, 3, 4, 8 and 19.

[4] *Ibid.*, pl. X, 8; p. 277: 'The broad waist buckle found with skeleton no. 54. It appears to have been originally covered with some ornament, which has

perished.' This remark may, however, have been prompted by the textile remains which still cover the surface.

[5] Böhner 1951; Werner 1953a and 1956.

[6] Steeger 1937b.

[7] Breuer and Roosens 1957, fig. 15, 8 and 19, 12.

almost identical disposition of the cells is to be seen on the plate of the buckle from Kertsch, southern Russia.[1] A buckle of such simplicity, without a rectangular base to the tongue, must be early in the series. Apart from the Childeric grave, there is no lack of other dated contexts for this type of cloisonné work, e.g. Lavoye grave 319 which contained, as well as a copy of a coin of Zeno (474–491) a glass bowl, gold-hilted sword, and bronze-covered ewer with Christian pictures.[2] The sword, axe and buckle in Petersfinger grave XXI are all Frankish of the last half of the fifth century, and since the group is a harmonious assembly, the owner buried there must have been a Frankish leader of that date.

Other recognizably early objects in this cemetery do not belong to graves where the furnishings are so full or so distinctive, but they are most likely to indicate con-temporaneity, e.g. the square-looped buckle in grave LXIIIa with its plate so near to the inlaid plate at Croydon.[3] In the same grave was a second skeleton accom-panied by an inlaid iron buckle loop,[4] no doubt completing a double grave of the fifth century (lying S–N at the edge of the cemetery). The inlaid iron buckle of grave XXIX with a pair of bases of applied brooches,[5] bronze pin and beads, bronze wire bracelet, finger ring, knife, iron ring and fragments; the buckle with heart-shaped plate in grave XXXIII with knife and spear; the bronze belt-slide in grave XLVIII with a Roman Aesica brooch, ivory purse ring, iron fragments and amber beads, are all of the fifth century. Three of these graves were lying W–E on the south-western edge of the cemetery, while grave LXIII was S–N on the eastern out-skirts. This suggests that the cemetery was begun in the south-western part, although some graves may have been lost at the edge of the chalk pit.

An excavation in 1960 at Winterbourne Gunner[6] near Salisbury disclosed still another early cemetery in this part of the country, and there, too, was a grave which preserved the remains of a fifth-century Frankish warrior (Fig. 20). Again there is the inlaid buckle loop with oblong plate, a bronze strap-end with animal decoration, tweezers, iron fragments and a francisca of the type ascribed to the period A.D. 450–525 (cf. Fig. 5, 17).[7] Such an assemblage can only be the personal possessions brought by the man from Belgium or northern France, and the animal style points to the earlier part of the fifth century (see p. 60).

Continuing in a northerly direction we come upon the valley of the Kennet, where a cemetery at Bassett Down, Wilts., provides material mostly of an early date, e.g. shield bosses with concave sides to the dome, star-decorated saucer brooches, and in particular a semicircular-headed bow brooch and a spoon of the type current in the

[1] Breuer and Roosens 1957, pl. IX, 1.
[2] Chenet 1935.
[3] Evison 1958, pl. XXVI, c and d.
[4] Evison 1955, p. 40, item 31.
[5] Cf. Krefeld-Gellep grave 1076, Pirling 1959, p. 227, Abb. 14.
[6] J. Musty, *Wilts. Arch. Mag.* (1964) (forthcoming).
[7] Böhner 1958, pp. 166–7.

late fourth to early fifth century with an animal head between the shaft and the bowl.[1]

At West Overton, Wilts.,[2] some prehistoric barrows very recently excavated have produced four Saxon graves and evidence of further disturbed graves. Two of them probably belong to the sixth century, but a woman's grave, Skeleton IV, most likely belongs to the fifth century (Fig. 21). It contained a Roman bronze key and iron keys, knife, iron buckle, bronze strap fragments and a bronze penannular brooch with iron pin, one blue glass bead and ten amber, and on this necklace was also a small bronze ring and a semi-sphere of bronze perforated. The brooch has returned and flattened terminals, notched in a way suggesting a degenerate animal head, and is a type found on late Roman sites, e.g. Richborough.[3] The Roman key, the perforated bronze and blue glass bead are all early signs. A loose find in the barrow complex was the triangular lug of a bronze cauldron of the type manufactured in the Meuse valley.

The upper Thames

Returning once more to the upper Thames valley, another Frankish warrior with a Krefeld-Oberlörick sword was buried at Abingdon[4] in grave B42 (Fig. 22). The scabbard mouth fitting is the same type as that at Petersfinger, and the human mask with birds' heads chape matches the continental ones (cf. Pl. 4, b). A ring-strap distributor and four bronze studs were also attached to the scabbard, and there was a knife, an iron buckle with bronze plate, a second iron buckle and a flint, and a long, curved strip of bone with perforations. This last does not appear to have been part of a comb, and may be the remains of a musical instrument such as a lyre. The later graves of Taplow and Sutton Hoo show that it is in a chieftain's grave that we may expect to find a musical instrument. The ring-strap distributor held three bronze tabs, doubled over the ring, and with disc ends, the top ones wider than the lower, which were riveted on to straps. One tab of exactly this shape was amongst the scabbard fittings found with the early fifth-century hoard of coins at Wiesbaden-Kastel.[5] Another grave, no. 49, also contained a sword, and although it has no bronze mounts, its iron fittings and chape seem to be very similar to those of grave 42. There were with it a large bead and a spearhead and ferrule. These two graves contained the only

---

[1] *Wilts. Arch. Mag.* XXVIII, 104–8; XXXVIII, 282. XLVI, 155; Brown III, p. 254, IV, p. 407, 655–6 and pl. CLV, 12 and 14; *Devizes Museum Catalogue*, II (1934), pp. 243–7, fig. 36 and pls. LXXXIII, LXXXIV. The animal head on the spoon is clearer than appears in the drawing, pl. LXXXIV.

[2] Excavated by Miss Isobel Smith, and published by her kind permission.

[3] Bushe-Fox 1926, pl. XVI, 8. It appears to be similar to the type H 3 of Fowler 1960.

[4] Leeds and Harden 1936, pp. 38–9, pls. IX b, c, d, XIX.

[5] H. Schoppa, 'Ein spätrömischer Schatzfund aus Wiesbaden-Kastel', *Fundberichte aus Hessen*, 2 (1962), 164, Abb. 2, 4.

swords in the cemetery; they were near to each other and lying W–E in the same row. The accompanying objects are not so distinctive as at Petersfinger and could have an origin on either side of the Channel. There is no doubt that the cemetery started in the fifth century, for apart from these swords there is the important find of the fourth-century tutulus brooch in grave 106. Its accompanying objects suggest that this can have been no more than a generation old when buried, and both this and the spiral-decorated applied brooch with it must have come from the continent. The tutulus brooch is found between the Seine and the Elbe,[1] but the finger-rings also found in grave 106 suggest Frankish land as the immediate source.

Essex

North of the Thames, a man with the possessions of an early Frank was buried in grave 115 at Great Chesterford, Essex, and in the digging of this an earlier woman's grave, with a pair of small square-headed brooches, beads and bone pin, was disturbed. The man had an angular spearhead with bone ferrule, knife, small whetstone, iron purse mount, small bronze and silver strap-end, and the iron buckle with kidney-shaped loop and rectangular plate inlaid with circle and star motifs.[2]

Discussion

Some of the more recently excavated cemeteries have been omitted from the survey, e.g. Portsdown, Hants. and Winnal near Winchester, since they are exclusively late. Alton, Hants. was probably begun before A.D. 500, but has yielded nothing clearly Frankish of the fifth century. Like a new excavation at Worthy Park, Hants., it is important for revealing the use of cremation to a considerable extent in this area between the upper Thames and the south coast, an area previously regarded as thinly populated in the early period and devoted to inhumation as a burial rite.

The study of individual graves, therefore, has produced more information to be added to that already garnered from a review of the distribution of fifth-century Frankish objects in England. That review has already suggested that some of the Germanic members of the Roman army in Britain may have returned to this country with the first wave of invaders in the south, that a considerable amount of material manufactured in northern Gaul was imported to the south of England, and that with this material were imported less tangible things such as knowledge of art motifs and techniques. It must now be considered whether the evidence of individual graves supports the proposition that there was an actual migration of Franks to the south of England in the fifth century.

[1] Werner 1950, Karte 6.   [2] Evison 1955, pl. III, g.

The orientation of the bodies varies, but of mainly W–E direction are the cemeteries of Mitcham, Lyminge, Harnham Hill, Alfriston,[1] High Down and Dover. Cemeteries where the graves are partly W–E and partly S–N are: Petersfinger, Winterbourne Gunner, Abingdon and Riseley (Abingdon is partly a cremation cemetery, and Riseley has a few cremations, one of them in a Roman pot). The four graves at West Overton were: two S–N, one E–W, one SSW–NNE. Chessell Down was unusual in being mainly NE–SW with four SW–NE and six W–E or E–W (which end the head was at is not clear). At Long Wittenham the heads were W or SW, with a few NW or S, and one child N. Brighthampton, too, varies between W and SW, with a few in every other direction. Chatham Lines stands apart, for of the thirteen graves, six were recorded as N–S and two S–N.

Of the graves discussed in detail above, Brighthampton grave 31 was placed with head NNW, i.e. it may be regarded as a N–S grave. This direction is unusual at Brighthampton and rather rare in England, but it was the one used at Haillot and Furfooz in the Namur region. Surprisingly enough, this was also the most usual direction at Chatham Lines where, although some of the burials may be dated late in the sixth century, there were no W–E graves.

Besides the similarity in orientation, Brighthampton, grave 31 and Chatham Lines, tumulus XVII are alike in being amongst the very earliest of the post-invasion graves; they can hardly be dated later than the middle of the fifth century and are possibly even earlier. Another warrior's grave of the same date is Winterbourne Gunner VI, where there was no sword, but the francisca and inlaid buckle are of Frankish origin; animal ornament on the strap-end indicates a date in the first half of the century. The Petersfinger and Abingdon swords are undoubtedly products of the second half of the fifth century, a date confirmed by the associations of the Petersfinger sword. The Strood warrior could be as late as the sixth century, but the bronze-covered vessel with it of about A.D. 400 and the position of the grave alone by a Roman cemetery suggest that the fifth century is more likely. The Long Wittenham boy's grave with cauldron and stoup is exclusively Frankish and of the fifth century. Most of these graves would not have appeared in any way incongruous had they been located among fifth-century graves in northern France or Belgium.

It is perhaps surprising that Frankish pottery (except for a bowl at Chessell Down and a bottle at Howletts) is absent, and where pottery is present it is Anglo-Saxon, e.g. the horned pot in Alfriston grave 52, the bowl in Long Wittenham grave 57 and the pedestal pot in Reading grave 13. The reason for this may be that pottery brought by the invaders would be in constant use and broken sooner than metal possessions. As Frankish pottery was wheel-turned and produced by commercial kilns in the

---

[1] Except six S–N, one N–S and three NE–SW or vice versa.

Rhineland or northern Gaul, there would be no replacements to hand. Pottery in Anglo-Saxon England was all made by hand until the middle of the seventh century. By then trade was bringing in continental Frankish pots to Kent, but while it would not have been impossible for a kiln to be established in that county, there is as yet no evidence for this, and the comparatively small number of wheel-turned pots in existence, and their similarity to continental types, suggest importation rather than native manufacture. In the fifth century, then, replacements of domestic ware would have been supplied by Saxons working in the simple hand-made tradition, and it is worth noting the appearance of the odd Germanic type of pot already at Furfooz.[1]

The traces of Christianity are also important, for the power of the bishops in northern Gaul did not wane, in spite of the incursions of pagans,[2] and the manufacture of various articles such as glass bowls with Christian symbols[3] and the repoussé metalwork with Christian scenes continued. The Franks were therefore able to acquire the material trimmings of Christianity, even if the spiritual values were lost on them. It is this connection with Christianity that presents us with the most striking evidence regarding their origin. The fact that the method of burial in this area of England is predominantly inhumation in the W–E direction shows clearly that many of the invaders must have come from that part of Europe where this custom was in force, and certainly not from the coastal areas north of the Rhine mouth where cremation was the main rite with some admixture of S–N inhumation. These were the people who crowded into the rest of England via the Wash, and the eastern coasts of East Anglia. It has been supposed that W–E orientation in the south of England was caused by connections arising in the sixth century from geographical proximity to the Franks on the continent, but as some of the graves are of fifth-century date it must be realized that the custom was founded early and by migrants.

Cremation also occurs sporadically throughout the south, many of the pots being certainly quite as early as the inhumations, and this confirms the mixed nature of the invading bands. An indication of the beginning of the mixture is given at Furfooz, where a cremation in a Roman pot was carefully placed amongst the fourth-century burials in the hypocaust of the bath. Also, there are graves throughout the area with belongings such as early saucer brooches which would be at home in Saxon areas on the continent. Amongst the fifth-century goods in all these regions there seems to be nothing one may regard as specifically Jutish, unless it is the early type of cruciform brooch which also appears in other parts of the country, but south of the Thames only in Kent. Other direct Jutish connections, such as bracteates and square-headed

[1] Nenquin 1953, fig. 10, A, 48.
[2] J. M. Wallace-Hadrill, *The Long-haired Kings* (1962), p. 166.
[3] Breuer and Roosens 1957, pp. 307–11, fig. 28.

brooches, do not begin until a little later, in the sixth century, and represent a secondary wave of immigrants. The amount of fifth-century Frankish material in this area is remarkable, but amongst the sites Alfriston stands out as the place where most material exists and where there are most graves of individuals whose possessions were entirely Frankish. More far-flung sites such as Great Chesterford in Essex and Bidford-on-Avon in Warwickshire, where the same kinds of objects have been found, may show traces of the same people who elected either to penetrate further into the country or to follow a different route.

These facts show that parts of Kent, Sussex, the Isle of Wight, Surrey and the upper Thames were invaded in the middle of the fifth century, and that some of the settlers possessed the same types of worldly goods as were owned and produced by Franks living between the Meuse and Seine. There is also evidence of the continuance and development of a Frankish metal-working tradition. Graves of Saxon type, and occasional intrusion of elements of this and other tribes into Frankish type graves, show a mixture of peoples. If one attempted to relate these facts to the Chronicle story, one would have to assume that a tribe of Jutes (who, we are told, invaded Kent, the Isle of Wight and the mainland opposite) and a tribe of Saxons (who invaded Sussex and Wessex) had been living with the Franks on the continent for at least a generation, so that they had become materially indistinguishable from the Franks and from each other, although they remembered their own tribal traditions. There is no evidence for this. The simpler and more obvious explanation is that the invaders were actually Franks who had come from northern Gaul.

The Franks are a people who were not mentioned at all in the records of the invasion in the Chronicle, or by Bede, but the archaeological traces of them in the south of England have long been recognized for the sixth century, and their entry may now be pushed back to the fifth century. Nor does the Chronicle allow of any Germanic settlement of the Isle of Wight or penetration northwards from Southampton before A.D. 495 whereas the archaeological evidence shows invasion beginning in the middle of the century. We may remember that the historical records are scanty, and no doubt many facts of equal importance have been omitted.

So far we have been studying the customs and possessions of the invading Germanic people but there is one more avenue to explore. Throughout the first millennium A.D., Germanic craftsmen were fascinated by the use of animal design for ornamentation. In this sphere they adopted and developed motifs and techniques, going indefatigably from one treatment to another with unflagging inspiration and invention, touching in the process such high peaks of accomplishment as the carpet pages of the Lindisfarne Gospels. It is these gradual and subtle changes in art forms which often give the student a firm indication of the sources of inspiration available to the craftsman, and lead to a method of dating.

This vital source of information has so far been left untapped, for it is much more complicated than the other evidence adduced. It is indeed fortunate that the style of animal ornament in vogue in the south of England at this time is not only an attractive one, but is particularly distinctive, and since the interpretation of the evidence given here diverges radically from previous theories, it will be set out in full.

V

The Quoit Brooch Style

Theories of origin

THE most important and distinctive group of objects of the half century preceding A.D. 500 are those with an unusual animal style which has been discussed by Leeds,[1] and attributed by him to Romano-Britons working just before the
invasion. In his study he brought forward Gallo-Roman comparisons for the animals.
The subject of this style was reopened in 1958 by E. Bakka,[2] who suggested the name
Quoit Brooch Style because of its use on these comparatively rare brooches, and
regarded it as originating in south-east England under the hands of the Anglo-
Saxons. In 1961, S. Hawkes, convinced that the craftsmen were Jutes, suggested the
term 'Jutish Style A'.[3] This has the drawback of presuming to define nationality in
a period of migrations when many tribes were broken up and amalgamated with
others, and the term Quoit Brooch Style is preferred here. It is generally agreed that
the style, because of the way in which it fits in as a stage in the long development of
animal style from Romano-Germanic beginnings must be of Germanic origin, and
that there are no grounds at all for Leeds' attribution to Romano-Britons. His attention to affinities with 'Gallo-Roman' bronzes, however, is a different matter, and an
attempt will be made here to show that, although Leeds did not have the benefit
of the results of recent wide research, his usual perspicacity brought him near to the
truth.

S. Hawkes' summary (p. 71) shows her thesis to be that this style was the work
of Germanic craftsmen with south Scandinavian traditions who were working in
Kent, in the region of Canterbury, in the late fifth to early sixth centuries. She labels
it 'Jutish Style A', although the nearest examples in time of a possible antecedent
animal style in Jutish lands date to the third century A.D., and the only other com-
parative style is to be found in Norway of the fifth century. This is the first time that
a case for the style has been presented at such length, and it merits close examination.

At the outset, consideration must be given to some weak points in the argument

---

[1] Leeds 1936, pp. 3–7.   [2] Bakka 1959, pp. 9–14.   [3] Hawkes 1961.

which immediately spring to the fore. First, if the craftsman was a Jute, one would expect him to use this type of ornament on the jewellery forms already familiar to him, the square-headed brooch being the most obvious candidate as it is undoubtedly of Scandinavian origin and later became widely used in England. Secondly, the preponderance of late Roman, rather than Germanic techniques is of paramount importance, and has not been accorded the full weight it demands. Thirdly, it was not noted that the artist's eye is pleased by arrangements sufficiently classical in style to show that he is not obsessed by the barbarian's ingrained *horror vacui*. Fourthly, important points ignored are the excellent rhythm of outline of the creatures, and the flat treatment given to them, which differs radically from preceding and ensuing styles. It must also be kept in mind that this work was produced for a short period only, in a limited field, and seems to have died out without having any appreciable effect on any style that came afterwards.

The form of the objects on which this type of ornament is to be found is the first and most important point to be considered. The brooch form which we can be certain was well known to Jutish craftsmen is the square-headed brooch, for it is of Scandinavian origin; there are a few Scandinavian brooches of this period adorned with a closely related animal style, and the form continued in production after the settlement in England. However, no square-head in this country is so decorated. Moreover, none of the objects bearing this style can be of Jutish origin. A possible exception appears to offer itself in the quoit brooches themselves, but it will be seen that this may be dismissed.

The form of English quoit brooches is the result of the amalgamation of two different types of earlier ring brooches, the penannular and the annular. The former has usually been quoted as the source, and as this type was in use in Roman Britain, Leeds used this point as evidence for Romano-British manufacture. The penannular brooch is a narrow band or ring of metal, often wire-like or round in section, which is interrupted at one point where the ends are rolled back, leaving a space for the pin to pass. On some brooches the rolled-back ends stand above the plane of the ring (they are often ornamented, perhaps as animal heads), and are functional as pin-stops. The inner ring of the Sarre brooch (Pl. 12, *c*) on which the pin slides is, in fact, a penannular brooch affixed to an ornamental surround, and the same arrangement is visible on the fragmentary Howletts brooch (Pl. 10, *c*). The inner part of the Alfriston brooch is an incomplete penannular brooch (Pl. 15, *a*). The form of a penannular brooch occurs frequently on Romano-British sites from the second century A.D.; simple in shape, it changes little, but by the late fourth or early fifth century the terminals sometimes become zoomorphic,[1] a trait interpreted as being caused by

---

[1] Studies on this subject are: Kilbride-Jones 1937, Leeds 1945, Savory 1956, Fowler 1960.

contact with Germanic taste. The form, however, is not unknown on the continent, it occurs e.g. at Westerwanna,[1] and Abbeville, Aisne (a fourth-century grave),[2] and Monceau-le-Neuf.[3]

The penannular aspect of the English brooches is the least important, for the outer or main part consists of a broad, flat band which bears decoration, and is interrupted only by a short slot in the inner circumference for the passage of the pin. Even where the form is actually penannular, e.g. Lyminge, Alfriston and Riseley, the flat decorated band of such a width is not something which could have been inspired by the wire-like Romano-British penannular brooches. There are other types of ring brooch which were in use on the continent and Scandinavia from the third to fifth centuries A.D., and which must provide an immediate source.

Many of the Anglo-Saxon brooches are in the form of a flat band, with a pin-slot and decorated with circle-and-dot punch marks, e.g. Holywell Row, Suffolk, grave 45,[4] Mitcham, Surrey, graves 116 and 229,[5] and this form of decoration also occurs on the Riseley penannular brooch. A brooch of exactly this annular form and decoration was found in a grave at Steine, Bö, in northern Norway, with a fourth-century bow fibula, comb, etc.[6] Another annular brooch, but without pin-slot, was found at Skogöya, Steigen,[7] with a sixth-century cruciform brooch. Further south, a pair of flat, annular brooches without slot accompanied some beads and two early migration-period cruciform brooches (and the knob of a third) in a grave at Tude Mark, Ribe, Jutland,[8] and another annular brooch was found in a late fourth-century grave, again in Jutland, at Fannerup, Randers, with a Nydam fibula, two bronze plate brooches, two needles, beads and pendant.[9]

In Scandinavia a variant of the ring brooch, which began at the end of the Roman period, is known as a key-ring.[10] for it is sometimes found with keys attached. It has a pin like the annular brooch, but also a projecting tab attachment to the ring for suspension. This is the form of the ring from Hol, Norway, with animal decoration.[11]

On the continent, another type of ring brooch, fairly rare and found first in Germanic territory at the beginning of the fourth century,[12] also has an extension to the ring, but its purpose is decorative rather than functional; this type has a pin-slot and pin-stops at a point where the ring is flattened and spread out into a spatulate shape. A later version of this as a narrow circular band (one has circle-and-dot decoration),

[1] Plettke 1921, pl. 14, 15.

[2] Pilloy 1880, I, pl. V, 9.

[3] Pilloy 1912, III, pl. VII, 12.

[4] T. C. Lethbridge, *Recent excavations in Anglo-Saxon cemeteries in Cambridgeshire and Suffolk* (1931), fig. 11, E.

[5] Bidder and Morris 1959, pl. XII.

[6] Sjövold 1962, pl. 23, p. 154.

[7] *Idem*, pl. 7.

[8] Åberg 1956, p. 175.

[9] Åberg, p. 172, Randers Museum 3577–96.

[10] Sjövold 1962, pls. 9f, 22c, 28c, 32c, 39a–c.

[11] Hougen 1936, fig. 13.

[12] J. Werner, 'Ein frühalamannischer Grabfund von Böckingen, Württemberg', *Germania* 1938, pp. 114–17, Abb. 1. 4.

with pin-slot and stops, has the area outside the slot extended into animal heads. All these features are to be found on the English quoit brooches. Three of these brooches have been found in Frisia, two of them coming from Ezinge; their dating to the late fourth or early fifth century is assured by the similarity of the style of projecting animal-head decoration to that on the late Roman bronze strap-ends, etc. and the Saxon equal-armed brooches. Some are endowed with bull-like horns, and as this is not a late Roman trait, it is concluded that these brooches are of local manufacture.[1] The additional trait of longitudinal grooves on the griffons' necks at Ezinge recurs on other objects to be discussed, including the brooch of the same type kept in the museum at Laon in northern France (Fig. 23, a).

Surprisingly enough, however, it seems to have escaped notice that the exact structure of the Sarre quoit brooch and an extraordinarily close relation to the form of the Alfriston penannular brooch were already in use in late Roman workshops producing openwork bronzes. An annular brooch from Enns, Austria (Pl. 8, a)[2] has a decorative outer border of openwork pelta shapes, each of which is attached to a plain inner penannular ring, with the exception of three peltas opposite the opening in the ring. This part of the ring must have been left free to give space for the base of the pin to slide. Another brooch, from Linz, Austria[3] (Pl. 8, b), has an outer openwork border of alternating spirals fixed to a plain inner ring at three-quarter points. This ring is recessed at the fourth point for the passage of the pin, and the loop by which the pin was fixed to the inner ring is still in situ. These are certainly the immediate forerunners of the English quoit brooches, and the Alfriston brooch retains both the openwork border and the spiral pattern.

The fine English quoit brooches, then, from Sarre, Howletts and Alfriston owe their intricate construction directly to a Roman workshop. The penannular brooch from Riseley, Horton Kirby (Fig. 28, i), also shows connection with the family of broad-band annular brooches with ring-and-dot ornament found in Denmark and France. These forms and methods must have been in use in the bronze workshops of northern Gaul, whence they spread to England and the north.[4]

No other form of object bearing Quoit Brooch Style has connections with the Jutes. Late Roman forms may be recognized in the large disc brooches with a central stone en cabochon, i.e. Faversham and Higham (Pls. 10, a; 15, b). An amber glass cabochon appears on the plate of the buckle from High Down (Pl. 14, d) and cabochon

[1] A. Roes, 'A travers les collections archéologiques de la Hollande', Berichten van de Rijksdienst voor het Oudheidkundig Bodemonderzoek in Nederland, IV, 28–30, figs. 4 and 8; Germania 1936, Beilage 3, fig. 1, 232; P. C. J. A. Boeles, Friesland tot de elfde eeuw (1951), figs. 59, 2; 79, 232, pl. XLVI, 5.

[2] Reigl 1927, pl. XV, 6; Oberösterreiches Landesmuseum, Linz, no. B. 242.

[3] Ibid., pl. XV, 7; Oberösterreiches Landesmuseum, Linz, no. B. 636.

[4] Cf., for example, an annular brooch consisting of six openwork birds' heads in Copenhagen museum, no. C. 2935.

E

stones form the centre piece of the pendants from Bifrons (Pl. 12, *a*). The use of cabochon stones was ignored by the Anglo-Saxons for the next century until the Ribbon Style had been in vogue for some time. Round or oval brooches with a raised glass paste centre are fairly common on sites in use at the end of the Roman period, and also occur in early Saxon graves,[1] so that they were being worn just before and just after the beginning of the invasion.

The square plaque from Bishopstone, the plaque from Howletts re-used as a brooch, and the strap-slide from High Down cannot be exactly paralleled, but are in general the type of metal fixtures used to stiffen and secure attachments to the wide leather belt of the Germanic soldier in the Roman army.

So far our search for the origin of these objects has drawn attention to Germanic people in close contact with Roman culture, and some of the other objects recently considered to belong to this group are even more informative. Standing out amongst these is the francisca from Howletts which must have been the weapon of a Frankish warrior. The drawing given of this in *Antiquaries Journal*, IV, 276 cannot be a true representation of its shape, and the present whereabouts of the ornamented plate is unknown.[2] Amongst the material from Howletts in the British Museum[3] there is a francisca, the shape of which might possibly be equated to this illustration, but investigations made since accession have not been able to elucidate this point (Fig. 27, *l*, Pl. 6, *b*).

The animal mounts from Bidford-on-Avon (Fig. 24, *f–j*) were fitted on a bucket which has bronze bands with arcading and dots in repoussé after the fashion of the Frankish buckets of the late fifth century.[4] This bucket must have been produced in the same centre, and is closely connected with others in England of the same type (Map 8).

The Bifrons strap-end (Pl. 11, *a*) is a type met with in Germanic graves in Belgium and Germany of the late fifth century;[5] the type usually consists of two plates, rounded at one end, and squared at the other, with two rivets at the squared end and sometimes one at the tip. Similarly, the Bifrons pendants (Pl. 12, *a*) recall earrings in a grave at St Quentin of the late fourth century.[6]

The unique mount from Croydon (Pl. 13, *a*) is for a belt, to allow a strap to join it at right angles, other movable straps to take off from the rings, and for a knife sheath or similar equipment to be suspended from the hinge in the middle. Although unique as it stands, it is composed of four tubular elements which occur singly elsewhere,

---

[1] See Chapter III, p. 28.

[2] Reproduced by Hawkes 1961, p. 38, fig. 4, with the scale stated as 1/1 and 2/1. None is given in *Ant. Journ.* IV, but presumably the axe is meant to be about 1/2 and the plate 1/1.

[3] Evison 1955, page 37, no. 11; B.M. Reg. No. 1938 10–6 1.

[4] See Chapter III, pp. 22–3.

[5] Breuer and Roosens 1957, fig. 4, 7; Figs. 5, 13 and 17, *g*.

[6] Eck 1891, pl. 1, 23.

some without known associations, e.g. Droxford, Hants.,[1] Bifrons, Kent, Barrington, Cambs., East Shefford, Berks., Orange Terrace, Rochester, Horton Kirby and Willsborough, near Ashford, Kent. At High Down, grave XXIX, there were also two iron buckles with square plates—probably inlaid,[2] and a knife. At Petersfinger, grave XLVIII, a large tube was with an Aesica brooch, ivory ring, beads, and iron fragments. Reading, grave 13, is an early grave with, amongst other things, a pedestal pot, zoomorphic buckle and Haillot type of strap-end. At Barrington in Cambridgeshire there were beads, a perforated silver coin, tinned bronze fibula, ivory ring and iron buckle. At Chatham Lines in Kent, sixteen bronze tubes were found together, some containing traces of leather inside; with them were various bronze rings and fittings, beads, knife, a small radiate brooch and a pair of small square-headed brooches. Grave XCVII at Riseley, near Horton Kirby, Kent, contained a bronze tube of half length. With it was an applied brooch with heart-shaped motifs and egg-and-dart border, a pair of saucer brooches with whirligig leg ornament and egg-and-dart border, also a knife, bronze buckle, small bronze loop and one amber bead. A number occurred at Alfriston. In grave 91 there was also a small francisca, a horse's bit, inlaid purse mount, etc. (Fig. 23, b–e). Grave 103 had beads, an iron buckle, an iron(?) punch, and an openwork bronze mount of Roman type but with animal heads (Fig. 23, f–h). Grave 14 had a Roman coin, disc brooch, knife, spear, iron ring and iron rim, and also the zoomorphic buckle with fixed plate of fifth-century type already mentioned (Fig. 24, a–e, p. 27). Two points from this list are striking (list, p. 99, Map 10): firstly that the distribution is very similar to the distribution of Frankish objects mapped in Chapter III, and, secondly, the accompanying objects at Alfriston (3 graves), Chatham Lines and Reading include recognizable Frankish fifth-century imports. The Chatham Lines grave belongs to the early sixth century, but the Petersfinger grave contained a Roman brooch. I do not know of any of these bronze tubes on the continent, but if they are not Frankish, they are certainly very closely associated with the early invaders from that direction.

The flat U-shaped chape to the scabbard of the Brighthampton sword (Fig. 11, a, c) is a development of a type which began early among the Germanic peoples, and occurs, for instance, on one of the Snartemo swords.[3] The type also makes its appearance in the grave of a Germanic warrior at Kostheim.[4] Of the two buckles bearing Quoit Brooch Style, the unusual rectangular loop of the High Down buckle (Pl. 14, d) is the form often adopted by the Frankish buckles carried out in large-cloison technique of the fifth century (Fig. 7, 4).[5] The heart-shaped plate belonging to it is also a fifth-century type and the cabochon is in glass of the amber colour most usual in

---

[1] This has a loop attached to one side.
[2] *Arch.* LIV, 377–8; Evison 1955, p. 39.
[3] B. Hougen, *Snartemo Funnene* (1935), pl. IV, 9.

[4] Werner 1959, Abb. 20.
[5] E.g. Breuer and Roosens 1957, pl. IX, 2.

the migration period. The Alfriston bronze buckle (Pl. 14, *c*) falls closely into line with the series of inlaid iron buckles from the Meuse area, with its kidney-shaped, fluted loop and oblong plate divided into three longitudinal panels. Consideration of the forms alone, then, shows that practically all of them are known, and some of them exclusively, in Frankish graves of northern Gaul at the beginning of the fifth century.

The second point which has not received sufficient consideration is the great preponderance of jewellery techniques which were commonly used by craftsmen in the Roman empire but which were not in the normal repertoire of the Germanic workers. Gilding was of course used by both, and even parcel-gilding to some extent, but not in the way it is used here. It became routine for a Germanic craftsman to gild the whole of a chip-carved surface, leaving only a border in reserved silver to provide a background for niello inlay. Parcel gilding as it is used here was unknown, i.e. in zones on the quoit brooches, and to pick out animals against a background as on the Brighthampton sword chape, or parts of the birds on the Sarre brooch. It was only on imported Byzantine pieces such as the ladle with gilded triangles in the Sutton Hoo ship burial that the heathen Anglo-Saxons ever saw this technique. Other techniques such as the milling of borders do not appear in pagan Saxon work. The use of bird figures in the round is certainly Roman, appearing as part or whole of a brooch,[1] and as a pin-head in the Germanic grave 85 at Abbeville.[2] The chip-carving on the Howletts belt plate no. 14 (Pl. 13, *b*) has been referred to the Nydam style, but the main characteristic of the Nydam chip-carving is its extraordinary depth. The Howletts plate is thin and the chip-carving shallow—much more like the shallow chip-carving of the late Roman period on the Snodland buckle, for example, or more nearly for pattern, a plate illustrated by Riegl.[3] It is also more satisfactory to regard the polished excellence of craftsmanship evident in the Sarre brooch, and for which there is no precedent in Scandinavia, as the outcome of direct association with a workshop producing late Roman silver vessels.

The third point to be noticed is that the artists' conception of design, on the complete Howletts brooch, the Sarre, Higham and Faversham brooches and the Bishopstone and Howletts plaques[4] is far nearer classical ideals than the Germanic craftsman ever attempted to get. Instead of all-over designs filling every nook and cranny, the decorated surfaces are limited to bands, separated by zones severely plain. Not only is this reminiscent of the products of Roman craftsmen, but it recalls in particular the decoration of bowls, dishes and platters, e.g. from Mildenhall,[5] and the maker was surely influenced by this sort of work. A detail to be noted is that the

---

[1] E.g. from Naix, Liénard 1881–5, pl. xxix, 3 and 4; and Verdun, pl. xxxiii, 3.

[2] Roosens 1962, pl. ix, 6.

[3] Riegl 1927, Taf. xxii, 2.

[4] The Howletts plaque was omitted from Hawkes 1961 list of objects connected with this style.

[5] J. Brailsford, *The Mildenhall Treasure* (1958), pl. 3a, pl. 4, p. 17, b.

scrolls used on the Alfriston penannular and High Down square quoit brooch are near to classical originals by reason of the tendrils which were usually omitted by the more geometrically-minded Germanic people (cf. Pls. 15, *a*; 16, *a–c* and Fig. 11, *b*).

Amongst the elements of the Quoit Brooch Style are schematized human masks which sometimes appear at intervals between the animals, e.g. the two Howletts brooches and the penannular from Alfriston. From these we may turn our eyes to the Mildenhall treasure which is a scatter of plate produced in late Roman workshops of different countries, some coming from the east, and some from Rome, e.g. the Neptune dish.[1] The cover of the flanged bowl[2] has a border of profile Bacchic heads spaced at intervals, eight centaurs fighting beasts in between. On four other bowls the flange has four equally-spaced profile heads with hunting scenes between.[3] A late fourth-century date is assured for these by general affinities of the Mildenhall treasure with the coin-dated find from Traprain,[4] and by detailed comparison with the Hercules bowl at Traprain with its border of profile masks and hunting animals. Two similar bowls in the British Museum come from the Hill of St. Louis, Carthage,[5] but an indication of the location of the workshops producing this silverware, and which is generally accepted, is given by the lanx from Riseley Park.[6] This lost, but well-recorded plate bore an inscription showing that it was presented by a bishop of Bayeux to his own church, and it may well have been made near the church where it was kept. The centre of production of silverware with borders of animals and masks is therefore in all probability to be placed in northern Gaul in the late fourth century.

Regarding the fourth point, the flat treatment of the animals in this style (with the exception of the Bidford bucket, the reason for which will be discussed later) is completely strange to the perpetual striving for three dimensions which may be witnessed in works of the Germanic craftsmen. The animals of earlier periods are carried out in three dimensions, either in repoussé[7] or in chip-carving or moulded relief, and later developments in England are in the chip-carving relief of Style I or the relief or filigree-crested repoussé of Style II. This flatness may have been inspired also by late Roman silver plate, but it is bound up with the next point to be considered.

This is the style of the animals themselves. They have been called naturalistic by

[1] J. M. C. Toynbee, *Art in Roman Britain* (1962), pl. 117, p. 170.

[2] J. Brailsford, *op. cit.*, pl. 2, b.

[3] T. Dohrn, 'Spätantikes Silber aus Britannien', *Mitteilungen des Deutchen Archaeologischen Instituts*, II (1949), pp. 67–139, Taf. 18, 19.

[4] A. O. Curle, *The Treasure of Traprain* (1923).

[5] British Museum, O. M. Dalton, *Catalogue of Early Christian Antiquities in the British Museum* (1901), p. 79, nos. 356–7 with fig.

[6] Cabrol Leclerq, *Dict.* IV, 1.1180, fig. 3777.

[7] Himlingøje beakers, Forssander 1937, Abb. 14 and 15.

various workers in the field because, although they are of formal design, they are in a totally different class from the exploded mosaics of Style I and the interlacing, elongated intricacies of Style II; by comparison they are far nearer to the works of nature since their heads and limbs are not only fitted on to their torsos in the right places, but they are roughly of the correct proportions. Within these limitations, the way in which the various animals are conceived by the artists varies considerably. To jettison the term 'naturalistic' is perhaps a praiseworthy action, but the reasons so far given for doing so are not sound. It is essential to attempt to distinguish between a barbaric artist who is doing his poor best in an intractable medium to give a picture of a beast as nature made it, and a barbaric artist who makes no attempt to do this, but intends instead to achieve a pleasing abstract impression of line and rhythm. To take examples already given in this connection,[1] the animals on the late Roman mosaic pavement from Rudstone, Yorks., the animals and humans are all provided with the correct number of limbs, the leopard with its spots, the deer with antlers, and even the warped vine with grapes. The artist was trying to copy classical and naturalistic models, but because of his innate lack of sympathy with the system, lack of training in performance, and difficulty with his medium, the results are not recognizable as real creatures and plants. It is not always so easy to distinguish an artist's intentions, perhaps because sometimes he was not sure of them himself. In the two-dimensional efforts of the late fourth century, the artist is sometimes using classical works only as a general guide and strong tendencies towards balance and pattern may be perceived as a result, e.g. the plate with inscriptions to the second and twentieth legions recorded in the seventeenth century, where the soldiers and animals are grouped and disposed as a formal symmetrical design (Fig. 25).[2] The soldiers are portrayed by disembodied rows of heads and legs above and below rows of transparent shields. The animals are mostly fanciful rather than natural, and the peacocks appear as if embroidered in herringbone stitch.

The chip-carved bronze buckles of the fourth century show another phase of this two-dimensional method developing. Some of the Snodland type carry portraits[3] and roundels of portrait busts, the copies attaining varying degrees of pictorial success. The same applies to naturalistic hunting scenes.[4] It is in a technique two-dimensional such as this that the Quoit Brooch Style must first have arisen, and an investigation beginning in this quarter is likely to prove fruitful.

These neglected aspects of the Quoit Brooch Style make it quite clear that the Jutes had no responsibility in the matter because the forms of the objects were not

---

[1] Hawkes 1961, 58; T. D. Kendrick, *Anglo-Saxon Art* (1938), pl. xxv.

[2] P. Buonarotti, *Osservazioni istoriche sopra alcuni medaglioni antichi* (1698), p. xvii. A bronze bowl with a hunting scene in the same type of stylization was found in a Frankish grave of c. A.D. 400 at Saint Rimay, Loir et Cher, *Bericht der Römisch- Germanischen Kommission*, 31 (1942), 72–5, No. 64, Abb. 12, 3.

[3] Behrens 1930, Taf. 31 and 32A.

[4] *Ibid.*, Abb. 8.

known to them, nor did they practise to such an extent the late Roman techniques or composition, and, furthermore, effects limited to two dimensions had no attractions for them. The majority of pointers have been in the direction of northern Gaul where Roman traditions survived amongst craftsmen.

Germanic animal ornament of c. A.D. 400 on the continent

All of the points raised in the preceding pages are serious objections to the rise of the Quoit Brooch Style in Kent under the hand of the Jutes. Prompted by findings so far, the theory is now put forward here that all the requisite conditions were present in the north of Gaul in the middle of the fifth century for the beginning of the style. It has been seen that the object forms on which it appears in England are in the late Roman tradition continued by the Franks, the techniques are those of late Roman craftsmen working on plate, and so is the artistic composition; moreover, the flat treatment, together with the stylization, is only to be found in northern Gaul. It has been shown earlier that there was a migration to southern England in the middle of the fifth century by people who took with them to their graves glass and metal goods which had been made in this part of Gaul. There is no doubt about the intimate connection between the Quoit Brooch Style objects and the chip-carved belt mounts worn by Germanic warriors in the last days of the army of the Roman empire. The technique of chip-carving itself is to be seen on the High Down strap-slide, the Howletts bronze plaque, the Bishopstone plate, etc., and the motifs used on the Roman bronzes, especially the geometric spiral scroll, are transferred to English pieces, without modification. Amongst other metalwork techniques are incising, also often used to render spirals, but this is a more tractable method in which it was possible to include the original naturalistic fussiness of tendrils, as on the Howletts re-used plaque, the Alfriston penannular brooch and the High Down square brooch. Punched patterns in a variety of shapes are another decorative feature, e.g. annulets, crescents, ball-in-triangle. Rows of tiny triangles, base to apex to form a line carried out in 'niello' on late Romano-Germanic brooches made in France,[1] appear in the Quoit Brooch Style as incisions or stamps, and in metal insertions in the inlaid buckles.[2]

Turning to the zoomorphic decoration, we note that the motif of a pair of horses' heads back to back was used on a number of late Roman objects, e.g. strap-ends,[3] and found its way both to Scandinavia and to Britain. They decorate the edges of strap mounts at Sösdala in Sweden[4] and a sword scabbard in Norway,[5] and a series

---

[1] Werner 1959, p. 376, Abb. 4, 2. The inlay is said to be niello, but it does not seem to be possible to inlay niello on bronze; A. A. Moss, 'Niello', *Conservation*, I, 2 (1953) 57–8.

[2] Evison 1955, pl. IV, d and pl. VI, d.

[3] Behrens 1930, Abb. 10 and 12.

[4] Forssander 1937, Abb. 1.

[5] Hougen 1936, fig. 3.

of late Roman buckles in Britain.[1] With hardly any alteration, they appear on the post-invasion strap-slide from High Down (Pl. 13, c) and on strap-ends from Chessell Down (Pl. 14, a) and Croydon (Pl. 14, b). These horses' heads are all seen in profile, but occasionally they are represented full-face. An easily recognizable head, flat and splay-snouted, is the shape taken by the terminals of the Alfriston penannular brooch (Pl. 15, a) and also by those of the brooch from grave XXII, Riseley, Horton Kirby, Kent (Fig. 28, i). These horses' heads are seen full-face, but may be clearly recognized from their close relations in earlier profile versions, for instance on the ends of the loops of chip-carved buckles, e.g. Vermand[2] and Mainz.[3] The closest parallel to the English heads, however, is to be found on a strap-slide of the late fourth century. It is to be noted that animal heads in relief occur on triangular- or semicircular-ended strap-slides like those found, e.g. at Furfooz, Rhenen[4] and Tournai,[5] but it is only at Furfooz, Belgium,[6] that these full-face heads occur in a flat version exactly like that on the English brooches (Fig. 28, i).[7]

These horses' heads are part of a system of stylized animal ornament already formulated in the late Roman period, and displayed to the best advantage as a border ornament on belt fittings. The belt mounts at Rhenen, for instance, include amongst the motifs, forward-creeping 'lions', running slender-waisted lions and backward-glancing quadrupeds (Pl. 4, c).[8] A backward-glancing sea-lion with no hind legs but curling tail appears on the buckle from Chécy[9] and on the spear from Vermand (Pl. 1, a).[10] All these are carved in relief and are stylized with patterned decoration of the body by means of regular punch-marks. These same animals were adopted by the Saxons to adorn the edges of their equal-armed brooches.[11] Here are most of the ingredients for the Quoit Brooch animals—missing is the flat treatment and an untrammelled flowing rhythm of outline.

For the most part, the extensive production of chip-carved belt ornaments was entirely in relief, but by the fifth century a change had begun to take place. Border animals, for instance, shed their rotundity and became flat, but any feeling which was lost in depth was regained in the smooth flow of the contours. On a strap-end from Mahndorf[12] the sea-lion has turned into a quadruped with curly tail, and the tip is finished with a human mask. A strap-end from Kreuznach,[13] decorated mainly by

[1] Hawkes and Dunning 1963 (fig. 15).

[2] Fig. 26, c. [3] Behrens 1930, Abb., 4.

[4] Pl. 4, c; Roes 1953, pl. VII, Afb. 5, 2, and pl. II, 2, pl. VI, 2.

[5] Faider-Feytmans 1951, pl. IV.

[6] Nenquin 1953, pl. VI, D 1 C.

[7] The Germanic character of this grave group is emphasized by the pot of Argonne ware which emulates a Germanic shape; Nenquin 1953, Tombe III, pp. 88–9, Fig. 10, A. 47, pp. 42–3.

[8] Roes 1953, pls. II, 2, V and VI.

[9] Gricourt 1958, pl. I, I.

[10] Ibid., pl. IX.

[11] A. Genrich, 'Die gleicharmigen Fibeln der Völkerwanderungszeit im Gebiet der unteren Elbe', Hammaburg, 3 (1952), 181.

[12] Grohne 1953, Taf. VIII, 2, Abb. 46, g.

[13] Behrens 1930, Taf. 32, 2; H. Schoppa, Die Kunst der Römerzeit (1958), pl. 138, 2.

stamps, with chip-carving relegated to mere rows of triangles, is bordered by a pair of dog-like creatures, whose descent from the curly-tailed sea-lion is betrayed by the disc in their haunches and their long tail. A lightness of touch and delicacy of line distinguish this piece from its more compact and angular predecessors.

Tendencies in the same direction are to be seen on buckles from among a group of objects, which from their assortment would appear to constitute the contents of one grave, and which were illustrated by E. Fleury under the 'époque carlovingienne'.[1] They were found at Landifay (Canton de Guise) and include a buckle and counter plate (Fig. 27, a–i). The loop is ornate, with zoomorphic terminals, and the tongue has a zoomorphic tip and square base with affixed S-shaped animals. The plate is divided into two compartments, one filled by the bust of a woman, the other of a helmeted soldier with spear. These portraits are abstract in quality, notable details being the circular eyes, pear-shaped noses, and dotted contour lines over head and drapery. On the counter plate the two sitting animals are also stylized to a certain extent, with decorative bands and dots on the body, but are less simplified in outline. The other objects are a second zoomorphic buckle loop, two arrowheads, two rectangular mounts, a scabbard-tip mount and a knife. This is yet another knife of the Richborough type, and the information provided by the drawing, supplemented by Fleury's description,[2] reveals that it must have been the best preserved of the group known from Mainz, Greiffenklaustrasse, Grab 2; Vieuxville near Liège; Misèry,[3] Somme; and Sissy, St. Quentin, where it was found in a warrior's grave in each case, and Winchester, Hants.,[4] for it had an 'ivory' handle encircled with silver, quadripartite pommel and metal-inlaid blade.

Further examples of this animal style may be noted. The lion on the plate in the warrior's grave at Misèry (Fig. 2, 2, Frontispiece) has only one hind leg, but is endowed with two front legs as his head is turned full-face. All the details of the body are formal patterns, ring-and-dot eyes, a triangle above the dotted nostrils, arced stamps in a row round the face and dashes between two lines along the back to represent the mane, other curved lines and dots to section off the hindquarters and ribs. A row of dots follows some of the lines of the body and also the border of the rectangle. The animal on the back of this plate (Fig. 2, 3) is even more stylized; it is backward-glancing, with one hind and fore-leg only, a bifurcating tail, ring-and-dot eye, lenticular ears with ring-and-dot terminals; the body divided into compartments containing dots and hachuring. The sea-lion on the buckle-plate is in

---

[1] Fleury 1877–82, II, 250.

[2] 'Le poignard H est pour nous de forme absolument nouvelle et attribuable a l'Orient, avec le renflement et la courbure de sa lame d'acier guilloché d'or et damasquiné avec son manche d'ivoire cerclé d'une virole d'argent ciselé.'

[3] Fig. 3, 6.

[4] Werner 1958, Abb. 1, Abb. 19 Grab 2, Taf. 72, 10; Taf. 82, 1 and 2 and p. 396 note 53. *Ant. Journ.* XXVI, fig. 11a.

the same style with undulating body and tri-lobed tail, again with ring-and-dot terminals to ear and tail, and dots and hachuring on the body. One of the Vermand lions (Fig. 26, *e*) obviously comes from the same jungle, together with the backward-glancing animals (Fig. 26, *a, b*). One buckle plate has a full-face human head and running animal (Fig. 26, *c*) (the main components of the Quoit Brooch Style) and another plate (Fig. 26, *d*) has a standing animal with head to ground (cf. the Croydon mount, Fig. 30, *o*). A flat treatment, incising and stamping, is used for all of these, and they are intended to be patterns rather than portraits.

It was the animals from Vermand that Leeds saw as the forerunners of the Quoit Brooch Style. S. Hawkes objected on the grounds that this kind of bronze work was widespread in the Roman empire, and 'other buckles with naïve and amusing engraved animal figures are unusual, but do none the less occur elsewhere in Roman frontier districts, even as far away as Hungary'. It is true that chip-carved bronze work of this general type was widespread, but, although there is no recent corpus of the material to provide tabulated evidence, it looks as though there were very few bearing a stylized animal of this type in two dimensions only. The one in Hungary referred to is almost the twin of the one from Sédan, France (Pl. 9, *c*), and it has already been pointed out by Forssander that they must have been produced by the same workshop.[1] Another, from Colombier-sur-Seulles, near Bayeux (Pl. 9, *b*) bears on the plate a griffin with an animal head at the end of the tail.

A plate of unknown provenance in Oldenburg Museum (Pl. 18, *a*) bears a backward-glancing beast nearly identical to that on one of the Misèry plates (Fig. 2, 3); the diverging lenticular ears, single hind and fore-leg, the curve of the tail and the hachured banding on the neck are the same. The distribution of five in a limited district between the Somme and the Meuse, with one near Bayeux and outliers in Hungary and Oldenburg, suggests that the last two are not in their place of origin (Map 11). In support of this, it may be noticed that also at Oldenburg, found in Herbergen, is a chip-carved type of zoomorphic buckle which has a very similar tongue to the Vermand type (except that it is double), i.e. zoomorphic tips, rectangular base and zoomorphic side extensions (Pl. 9, *a*).[2] These latter are surely not backward-glancing animals as suggested by Behrens, but are on the same lines as on the Vermand and Budapest Museum buckles, i.e. the forepart of an animal biting the square base of the buckle tongue, with the back of its body curling round and the additional conceit on the Budapest and Oldenburg buckles of ending in an animal head. This type does not seem to be very common, and Behrens could only cite one parallel from Kent,[3] and the one from Mainz already mentioned. It is probable that these buckles with chip-carved plates also come from the same workshop in northern France.

[1] Forssander 1937, p. 216.
[2] Behrens 1952, Abb. 19, 4.
[3] Behrens 1950, p. 16.

We need not be delayed here by the Snodland type which has busts in medallions, or the hunting scene type from Dunapentele, for these are at their best obvious portraiture, and at their worst inept copies. They have not been subjected to deliberate formalization.

The evidence of these belt fittings, then, shows that there was a workshop in northern France in the first half of the fifth century, producing abstract animal ornament of two dimensions, which was used to ornament the types of belt fittings worn by Germanic soldiers, probably Frankish *laeti*.

The transference to Britain of the double horses' head motif has already been commented on, and it would not be surprising if this new flat pictorial technique also made its way across the Channel before the invasion. In fact, it does actually occur on the plate of a buckle of which the loop bears a pair of horses' heads. It comes from Stanwick, Yorks.,[1] and on its plate are two peacocks beside a tree of life carried out in crude incising and with annulet and crescent stamps, the latter forming a bordering row along the peacocks' backs as on the Misèry lion. The extreme rarity of this kind of Christian subject in late Roman Britain is in favour of its being the result of influence from abroad.[2]

The style may also be traced in some strap-ends (or toilet implements),[3] which are a development of a late fourth-century continental type as at Vermand,[4] and occur both on late fourth-century sites in Britain and in Anglo-Saxon contexts. Three were found at Richborough;[5] two have ornament in the shape of a pair of birds' heads, and geometric ornament, one with the addition of arced stamps. Another (Fig. 27, *k*)[6] has a drawing of a kind of serpent, with a dotted collar and arced stamps representing scales on the body and a fringe of short lines to represent fur along its contours. The stamps and furry outline should be compared with the buckles at Vermand and Misèry. A nail-cleaner was found at Wor Barrow, Handley Down (Fig. 27, *j*),[7] again with arced stamps as a border and above a human face, this latter being surrounded by arced stamps to represent a whiskery outline, in the very same manner as on the Misèry full-faced lion. A strap-end with knobbed terminal has lately been found on a villa site at Rockbourne, Hants.,[8] and its design of human face

---

[1] A. B. Tonnochy and C. F. C. Hawkes, 'The sacred tree motive on a Roman bronze from Essex', *Ant. Journ.* XI (1931), 123–8, fig. 2; Hawkes and Dunning 1963, fig. 15, m.

[2] This buckle has recently been regarded as British-made, and the existence of other examples of Christian subjects presumed (Hawkes and Dunning 1963, p. 25). As these other examples do not in fact exist, the above explanation of direct influence from abroad, and Germanic manufacture, seems to me preferable.

[3] These objects are notched at one end and have also been described as nail-cleaners. The other end is either flat and split so that it can be riveted to a strap, or it is furnished with a ring for suspension.

[4] Pilloy 1895, II, pl. 16, 3a and pl. 21, 1b.

[5] Bushe-Fox 1926, II, pl. XIX, fig. 35 (from topsoil), Bushe-Fox 1949, IV, p. 217.

[6] Bushe-Fox 1926, II, pl. XIX, fig. 34.

[7] Pitt-Rivers, *Excavations in Cranborne Chase*, 1898, IV, 89, pl. 258, fig. 10.

[8] *The Journal of Roman Studies*, LIII (1963), p. 150, pl. XVII, 4.

with arc-stamped hair, and incised circles connected by tangents, shows it to belong to this group. Two of these bronze mounts were topsoil finds, and could be post-Roman like strap-ends of the same shape found in Saxon graves at Long Wittenham[1] and Harnham, Wilts.[2] The Long Wittenham, grave 111, also contained the inlaid iron buckle loop, so that a common Frankish origin for the two objects is not unlikely.

Another strap-end of this type is the one found at Rivenhall, Essex, which has an incised sketch of the peacocks-and-tree motif also on the buckle found at Stanwick, and which I have suggested is likely to be of Germanic origin because of its horses' head loop and Christian motif (p. 59).

A strap-end of rather different shape is the one recently found in a post-invasion cemetery at Winterbourne Gunner, Wilts. (Fig. 20, b), but the dragon adorning it is obviously of the same family as the Misèry sea-lion with its undulating body, its tail bifurcating like one of the Misèry animals (Fig. 2, 3) and the arced stamps marking the body and dorsal fur as before. There is also a compartment on the shoulder. The shape of the strap-end is unique, but the diamond-shape at one end shows connections with the strap-ends from Chessell Down and Croydon (Pl. 14, a, b). As the Winterbourne Gunner strap-end belonged to a Frankish warrior with francisca and inlaid buckle who was buried in an Anglo-Saxon cemetery, it was presumably brought over by him along with the rest of his possessions. It illustrates how Frankish animal ornament of the Misèry sea-lion style had developed in the first half of the fifth century, so that we are now in a position to leave the continental craft for the time being and explore the English style of the second half of the fifth century.

English fifth-century animal ornament

Before considering the Quoit Brooch objects in detail, it would be as well to examine the list as so far presented, add to it any examples which have been missed, and extract from it products which are now clearly of Frankish origin. Foremost among the latter, of which there are three, is the Howletts francisca (Fig. 27, l). The weapon is indisputably Frankish, and the hare on the ornamental plaque shows little concession to abstraction; it still has the lifelike ear and fur markings of the late Roman racing animal, but the single fore and hind leg and the compartment marking the shoulder illustrate the distinct advance already made on the continent towards the racing animal developed in England on the Howletts brooch.

The Brighthampton pommel and scabbard mounts (Fig. 11, a–c, e, f, i) are of common Germanic form and might have been made almost anywhere in Germanic territory. The disc-headed rivets must have been used to fix the suspension straps to the scabbard, and the method may be seen from the sword in the grave 43 at Krefeld-

[1] Holmqvist 1951, Abb. 27.   [2] *Arch.* xxxv, pl. xi, 9.

Gellep (Pl. 4, *a*), where they are still *in situ*. The Krefeld sword comes from a Meuse factory, and the probability of the same origin for the Brighthampton sword is strengthened by its rivet decorated with a Christian cross. The animals on the scabbard mount have little in common with the Quoit Brooch Style. The birds' heads with curling beaks at the end are frequent in Frankish work, e.g. as terminals on purse mounts of the type found in Childeric's grave (Fig. 8), and they had already occurred on belt mounts at Belleray (Pl. 2, *b*) on the Meuse, but in the Quoit Brooch Style they are completely absent. The two animals are simple, with lumpy, irregular outline as opposed to the streamlined English drawings, and there is no trace of the sophistications of double contour and patterning on the bodies. The animals have been picked out in a different colour from the background, although the technique is not that of metal inlay but of particularly thick gilding on silver. Heavy gilding of this kind covers the central panels and other parts of the Misèry buckle and plates.

The Bidford-on-Avon bucket (Fig. 24, *f–j*) is bound with bronze bands decorated in repoussé in arc-and-dot motifs, so that it must have been produced in the same area as the other buckets of its kind in northern Gaul in the fifth century (Map 8). Only the appliqués of animal shape depart from the normal practice, and these are decorated with the same arc and dots, among other motifs. One of these also has already developed a shoulder compartment, the body is covered with patterning, and the trait of a border of rows of stamped arcs between double contours is carried on from the Misèry creatures. The essential difference between these animals and the style as produced in England is the existence of the third dimension, for the medium used on the bucket is that of repoussé bronze, while all the other creatures are flat.

These three examples, then, together with the Winterbourne Gunner strap-end, represent the stage of development already reached in Frankish animal ornament in the middle of the fifth century when they were brought to England by their owners, and it is a stage half-way to the full stylization and mastery of rhythm reached in the best Quoit Brooch work. The continuation of this Frankish style on the continent will be followed in due course, but now it is time to state the main elements of the Quoit Brooch Style in England and enumerate the examples. It must be remarked that some of the English animals are so similar to their continental predecessors that the line of demarcation is faint, and this is only to be expected, as the development can be traced stage by stage.

Quoit Brooch animal ornament[1]

1. Bowcombe Down roundel (Fig. 28, *a*)
2. Lyminge penannular brooch (Fig. 28, *g*)
3. Howletts plate (Pl. 13, *b*)
4. Alfriston buckle (Pl. 14, *c*)
5. Croydon strap distributor (Pl. 13, *a*)
6. Bifrons pendants (Pl. 12, *a*)
7. Bishopstone plate (Pl. 12, *b*)
8. Bifrons strap-end (Pl. 11, *a*)
9. Faversham disc brooch (Pl. 10, *a*, *b*)
10. Howletts complete quoit brooch (Pl. 11, *b*)
11. Howletts fragmentary quoit brooch (Pl. 10, *c*)
12. Sarre quoit brooch (Pl. 12, *c*)

Closely allied to these are objects with the same techniques, forms and patterns, which were made at the same time by the same people, but on which the complete animals do not figure. The first group may still be regarded as zoomorphic, for it includes horses' heads and human masks, while the second group is non-zoomorphic.

Quoit Brooch ornament—horses' heads and human masks

13. High Down slide (Pl. 13, *c*)
14. Chessell Down strap-end (Pl. 14, *a*)
15. Croydon strap-end (Pl. 14, *b*)
16. Alfriston penannular brooch (Pl. 15, *a*)
17. Riseley penannular brooch (Fig. 28, *i*)
18. High Down buckle (Pl. 14, *d*)
19. Higham brooch (Pl. 15, *b*)

Quoit Brooch ornament—non-zoomorphic

20. Howletts square brooch (Pl. 16, *a*)
21. High Down square quoit brooch (Pl. 16, *b*)
22. Alfriston rectangular plaque (Fig. 28, *j*)

[1] For descriptions, etc., see lists of Figures and Plates, pp. 101, 119.

Most of these objects have been described and discussed in detail by others,[1] so that it is necessary only to concern ourselves here with the most important characteristics of the style.

The twelve zoomorphic works are placed in an estimated order of development, whether of chronology or expertise it is impossible to say; suffice it to remark that the first six are only slightly removed from late Roman continental metal craft, and the last six reveal an enthusiasm for, and mastery of, unreal, dotted and hachured creatures of the imagination which nevertheless leap and crouch in a lively rhythm. No doubt many other objects were produced by the same workshops, e.g. annular brooches as at Broadstairs and Alfriston, and the two tendril-decorated buckles from Bifrons and High Down (Pl. 16, c), but the decoration is far less ambitious. These two buckles are regarded by Hawkes and Dunning[2] as being copied from the dolphin types current in Britain at the end of the Roman occupation. This is impossible, for all the examples produced in Britain are rather crude and clumsy copies of continental products, while the High Down and Bifrons buckles are of first-class execution and design. Moreover, the loop shows no sign of the British dolphin heads. These two buckles must owe their origin directly to continental buckles such as the one from grave 1 at Furfooz,[3] which possesses all the considerable number of elements necessary, i.e. loop with curling tail but no dolphin heads, tongue with lateral projections, one bar to hold the tongue, and a second for the attachment of the belt, projecting animal heads from the base of the loop and the second bar. The penannular bracelet at Chatham Lines (Fig. 15, c) is probably also a product of the Quoit Brooch school.

The first item mentioned is one which has not before been recognized as belonging to this group, and it has been ignored, except by Leeds,[4] who took it to be a Roman hare-and-hound motif. A bronze mount found in Burial 13 at Bowcombe Down, Isle of Wight[5] is planned with the same alternation of decorated zones and plain zones which is the outstanding characteristic of the group, and this is the main reason for regarding it as non-continental. Here the plain zone is raised, and the centre is an openwork cross with curled terminals, recalling the centres of the mounts from High Down, Howletts and Bishopstone. The animal border is flat and also carried out in openwork. These creatures are very similar to the animals of fourth-century chip-carved bronzes, but are stylized and flat rather than in relief. There are three pairs, tail to tail, with noses touching curving shapes, which project in a hornlike way to frame circular spaces, as on a pendant with chip-carved central scrolls at Richborough.[6] The Bowcombe piece, too, was probably a pendant when complete, for it

---

[1] Detailed descriptions are given in Hawkes 1961. It may be noticed from the lists of Figures and Plates below, pp. 101, 119, that there are a number of important points on which I disagree with these descriptions.

[2] Hawkes and Dunning 1963, p. 35, figs. 19, c and d.

[3] Nenquin 1953, pl. VII, D 10; cf. *Mainz. Zeitschr.* 12–13 (1917–18), p. 28, fig. 8; 1, 2.

[4] Leeds 1913, p. 47, fig. 6a.

[5] *J.B.A.A.* (1860), p. 255, pl. XX, 4.

[6] Bushe-Fox 1926, II, pl. XIII, 11.

was found on the chest of a skeleton (reported to be male). Although the animals are quadrupeds, they are executed in much the same way as the sea-lions on the edge of the Kreuznach strap-end with large spaces between their bodies and the main part of the object, and further, their noses are also touching a horned shape as on the Kreuznach strap-end, this presumably being a perforated version of the disc terminal frequently found in this position.[1] A fifth-century brooch at the museum at St. Germain has a bow decorated with two animals, their snouts touching a similar shape.[2] The use of whole animals or the heads only as decorative borders was common in the fourth century on bone combs as well as on bronzes, and the spread of this idea in Germanic lands is evident on this Bowcombe mount, and also in Scandinavia at Sösdala. A close parallel of animals in openwork appears on a key ring found in the grave at Hol, Norway, but there the animals are unrhythmical and static. A late Roman circular pendant with openwork dolphin border surrounding a chip-carved centre with star and scroll design was found at Gelbe Burg near Dittersheim, Mittelfranken,[3] and this must be the immediate predecessor of the Bowcombe pendant.

The Bowcombe creatures themselves are very worn, but still retain their sweeping greyhound-like outline with the long fore-paws of the Bidford animals and an inner contour line visible here and there, particularly on the legs. On the front shoulder of one a curving compartment is clearly visible (cf. the animals in the outer zone of the Howletts fragmentary brooch (Fig. 30, *f, j*)) and on the hind-quarters of its neighbour there is an S-curve. The other finds from the Bowcombe grave include a buckle with three kite-shaped rivets, a lead bead, disc brooch, bronze fragments, two iron rings and pottery and glass fragments; of these the buckle, rivets and glass alike point to a continental origin. The kite-shaped rivets must be an earlier version of the shoe-shaped rivets so common among the Franks of the sixth century for fastening the end of a belt over a shield-on-tongue buckle. As the shoe-shaped rivets were already in use in the period A.D. 450–525, a fifth-century date is reasonable for their predecessors.

The Lyminge brooch horse's head terminal is flat, but in profile, and this detail, together with the panel of cross-hatching and the heart-shaped leaves on the ring, harks back to Roman buckle decoration. But the complete animal is an advance on the Howletts francisca hare; its body is divided into segments by panels of hachuring, with dots in the segments; the contour is broken in places, but achieves a fine flow from the back of one creature's neck to the tip of its tail, where three dots recall the foliate tail tips at Misèry and Vermand (Figs. 3, 8 and 26, *a*) and the tongue of the Richborough dragon (Fig. 27, *k*). The chip-carved centre panel of the Howletts plate

---

[1] Behrens 1930, Abb. 8, 5, Taf. 31, 5.   [3] Information from Prof. J. Werner.
[2] *Acta Arch.* v, 137, Abb. 30.

(Pl. 13, *b*) might have graced a late Roman belt mount, except that the cruciform motif may point to a Christian production centre, but the border animals have clear double contours and body ornamentation.

There are many elements in the Alfriston buckle which are characteristic of a Frankish buckle: the form of a kidney-shaped loop and rectangular plate is the one favoured by inlaid iron buckles, many of which must have been made in northern Gaul. The backward-glancing animals are almost replicas of those on the Bidford-on-Avon bucket, except that they are in two dimensions instead of three. The evidence for the production of the Alfriston buckle in England consists of the fact that, so far, glass insets and silver inlay on bronze have not been found in continental works of the period, and also that this animal type appears on another plate found in England: no. 7, at Bishopstone.

At Bifrons, the sea-lions on the pendants (no. 6, Fig. 30, *b*) are crudely drawn, with square jaws, slit mouth, round eyes and tubular tail, but the strap-end quadruped (no. 8, Fig. 30, *h*) can vie with the best of the Quoit Brooch Style. In the Faversham disc (no. 9, Pl. 10, *a*) and the quoit brooches from Howletts (nos. 10, 11, Pls. 11, *b*, 10, *c*) and Sarre (no. 12, Pl. 12, *c*), we come to the finest pieces of the group, presumably the products of one workshop.

In the next section, curving horses' heads back to back project from the ends of the High Down slide (no. 13, Pl. 13, *c*) and the two similar strap-ends from Chessell Down (no. 14, Pl. 14, *a*) and Croydon (no. 15, Pl. 14, *b*). The Alfriston (no. 16, Pl. 15, *a*) and Riseley (no. 17, Fig. 28, *i*) pennanular brooches are on the lines of the Lyminge brooch but without the quadruped, and with full-face horses' head terminals. The circle-and-dot motif on the Riseley brooch shows its connection with the continental ring brooches of the fourth to fifth century but its scroll-formed eyes are also found on a Howletts animal (Fig. 30, *a*). The Alfriston brooch has an openwork animal head border, a tendril scroll and human mask. The human mask, often between animals, was already in use on Roman chip-carved bronzes, e.g. on the strap-slide at Rhenen (Fig. 29, *a*),[1] and with flat treatment at the tip of the Mahndorf strap-end.[2] Human masks in a row have left their traces on the loop of the High Down buckle, and on the border of the Higham brooch.

In the last, non-zoomorphic section, only three objects are listed. The square bronze plaque at Howletts (no. 20, Pl. 16, *a*) is decorated with tendril scrolls and inlaid wires, and was converted to use as a brooch. The High Down square quoit brooch follows the same circular zonal decoration as the other quoit brooches, simply extending the outer edge into the four corners of a square. The design is of tendrils, lines of triangles base to apex and crescent stamps. The triangular belt mounts in Alfriston, graves A and 17, were both cut from a single sheet of bronze which had

[1] Roes 1953, pl. II, 2.   [2] Grohne 1953, Taf. VIII, 2, Abb. 46, g.

F

been ornamented in this manner. The bronze sheet had been rectangular (Fig. 28, *j*), and was probably a buckle plate as its size corresponds very closely to the one in this grave and to the inlaid iron buckle plates. The design is based on a rectangle in the middle surrounded by two outer zones, the rectangle and the outermost zone bearing spiral decoration and the inner zone being plain. Annulet and ball-in-triangle stamps also figure in the pattern. The arrangement and the motifs strongly recall the Bishopstone plaque (Pl. 12, *b*), the belt-slide from High Down (Pl. 13, *c*) and the re-used plate from Howletts (Pl. 13, *b*). The square quoit brooch from High Down (Pl. 16, *b*) has an inner zone of wave motifs, and also diagonal rows of minute triangles as in the rectangle of the Alfriston mount. The inner zone of the Faversham brooch (Pl. 10, *a*) with its sharply incised waves and intervening carved triangles is very close, and the ball-in-triangle stamp is also used on the Chessell Down strap-end (Pl. 14, *a*) and the High Down buckle plate (Pl. 14, *d*). The ball-in-triangle stamp appears on both sides of the Alfriston triangle mount, so that it is obvious the craftsman was re-using a plate first manufactured in his own workshop.

A study of the illustrations emphasizes the fact that the main characteristic of the Quoit Brooch Style is the restraint shown in not covering the complete object with decoration, but in limiting it instead to zones or panels. Alteration of plain zones with decorated ones, either circular or rectangular, is to be seen in items 1, 4, 7, 9, 10, 12, 19, 20, 21 and 22, and confined to panels on 7, 8, 9 and 18. In the same tradition, the surface of the loop of the High Down buckle is fully ornamented, but the plate is comparatively austere, with only its central cabochon set in a plain field bordered by small stamps. On the quoit brooches alternate zones are gilded, a technical procedure already followed on the Misèry plates, where reserved silver and niello bands alternate with gilded zones beaded or moulded, surrounding a central gilt rectangle.

Previous students of this style have laid stress upon the trait of placing animals in rows, back to back or face to face, often in a symmetrical arrangement, but this is the inevitable result of the demands of the style. Spaces of any shape could be filled by workers in zoomorphic ornament of subsequent periods by means of tearing the animal into pieces, and distorting the resultant disarticulated members or by interlacing elongated limbs and torsos. All these tricks, however, had no place in the Quoit Brooch Style which demanded that the animal should be complete, integrated, and of recognizable proportions, although formalized. Where a small panel was concerned, it could be filled by one animal—e.g. the Bifrons strap-end. Where a larger space was to be covered, the artist preferred to take up a more classical attitude and leave zones undecorated. To fill the decorated strips there was no choice but to place the animals in rows, all facing one way, or opposite ways. Complete symmetry is hardly ever sought or achieved, for the details of body decoration vary even in creatures of the same contour.

The animals of this style fall into two categories: there is first of all a development of the classical hippocamp, and the rest are quadrupeds which assume a variety of positions. The hippocamp or sea-lion appears in its most nearly classical stage on the inner zone of the Howletts complete brooch (Fig. 30, *a*), though the convolutions of the tail have already been misunderstood by the artist, and a hind leg added with a residual spiral or ring on the rump to indicate the twisting. A simple version with tail curled under belly occurs on the Bifrons pendants, and a more sedate type with quadruped eared head on the Faversham disc brooch (Fig. 30, *b*, *c*), while the outer row on the complete Howletts brooch (Fig. 30, *d*) portrays a backward-glancing version.

The pair of creatures of the Croydon strap-divider (Fig. 30, *e*) have been misunderstood, and recently described as 'a pair of degenerate quadrupeds, or hippocamps confronted belly to belly, with pellets between their noses'.[1] Although the bronze is damaged at the position of the heads, the creatures can be recognized quite clearly as a backward-glancing version of the hippocamp as on the complete Howletts brooch (Fig. 30, *d*) for on each can be seen the definite outline of a fore-paw. They are placed back to back, the heads are less clear, but appear to be turned back to bite a crescent shape which reflects the hatched contours of the animals themselves.

Most of the quadrupeds are in couchant position (Fig. 30, *f–i*), some with their fore-paws curled up, e.g. Bifrons strap-end and the outer zone of the Sarre brooch (Fig. 30, *h* and *i*). Only one is running (Howletts brooch fragment, the outer zone, Fig. 30, *j*). Two of them have long, horse-like heads with noses touching the ground, giving the appearance of the act of grazing, i.e. the Croydon strap-divider (Fig. 30, *o*) and the Lyminge brooch (Fig. 30, *p*). The rest are backward-glancing (Fig. 30, *k–n*), including the serpentine creature of the inner zone of the Howletts fragment which has one hind-limb to reveal it as a part of a quadruped (Fig. 30, *m*). Several of the animals have roundels on or by the hind-quarters, probably indicating a stage of degeneration from the sea-lion.

All of these animals have their predecessors in late Roman work in bronze and silver. The chasing hound in full gallop and the pursued animal glancing back at its pursuer are well-known couples, e.g. the hunting scene on the plaque in the Louvre (Pl. 8, *c*). The sea-lion is a character frequently met in Roman art, and intermediate stages between classical versions and Quoit Brooch Style may be seen on the Misèry buckle plate (Fig. 3, 8) and the Richborough and Winterbourne Gunner strap-ends (Figs. 27, *k*, 20, *b*). The racing animal in conjunction with human mask appeared in chip-carved work such as the Rhenen belt equipment (Pl. 4, *c*, Fig. 29, *a*); on the Vermand buckle plate it is already reduced to two dimensions, and the same combination occurs on the outer zone of the Howletts fragmentary brooch (Pl. 10, *c*).

[1] Hawkes 1961, p. 36.

There is also a backward-glancing animal on a Misèry plate, and Vermand has an animal with head to ground. Even serpents are in evidence on the buckle plates from Chécy, Loiret and Rouvroy (Aisne),[1] where they are fighting sea-lions.

As to the techniques used, most of the products of the Quoit Brooch Style school are carried out in bronze, and a few in silver. A second colour was added to the silver quoit brooches by gilding the zoomorphic zones and parts of the birds. Silver wires or strips were inlaid in the Howletts bronze square and the Higham brooch, and sheet silver in geometric shapes on the Chessell Down strap-end and the High Down slide. On the Bifrons strap-end silver sheet covers the complete panel containing the animal, as it did on the High Down buckle-loop row of masks. On the other objects with sheet inlay the traces are too slight to show whether the sheet extended over the whole panel or the animal or mask only, e.g. Alfriston buckle, Croydon strap-divider and Faversham brooch. Apart from this, decoration is by incised patterns, with a certain amount of chip-carving and the use of stamps. The trick of following an incised line with a concurrent row of dots, which appears on the animals of the Alfriston buckle, the Lyminge brooch and the scrolls on the Alfriston and High Down brooches, is an echo of the treatment of the Bidford animals, and, at an earlier date, the busts of the warrior and woman on the Landifay plates and the animals at Misèry.

Other motifs and techniques which the Quoit Brooch craftsmen shared with the makers of late Roman chip-carving, such as spirals, etc., have already been mentioned at the beginning of this chapter. It may be further noticed that a variety of spirals found their way directly from late Roman to Anglo-Saxon work: geometric running or S-scrolls appear on the Landifay and Oldenburg buckles (Fig. 27, c, Pl. 9, a) and in the centre of the Howletts square brooch (Pl. 16, a); the tendril scroll of a Vermand buckle loop (Fig. 26, a) appears on the outer border of the Howletts square brooch; the running wave of the Vermand buckle plate (Fig. 26, c) can be seen on the Alfriston quoit brooch (Pl. 15, a) and on the High Down square quoit brooch (Pl. 16, b). In another composition one rolling wave element springs from one side of a border, and the next springs from the opposite side, e.g. the annular brooch from Linz (Pl. 8, b) and on the Faversham disc brooch (Pl. 10, a).

The story told so far, then, by the animal style on the personal belongings buried in Frankish graves in northern Gaul of the late fourth to early fifth century, and those buried in Germanic graves of the second half of the fifth century in southern England, is that a flat and stylized animal ornament with many of the Quoit Brooch Style characteristics was already developed on the continent before the invasion; some of these products found their way into England, and it was here that the style later reached its highest peak of rhythm and polish. The like of this does not appear

[1] Gricourt 1958, pl. I, 1 and pl. III, G.

on the continent, and even here its life-span was very short. These facts propose the actual migration of craftsmen who continued and developed the techniques and motifs they had known in France.

The development of related animal ornament in the fifth century on the continent

We must now turn our attention away from England and back to the continent, for surely there we must find further traces of such a pleasing animal style which stands distinct from all other Germanic treatment of zoomorphic ornament.

Applied disc brooches with repoussé decoration were manufactured in provincial Roman workshops, probably in Belgium,[1] by the late second and early third century, and some were worn by Germanic women on the continent before the invasion.[2] Two were also found in the firmly-dated woman's grave of the late fourth century at Vermand grave 24 (Fig. 1, g, h) with a solidus of Valentinianus (364–375), which contained a number of personal ornaments including the two disc repoussé plates, no doubt from disc brooches, for one of them still kept its separate rim, a usual finish affixed to this form. These were silver-gilt, and one shows a stylized lion's head full-face, surrounded by an *ovolo* border. The other has a central star motif, an antecedent to the numerous star centres on early applied brooches in this country.

The decoration of these disc brooches was usually geometric, stars, scrolls, etc., but two examples with animal ornament have been noticed. A later version of the Vermand lion with the mask quadrupled comes from Waben, Pas-de-Calais (Pl. 17, a), with rosettes in between and an egg-and-dart border. This has probably not wandered very far from its production centre in northern Gaul, but others of the same pattern have been found in S–N inhumation graves at Mahndorf, where they may be dated to the late fourth century.[3]

Four rather formalized backward-glancing sea-lions surrounded by a zigzag border adorn an applied brooch from Wehden (Lehe);[4] the head is a separate compartment and a lappet springs from the back. Three backward-glancing sea-lions at a stage of development nearer to the Roman originals are placed in circular procession on the applied plate of a brooch found at Sigy, near Neufchatel (Pl. 17, c). The vertical line decoration of the neck strongly recalls the sea-lions of Vermand, and the tripartite finial to its tail proclaims its recent descent from the classical sea-lion and the later type on the buckle plate from Misèry. Noticeable also is the ring-and-dot on the hind-quarters indicating stylized convolutions, and the lappet on the back

---

[1] Werner 1941, p. 29.

[2] Roeder 1927, 24 ff.; Steeger 1937 (a), 19 and 20.

[3] Grohne 1953, grave 8, Abb. 66; grave 14, Abb. 67 B. Grohne pointed out the similarity of this lion mask to that on the end of a tongue of a chip-carved buckle of the type produced in Belgium—his fig. 10, b; cf. also Åberg 1956, pp. 85–8.

[4] Roeder 1927, p. 22, Taf. 3, 3a, b.

of the head as at Wehden. The Waben brooch was recognized by Leeds as being immediately post-Roman on account of its egg-and-dart border, and this must apply also to the brooch from Sigy. They must represent the Quoit Brooch Style at the stage where it left the continent.

To clinch this point, there are the remains of a pair of similar brooches (Pl. 17, *b*) on which the animal design is the same as at Sigy, although slightly simplified (Fig. 29, *g*); the border is a simple raised line and a separate upright collar is soldered on the edge. These were found at East Shefford, Berks., grave XXIV, with a glass bead and a Kempston type glass beaker. The grave must be dated to the fifth century.[1] A general connection between these two brooches was noticed years ago by Baldwin Brown,[2] who saw the tripartite tail as a trident, but the details of their context are now clear.

A French origin for this type of brooch is stressed by another pair of disc brooches found at Muids (Eure).[3] Here the sea-lions are just as elaborate as on the Sigy disc, with curling tongue, lappet, tripartite tail and roundels below the body. The central roundel, however, here takes the form of a human mask, and the border a plait which is derived from the Roman guilloche. The plait border also occurs on some English applied brooches, e.g. on two from Fairford, Berks.,[4] where it forms the surround to degenerate lion-mask motifs.[5] When one finds a repetition of the lion-mask motif on an applied brooch from Reading, Berks.,[6] this time surrounded by a devolved egg-and-dart border, the cohesion of the group of English and French brooches becomes even more certain.

A very small mount in the form of an animal belongs to this period (Pl. 18, *b*);[7] it consists of two plates of bronze fastened together with a rivet; both outer sides are ornamented, and the space reserved by the length of the rivet suggests thick leather or wood in between. The creature is thin-waisted like some of the Quoit Brooch animals, and has a rudimentary ear and tail. Familiar details are the parallel line ornamentation of the body stopping short of the segment of the haunch, and also of the shoulder which is represented by the disc head of the rivet; the feet are feathered. The technique is chip-carving, and this, together with the feathered feet, recalls the edging of the bronze plate at Howletts (Fig. 30, *g*). It is of particular interest that this mount was dredged from the bed of the Meuse, at Heerenwaarde in Holland.

Most of the Germanic artists of the sixth and seventh centuries used animal orna-

[1] *Journ. Royal Anthrop. Inst.* XLV (1915), p. 92.

[2] Brown 1915, IV, p. 553.

[3] L. Coutil, *Archéologie gauloise, gallo-romaine, franque et carolingienne* (1895–1921), II, plate between pages 40 and 41, fig. 2.

[4] Leeds 1912, figs. 5 and 6.

[5] The lion mask must be the origin of these, and not the human mask as suggested by Leeds, or pelta shapes as suggested by Smith (Leeds 1912, p. 164).

[6] Leeds 1912, pl. XXVI, 1.

[7] A. Roes, 'Les trouvailles de Dombourg, Zélande', *Berichten van de Rijksdienst voor het Oudheidkundig Bodemonderzoek*, VI, 84, fig. 10. A Carolingian date is suggested for this mount by Dr. Roes.

ment to a great extent, but with very few exceptions it was in the stylized medium of the dislocated Style I or the elasticized Style II, and decoration consisting of a single articulated animal in recognizable proportions was very rare. The main exception is to be found among the Franks, and their earliest efforts in this direction show that an origin is to be sought in northern Gaul. This origin has been studied by Werner,[1] who has shown how the late Roman sea-lion with coiled tail and trefoil tip developed into the border animal on chip-carved bronzes, and so into a sea-lion brooch of northern French distribution (Fig. 29, b–d).[2] In his article of 1949 he regards these last as of Roman origin, but the sea-lion of the Sammlung Diergardt he dates to the early sixth century. This seems too late, and a date not too far divorced from the end of the Roman period would seem to be indicated by the objects associated with the Chassemy brooch (grave 139), i.e. melon bead and bronze ring. In these brooches the body is still coiled like a serpent, with the tri-lobed tail extending behind, but in the next stage of development the end of the tail is omitted and the coil only remains, sometimes with a roundel. This stage of the animal is extremely similar to the animals in the Quoit Brooch Style, and both stages may be seen on the two animals of the Douvrend hair-pin.[3] In the outer border of the complete Howletts brooch, the open-jawed creature is looking backwards, and the coiled hind-quarters end in a roundel (Fig. 30, d). The animals on the Bifrons pendants and the Faversham disc brooch have closed jaws and are facing forwards (Fig. 30, b and c). The quadrupeds in the inner zone of the Howletts brooch have a rather long and undulating body, with a curly tail and a roundel in the hind-quarters; this is an even nearer stage to the original classical sea-lion, showing how the convolutions of the body became misunderstood (Fig. 30, a). Some of the English Quoit Brooch animals therefore have much in common with this type of Frankish animal brooch (and hair-pins), and two of these imports have been found here—the pin at Faversham (Fig. 29, h) and one of the brooches at Alveston, Warwicks. (Fig. 29, i) (in grave 53 with beads, penannular iron brooch, fragments of two iron buckles, knife, bronze coin and fragments of bronze and iron).

Another import, a bronze mount, possibly for a box, is in the Ashmolean Museum (Pl. 18, c). Two appliqués, from the Arnold Collection (and therefore probably from Northfleet, Kent),[4] in the shape of similar animals might also be Frankish, but the development of legs and claws is more in keeping with the Quoit Brooch developments (Fig. 29, j). At the back of each of these mounts is a pair of projecting rivets, a form also adopted by an animal mount from Staxton, East Yorks. (Pl. 18, d),[5] where

[1] Werner 1949.
[2] Ibid., Abb. 42.
[3] Ibid., Abb. 44, 1.
[4] D. Wilson, 'A pair of gilt-bronze mounts in the Gravesend Museum', Arch. Cant. LXXVII (1962), pp. 156–9.
[5] Hull Museum Publications No. 195, 'second skeleton', pp. 8–10, pls. II and III.

it is said to have been a belt appliqué. The Staxton animal is likely to be Frankish as it has none of the characteristics of the Quoit Brooch animal and also it bears a top surface of thick white metal (? silver) plate—unusual in England, although one of the Alfriston quoit brooches is covered in this way.[1] A fragment of a radiate brooch at Staxton[2] emphasizes continental ties of this site in the direction of the Franks.

As Werner went on to point out, there are a number of other Frankish animal brooches developed from the Alveston type, particularly some of the S-shaped brooches with an animal or bird's head at each end.[3] In England, the use of well-proportioned and complete animals for decoration gave way almost without exception to the fanciful formalities of Styles I and II, but among the Franks they persisted in the form of brooches consisting of a horse, horse and rider, octopus and unidentifiable quadrupeds, not to mention the wide range of bird brooches,[4] of which the distribution centres on northern France and the Rhineland. Amongst this group we should include the pair of repoussé disc brooches found at St. John's College, Cambridge, with a bronze buckle inlaid with silver.[5] The animals portrayed on the disc brooches are unconnected with English animal ornament, but show similarities to some of the animal brooches of the Franks. The repoussé disc brooch is not a common Frankish form, but neither is it English in view of the central settings (now missing), and the Frankish origin of the associated inlaid buckle supports identification as imports.

The curvaceous quadruped continues as decoration on flat surfaces, for instance on the bezel of a ring found in Belgium, where it glances backward and still has a double contour line and shoulder and haunch compartments.[6] A formalized version of the backward-glancing animal may be seen on a bronze tag from Parfondeval (Pl. 18, e).[7] The outlines have become firm and geometrical, with circle-and-dot motifs, the one on the haunch being a relic of the curling sea-lion tail. Later developments of this, still with the circle-and-dot, but with an animal head on each end, occur on the ornamental plates of the sword from Normée in Épernay Museum. These two are incised on a flat surface.

Even later, a series of quadrupeds with curving outlines, and looking either forwards or backwards, are to be found decorating the flat surfaces of the large buckle plates produced in France during the seventh century.[8] Many of these 'Aquitanian' buckles were found in the Toulouse district, but some occur elsewhere, including the

---

[1] *Sussex Arch. Coll.* LVI, pl. IV, 7.

[2] *Hull Museum Publications No. 195*, pl. IX, 95.

[3] Werner 1949 and Werner 1961, Taf. 56.

[4] Werner 1961, Taf. 54 and 55.

[5] Holmqvist 1951, Abb. 26, 1 and 2; Evison 1955, fig. 4.

[6] Baron de Loë, *Belgique ancienne*, IV (1939), fig. 20, 2.

[7] L'Abbé Cochet, *La Normandie souterraine* (1854), pl. xv, 2.

[8] N. Åberg, *The Occident and the Orient in the art of the seventh century*, III (1947), pp. 41–64, esp. figs. 1, 3, 4, 5, 8, 9, and 21; distribution map p. 62: see also Behrens 1952, Abb. 23.

north of France, e.g. at Moislains, Somme.[1] These animals, according to Åberg,[2] 'largely contribute to the Mediterranean stamp of the style of ornament', but he does not explain in what way. It seems to me that if they do, it is at the end of a long line of development from the sea-lion through the fifth- and sixth-century Frankish derivatives. At the time of the earliest illuminated manuscripts, it was in the Frankish folios that the tradition of the animal portrait still flourished.[3]

Objects associated with the Quoit Brooch Style

By standing back and taking a general view of the jewellery bearing the Quoit Brooch Style in relation to the work produced in the late Roman period by both Roman and Germanic craftsmen, and in the following period by Anglo-Saxon and Frankish craftsmen, we are able to get a much better balance to our judgment than is to be gained by assiduously concentrating on minute points of decoration. Almost without exception, everything points to the region of northern Gaul or thereabouts as the only place possible for the very beginning of the Quoit Brooch Style. To recapitulate but a few of the main points: a number of the objects are of a type produced in this area, especially the inlaid buckle with rectangular plate, and the bronze-bound bucket with arcading decoration; the jewellery techniques come straight from a late Roman workshop producing silver plate, and so does the almost classical composition of the ornament, and these two features, together with the use of mask and animal design, are traced to northern France. The beginnings of the flat and formal animal ornament can be seen at Vermand, Sédan and Misèry, and later developments are only found in France.

With regard to the associations of the Quoit Brooch Style objects, it is immediately apparent that the cemeteries in which the style occurs are all sites where much of the early Frankish material was found. When we narrow down our view to the objects actually enclosed in the same grave, we must remember that unsupervised excavations such as Howletts do not always provide reliable associated groups, but there is no reason to suspect the records of the other excavations concerned. Frankish objects, as follows, were found in the graves containing the Quoit Brooch Style pieces:

1. Bowcombe Down roundel.   Bronze shield-on-tongue buckle and kite-shaped rivets.

---

[1] N. Åberg, *op. cit.*, fig. 8.

[2] *Ibid.*, p. 52.

[3] Sea-lions with tri-lobed tail, and quadrupeds, including a backward-glancing type, are to be seen in the Sacramentary from Gellone and in an Orosius at Laon (E. H. Zimmermann, *Vorkarolingische Minia-turen*, 1916, Taf. 135 and 144). J. Brøndsted, *Early English Ornament*, 1924, p. 305 ff., suggested a Coptic origin for these, but the animal portrait had already been in favour amongst the Franks for some time.

2. Lyminge penannular brooch.	Applied brooch with star motif and upright border (Fig. 28, *h*).
4. Alfriston buckle.	Strap-end, and no. 22 below.
10. Howletts complete quoit brooch.	Spiral silver finger ring.
11. Howletts fragmentary quoit brooch.	Pottery bottle.
14. Chessell Down strap-end.	Crystal ball, duck brooch.
16. Alfriston penannular brooch.	Glass cone beaker, spiral finger ring.
18. High Down buckle.	Purse mount.
20. Howletts square brooch.	(?) Sword and inlaid buckle.
22. Alfriston rectangular plaque.	Part in grave A, Alfriston, with bronze-covered rectangular buckle plate, purse mount; part in grave 17, Alfriston, with item no. 4 above.

All of these are objects which were current in the fifth century, and the star brooch with 2 is very like one possessed by the woman at Vermand (Fig. 1, *g*). This means that out of the fourteen objects which have recorded associated objects, ten were with fifth-century Frankish objects, a very high proportion. It must be added that no. 14 was in a grave which contained slightly later square-headed brooches of the early sixth century, and no. 16 also must have been deposited in the sixth century. Both were graves of rich women who had many possessions, and here one may well have to reckon with heirlooms or the girlhood possessions of old women. The strap-end 14 was well-worn.

Of the other associated groups, the beads and knife with 17 and the disc brooches with 21 are non-committal. The Style I buckle plate and button brooch with 3 are of the early sixth century, but the bronze plate is in any case a re-used, re-cut piece. An exception is 13 with a small-long brooch with horned head-plate and lozenge foot which has affinities with early north German types.[1] The distribution of this kind of small-long brooch in England is north of the Thames at Barrington and Linton Heath, Cambs., Luton, Beds., but besides the High Down example there is also one at East Shefford, Berks. The associations of the Quoit Brooch Style are therefore strongly indicative of the fifth century and the connections are overwhelmingly Frankish.

The importance of metal-inlaid work

To add to all this is the testimony provided by the technique of sheet metal inlay. By the fourth century it was by no means forgotten. Its use on bronze statues, particularly for the eyes, had continued. There is no reason why this source should have

---

[1] Leeds 1945, pp. 36–8, fig. 23, g.

supplied the models for Anglo-Saxon inlay any more than Norway, where line and geometric plate inlay was already in use. The Quoit Brooch Style, however, indulges in plate inlay which either fits into and follows the curving outline of the animal bodies, or is used as a complete cover for the panel containing the ornament. The use of sheet inlay in this way was unknown in the north, but silver- and copper-inlaid plate had been used for just this purpose by craftsmen of the Roman Empire in France and Germany and was still so used in the fourth and fifth centuries. A jug of the second century A.D. in the Metropolitan Museum, New York,[1] is an early example of plate outlining the animals. A box found in the Rhine,[2] besides having a row of inlaid leaves, is inlaid with a serpent in wires, its double-outlined mane-like back with rows of crescents recalling the Misèry animals. A box with compartments of this kind was found at Vermand,[3] so that a fourth-century date is possible.

The craftsmen of the fourth century working in the Roman tradition frequently used figure scenes, and particularly the hunt, in which the figures of humans and animals were picked out from the background by relief, but when the work was in a flat medium the figures were often picked out in a different colour—usually by the technique of parcel-gilding on silver. A very fine rectangular tray, the Ariadne tray recently found at Kaiser Augst, Switzerland,[4] with much other treasure, including three silver ingots bearing the stamp of the Emperor Magnentius (d. A.D. 353), has an interior rectangular panel and border panels of human and animal figures described as gilt, with a niello background. Actual inlay of another metal seems to be present at least in some of the border scrolls.[5] The central roundel of a circular dish from the same place bears a jostling and lively fishing scene, complete with octopus, carried out in gilt and niello.[6]

Occasionally a different method was used to pick out the figures to even greater effect, and sometimes in different colours. Instead of using parcel gilt, the craftsman applied a sheet of gold or copper exactly cut to the outline of the animal, and impressed on the background plate by means of the contour line and other internal markings, such as joint lines and fur dots. This may have been the technique used on the plaque with hunting scene in the Dumbarton Oaks Collection[7] said to have been found in France, carried out in bronze with silver inlay, showing a mounted hunter and three lions against a background of trees. In the Louvre (Pl. 8, c)[8] is a better-preserved rectangular bronze plaque in which the bodies of the animals in a hunting

[1] G. M. A. Richter, *Catalogue of Greek and Roman antiquities in the Dumbarton Oaks Collection*, 1956, No. 19.

[2] Lindenschmit, 1864–1911, IV, Taf. 16, 16.

[3] Pilloy 1895, II, pl. 17.

[4] *Illustrated London News*, 14 and 21 July 1962, nos. 6415 and 6416, vol. 241.

[5] *Ibid.*, no. 6416, p. 99, fig. 7, 8, 9 and 10.

[6] *Ibid.*, no. 6415, p. 71, fig. 8.

[7] *Handbook, Dumbarton Oaks Collection* (1955), no. 75. M. C. Ross, *Catalogue of Byzantine and early medieval antiquities, Dumbarton Oaks Collection*, I (1962), no. 58.

[8] D. T. Rice, *Masterpieces of Byzantine Art* (Edinburgh International Festival 1958), No. 22.

scene are inlaid with silver plate or copper plate and keyed with fur impressions just as on the Alfriston buckle. These two examples were both probably found in France, and a fragment of a third example was found in the Frisian terp of Winsum.[1] Now lost, it is said to have been of silver with applied gold or silver plates in the form of a man and a lion, but the basic metal looks dark in the extant photograph and may have been bronze. We cannot be certain whether all the sheet inlay in Quoit Brooch Style was spread over the entire panel concerned, or whether some was confined only to the outline of the bodies of the animals. In any case, it is designed to attract attention to the animals themselves, and the difference of method may be explained by the relatively smaller scale of the work.

These late Roman inlaid objects show by their figure style that they must be closely associated with the production of late Roman plate, such as some of the contents of the Mildenhall treasure and the Traprain hoard. We have already noted that evidence to suggest that silver plate with designs of masks and animals alternating was produced in northern Gaul in the late fourth century. These works are still in the full Roman tradition, but knowledge of the techniques was retained and passed on in the workshops in northern Gaul which catered for Germanic tastes at the turn of the century. The chip-carved buckle from Herbergen, Oldenburg (Pl. 9, a), is inlaid with silver on the scroll-decorated surface of the loop, and another similar, no doubt from the same centre, was found in a grave near Mainz.[2] A description given by Eck[3] indicates silver sheet inlay in the same position on the loop of a Vermand buckle (Fig. 26, a) and wire inlay to delineate the contours of the animals. A photograph of a similar plate in Oldenburg Museum (Pl. 18, a) shows the technique clearly. Other sets of Vermand buckle and plates have silver inlay only on the borders.[4] An ornate buckle with shield-shaped plate from Abbeville (Homblières) (Aisne) was also inlaid with silver.[5] The buckle and plates from Misèry (frontispiece) are not inlaid with metal, gold-plating and niello inlay being used instead. Nevertheless, a very close connection is apparent with the inlaid Droxford buckle as a quatrefoil motif appears on both, and two buckles at Alfriston (Fig. 16, d, h) which have a rectangular tongue base with inlaid metal grid are very similar to the Misèry tongue base inlaid with a niello grid.

Northern Gaul is the only manufacturing centre where, about the year A.D. 400, this special kind of metal inlaid work was carried out on buckles (see Map 11), and when this is considered together with the fact that the earlier forms of the animal art of the Quoit Brooch Style are to be found on the very objects produced in this

---

[1] Boeles 1951, pl. xx, 12. This fragment was found with a hoard of silver, p. 142.

[2] Lindenschmit 1864–1911, IV, Taf. 12, 1.

[3] Eck 1891, p. 216–17, pl. XVI, 8 and 9.

[4] Pilloy 1895, II, p. 228 ff. pl. 14, 1a, 2a and 3a; Eck, pl. xv, 1a, 2a and 3a). Fig. 26, c–e.

[5] Pilloy 1880, I, p. 190, pl. v, 1. M. R. Joffroy kindly informs me that the buckles from Colombier-sur-Seulles and Sédan (Pl. 9, b and c) have silver inlay.

technique, then there can be no doubt left but that connections are so close as to indicate actual migration of craftsmen from there to England.[1]

Early Norwegian animal style

If this thesis were accepted, one further outstanding problem would be solved. In all the Germanic world of the fifth century, there is only one area which produced an animal style analogous to the Quoit Brooch Style, and this is Norway. The astonishing likeness of these stylized figures to the Quoit Brooch figures has often been pointed out, e.g. by Holmqvist who suggested influence from Scandinavia to England,[2] and by Bakka who thought that the influence may have gone the other way.[3] Formalized Germanic animals of the third and fourth centuries as found on Danish beakers (Himlingøie, etc.) and are of a kind which could have been inspired in any part of the Roman empire by naturalistic art. A step further in stylization, development of rhythm of outline, sometimes with inner contour and patterned markings on the body, is apparent in a few pieces of Scandinavian metalwork which are exceedingly close to the English work in design, although the execution is divergent, being three-dimensional, usually in chip-carved relief. These are, principally, the two square-headed brooches from Nordheim and Hol in Norway, the gold collars from Sweden and various bracteates.[4] These, and many other objects found in Scandinavia, are inspired by late Roman chip-carved bronzes, as may be seen from the characteristics of the relief technique, border animals,[5] horses' heads, scroll patterns, etc. A continuation of these connections was ensured by the flourishing fifth-century trade between the Meuse and Norway which has long been recognized,[6] and this surely is the most likely way in which a Norwegian craftsman had his attention drawn to this type of animal decoration. The border animals of the bronze buckles worn by the Franks, the creatures on the Vermand spear, and the incipient Quoit Brooch Style would account for many of the ideas behind the ornaments constituting the grave-group of the Hol tumulus, for much of the work displayed on these objects is reminiscent of the fifth-century workshops of Gaul. The silver disc or quoit-shaped fragment has a beaded border like late Roman silver. The annular brooch with openwork animal border has already been compared with the bronze from Bowcombe Down and the Alfriston penannular brooch, all of which hark back to

[1] An additional detail is the use of blue glass stones inset in the eyes of animals at Vermand (Pilloy 1895 II, p. 229) and as centre stones to applied brooches; Steeger 1937a, 19 and 20, Grohne 1957, grave 30, Abb. 65, compared with the Faversham disc brooch and the Bifrons pendants.

[2] Holmqvist 1955, p. 25 (followed by Hawkes 1961, p. 67).
[3] Bakka 1959, p. 13.
[4] Hawkes 1961, pl. XIX a and b.
[5] M. B. Mackeprang, *De Nordiske Guldbrakteater* (1952), pl. 10, 15 and pl. 14, 19.
[6] Bjørn 1929.

Roman animal openwork borders. The S-shaped brooch in the find must be a fore-runner of the S-shaped bird and animal brooches later developed only amongst the Franks. The square-headed brooch with backward-glancing animals on the head also has closely-packed panels on the foot containing men and animals in a near-naturalistic style which must represent a Germanic interpretation of one of the closely-packed hunting scenes of late Roman silver. The remarkable similarity between the Norwegian and English Quoit Brooch animals, and yet the difference regarding their execution and the type of objects on which they are found, are both explained in a manner more satisfactory than so far achieved if they are interpreted as the result of craftsmen in different countries working on ideas which came from the same source in France. As the relationship between the French and English work is much closer than that between the Norwegian and French, this would be most reasonably explained by movement of craftsmen in the former case and the results of trade in the latter.

VI

Fifth-century Franks in England and the Anglo-Saxon Chronicle

THE archaeological material for the period before A.D. 500 in the south of England is revealed as being sufficiently plentiful to be used as evidence for historical events. It must not, of course, be discounted that some of the material produced here as evidence of a fifth-century date may be in the nature of heirlooms, and therefore misleading as to the actual date of deposition, but such a contingency cannot apply to the mass of facts assembled. On the other hand, there are no doubt many equally early objects and graves which might have strengthened the case but which have been omitted in this preliminary survey because of faulty records, or because of some of the many blind spots still to be overcome in research. Numerous graves with contents that are inconclusive either way have not been taken into account. The fifth-century material is scanty in comparison with the possessions of the dead which must have been laid down in the sixth and seventh centuries, but even so, there is an even sprinkling of it over the area investigated.

The survey of the archaeological material has shown that as early as the last part of the fourth century, while the Roman army was still in Britain, connections with northern Gaul are tangible in some bronze objects imported from the manufacturing centres there, and in the crude, stylized animal ornament which originated within the same industrial group. Very soon after the withdrawal of the legions, a Frankish woman was buried in a N–S grave at Chatham Lines, and a sword-bearing warrior in a N–S grave at Brighthampton. We have as yet no certain means of knowing whether the early fifth-century burials at Dorchester and Milton-near-Sittingbourne are pre-invasion or not, but if the contemporary military bronzes (buckle, rosette attachment and strap-end) which occurred at Croydon were contained in one man's grave (which, again, we have no means of knowing) his position in a post-invasion cemetery would establish him as a settler. The four bronze buckles with fixed plate which were made in the Meuse area in the first half of the fifth century (Figs. 12, *a*, 24, *d*, Map 7) are not likely to have reached the graves in which they were found at Sarre, ?Kent, Long Wittenham and Alfriston much after A.D. 450, and they were certainly made before that date. A proportion of the graves containing other fifth-century material, such as glass vessels, must be just as early.

Other Frankish material of c. A.D. 450–500 is spread over the area including Croydon and Mitcham, north and south Kent, the Sussex coast, the Isle of Wight, the upper Thames, and parts of Hampshire and Wiltshire between there and the south coast. The dating cannot be more precise within these fifty years and individual objects might be slightly earlier or later. Side by side with this, in the same spots, there is equally early material from other sources on the north-west coast of Germany, i.e. decorated urns, cruciform brooches in their earliest stage, applied and saucer brooches, etc., as well as more than a few occurrences of the cremation rite to show that other Germanic tribes were also taking part in the first assault. The grave of a man of rank or leader of warriors is distinguishable by his long sword, and these occur fairly frequently in the early cemeteries, but the associated objects have often been lost, or are not of a sufficiently individual nature to be accurately informative, so that only a small proportion provides intelligible evidence. Where a sword is accompanied by the specialized weapon of the Frankish throwing axe, the francisca, there can be no doubt of the nationality of a leader versed in the use of this type of missile. Alfriston grave 26 must have belonged to a Frankish leader who possessed a francisca and a sword with strap mounts on the scabbard similar to those preserved at Oberlörick. Petersfinger, grave XXI, contained the particularly complete and distinctive equipment of an officer of equivalent rank; a sword scabbard produced by the same workshop as was responsible for the scabbards at Oberlörick and Krefeld-Gellep, a Frankish cloisonné buckle and an axe, together with shield-boss, spear, etc. A grave at Abingdon also produced a sword from the same workshop. Frankish warriors of the fifth century were also buried at Brighthampton and Winterbourne Gunner.

The surprising number of fifth-century Frankish products which had arrived in the southern counties, together with some individual graves of inhabitants recognizable as Frankish, and the almost exclusive use of the rite of inhumation in a W–E direction show that a migration must have taken place from northern Gaul. This is further supported by the introduction to south Britain of Frankish animal ornament, together with the techniques of craftsmanship in which it was executed. Exact correspondences down to the minutest detail in form of object, idiosyncrasies in decoration and arrangement, and the specialized use of gilding and inlaid metals, leave no room whatsoever for any doubt. The difficulty of recognizing an ethnological group from archaeological remains must not be passed over lightly, however, and the view may be held by some that these people represent a tribe, such as the Saxons or Jutes, who may have been associated closely with the Franks on the continent for some time. This likelihood is not provable, and is the least probable, for their graves show the complete mixture of Germanic, Gallo-Roman and eastern elements continually present in the continental Frankish graves of the fifth, sixth and seventh centuries. The presence of Anglo-Saxon pots in otherwise Frankish graves is of no significance in this connection because, as pottery has a short life, the wheel-turned vessels brought over in the invasion trip would soon be replaced by the hand-made pottery available from some other element of the mixed tribal groups.

It is interesting to note that the peculiar Anglo-Saxon horned pot type found with an inlaid buckle at Alfriston (Fig. 16, *l*) occurs also at High Down, Horton Kirby and London, so confirming the distribution of Frankish material.[1] The find spots of the three similar animal-decorated applied brooches at Sigy (Seine Inf.), Muids (Eure) and East Shefford, Berks., could perhaps represent a stage of one of the invasion routes and one of the destinations. The fact that this method of ornamentation and its techniques lasted for only a short time suggests that the colonies were not revived by the arrival of subsequent batches of migrants from the same quarter. The Frankish element, intermingled as it was from the first with other elements, became submerged under the numbers of different Germanic tribes.

Some of the earliest archaeological traces are to be found on the Isle of Wight, and the Frankish objects, particularly swords, which were found at Petersfinger and Winterbourne Gunner near Salisbury, and Abingdon and Brighthampton in the upper Thames area, show that the course of invasion must have been in a northerly direction, starting from the south coast. A few of the characteristics of the southern area are also to be found north of the Thames, mostly along the course of the Icknield Way. Either a few of these people came in via the Wash, or they spread northwards after reaching the upper Thames from the south. But the amount of this material is comparatively small, and could be the result of local movements or trading.

The archaeological material is therefore not in accord with opinions quoted in Chapter 1. The distribution of cremation, mostly north of the Thames, does not indicate the limit of early cemeteries as Leeds thought, for there is plenty of evidence of fifth-century settlement to the south in Hampshire and the Isle of Wight, and while some of these people used cremation as a burial rite, a good number, possibly the majority, used inhumation. Future research may clarify this point, but much evidence was lost in unscientific excavations, particularly as regards cremation which

---

[1] The London pot (Brown 1915, IV, pl. CXXXVII, 3) is the earliest for the horned bosses are in their original zoomorphic state; the diagonal lines represent the bones of a fish or feathers of a bird radiating from a backbone on the spine of the boss, a circular stamp each side near the top represents the eyes, and at the top of each boss a depression indicates the mouth. The Alfriston pot lacks only the mouth at the top of the bosses. At High Down (Brown 1915, IV, pl. CXXXVII, 4) the bosses are smaller. The pedestal pot at Horton Kirby (Leeds 1913, fig. 24, top row, second from right) again has six sharply-defined longitudinal bosses, and the stamps used are the same kind of ring stamp, and the chequered stamp placed diagonally as at Alfriston.

G

leaves so little in the way of physical disturbance or relics in the ground. Contrary to earlier opinion, then, there are clear archaeological traces of fifth-century Franks in the upper reaches of the Thames and at various points towards its mouth, round the coastal fringe of the Weald, in the Isle of Wight and to the west near Salisbury.

This archaeological material can now be used in assessing the historical events, and conjectural interpretation on these lines will be attempted here. Armed with this archaeological evidence, we may turn back to the records of the Anglo-Saxon Chronicle and assert that the archaeological material makes it clear that the beginning of the events in each geographical division should be set at the same chronological point. That is, of course, if we are not to assume that the Chronicle records apply only to a limited section of the settlers, and that the presence of these other people was ignored by the annalists for some reason known only to themselves. There is a strong probability that the West Saxons compiling the Chronicle suppressed the Jutish identity of Stuf and Wihtgar,[1] and a Frankish contingent might easily have suffered the same fate at their hands.

There are many opinions on the way in which the settlement was actually accomplished; backed by the words of Gildas, the most generally held belief is that a heavy first attack led to a settlement of a considerable body of people, which was followed by smaller, occasional settlements throughout the following century. The Teutonic leader who arrived from over the sea would have been the well-known type of barbarian fighting man, well-built and of great courage, followed to the death by his small band of loyal retainers. He would be fighting against the Romano-Britons, who although now bereft of the Roman army would still be able to draw on Roman military tradition, no doubt retained much of the equipment, and were able sometimes to find leaders who had had a Roman military training, e.g. St. Germanus, and the victor of *Mons Badonicus* (?Arthur) who, from the indications of later tradition and the duties of his post as a kind of *Comes Britanniarum*, was able to command a force of armoured mounted cavalry. A formidable foe, indeed, to be faced by small bands of barbarians landing piecemeal from ships. It must soon have become apparent to those who made the attempt that the invasion, at any rate of the rich south, would need to be carefully planned and carried out with detailed efficiency.

This is surely the story that is told by the archaeological evidence. The Roman army withdrawn from Britain numbered a great many Germans amongst its ranks, and these troops were used in an attempt to resist the pressure of the Germans surging across the Rhine. The course of the earliest invasion of Belgium and northern France by the Franks is far from clear in the written records. Salian Franks had been settled as *laeti* by Constantius Chlorus in the area of Amiens, Beauvais, Troyes and Langres in 294–5, and by 357 Salian Franks were already settled in Toxandria,

---

[1] Collingwood and Myres 1937, 365–6.

between the Scheldt and the Meuse.[1] In 451 the Salians fought as *foederati* with Aëtius against the Huns. Only this much seems indisputable. A date of 446 is proposed for a battle by Aëtius against the Salians at *Vicus Helena*, presumed to be Helesmes (Nord). By 455 the Salians under Clodio were as far south as Cambrai and Arras. These few facts are not inconsistent with the archaeological evidence of the presence of Franks (as *laeti*) in the late fourth and early fifth century in northern France, and probably as independent settlers in Belgium in the middle of the fifth century.

If the continental records of the Salian Franks at this period are so slight, it is no wonder that an expedition to Britain should have gone unrecorded. Archaeological evidence, however, goes on to tell us that some of these people transplanted themselves in the second half of the fifth century throughout England south of the Thames in most of the parts not made uninhabitable by the forest of the Weald. If it was these men who undertook the leadership of the initial invasion, Frankish settlers, *foederati* and Franco-Roman soldiers, especially those who might already have served in Britain and so would know the terrain before them, then the result must have been a well-planned and co-ordinated operation carried out by the top-rank fighting men of the age. By deploying their forces from Kent to the Isle of Wight, and synchronizing their attacks, they would, indeed, have been able to overwhelm all resistance to the south of the Thames, causing Britons to flee to London[2] and over-running the land as Gildas would have us believe. There seems very good reason, then, for visualizing the events recorded in the Chronicle as portraying a single, concerted operation.

Bede[3] has recorded that Aelle was the first to have *imperium* over the peoples south of the Humber, and this would explain the strategy of the invasion. Aelle in command of and directing the attack, would have a central position in the flotilla, so that contact with the forces to his left and right could be more easily maintained. Cerdic and Cynric, with Stuf and Wihtgar, invading Hampshire to the west, and Hengist to the east in Kent. The story of invitation by Vortigern to Hengist and Horsa indicated they were already in occupation as *foederati*, but their revolt could have been timed to coincide with the arrival of Aelle as leader, and other forces. The attackers may have advanced as well up the Thames, so cutting off in a pincer movement the south-eastern segment of Britain—a strategy which was to be adopted once again in 892 when the Vikings established two large camps, one at Milton in the north of Kent, and one at Appledore in the south. Nevertheless, as traces of the invaders are sparse in the middle Thames, and as there is a close relationship between the Sussex and Surrey settlements, it looks as though the main force of the attack was launched from the south towards the upper Thames and the Croydon area.

[1] Verlinden 1954, p. 5.
[2] Anglo-Saxon Chronicle, year 456.
[3] *Ecclesiastical History*, II, 5.

We may then take the liberty of allocating the date of A.D. 449[1] to the arrival, not only of Hengist and Horsa's reinforcements, but of Aelle and his fleet in Sussex (instead of A.D. 477) and of Cerdic and Cynric in Hampshire (instead of A.D. 495) We may further take up Stenton's suggestion that there is evidence of duplication of events in the West Saxon annals, i.e. the arrival of Cerdic and Cynric in five ships at *Cerdices ora* and their fight against the Welsh on the same day (given as 495) is the same event as the arrival of West Saxons in three ships at *Cerdices ora* when Stuf and Wihtgar fought the Britons (given as 514). The arrival of Port and his two sons Bieda and Maegla in two ships at *Portesmutha* (given as 501) should also be placed at the same point of time, i.e. 449. The battle fought by Cerdic and Cynric against Natanleod (508) thirteen years after their landing, and by Cerdic and Cynric at *Cerdicesleaga* thirteen years after the other landing, Stenton suggested were identical.

Now the rest of the dates are not likely to be accurate, but the order of events is presumably correct. In allocating dates on the principles suggested above, therefore, it will be a useful procedure to base calculations on the Chronicle dates to obtain an idea of the sequence and possible spacing in time of events. The battles fought by Cerdic and Cynric thirteen years after landing would therefore be placed at 462, the battle of Old Sarum would become 487 and the Battle of Bedford 506. The reign of Ceawlin would have extended from A.D. 495 to 528, and the puzzling occasion when he and Cutha fought the Britons at *Fethanleag* and Cutha was killed, and Ceawlin 'returned in anger to his own', would have been in 519.

The reasoned alteration of dates in this way would solve a number of problems. It has always been quite clear from archaeological evidence that the areas of Bedford, Aylesbury, Limbury, Bensington, and Eynsham must have been settled by Saxons long before 571, the Chronicle date for the battle, and a remaining British enclave in this district has been proposed as the only possible solution. As early as 1925 Leeds thought that the battle should be put about a century earlier in order to fit the facts of archaeology.[2] The sites of Kempston near Bedford and Luton near Limbury were already settled in the fifth century, and the same applies to the upper Thames area where Eynsham is situated, while the Quoit Brooch Style plaque from Bishopstone, Bucks., and a fifth-century glass cone beaker at Dinton near by,[3] show the presence of Franks at the same time near Aylesbury. Even 506 therefore seems too late for important battles to be fought at these places.

Next in the list of kings to have the *imperium* over the kingdoms south of the Humber, Bede names Ceawlin, who was succeeded in this office by Ethelbert of Kent. Now, if one accepts the Chronicle dates of Ceawlin A.D. 560–593 and Ethelbert

[1] See Appendix, p. 88 for the relevant entries in the Anglo-Saxon Chronicle.

[2] *History*, X (1925), p. 105.

[3] Douglas 1793, pl. XVI, 5.

A.D. ?560–616,[1] it will be seen that their reigns would be practically contemporary and we would have to assume that Ethelbert took over the office while Ceawlin was still living and ruling his kingdom. Ethelbert's dates are confirmed by external records, but Ceawlin's are not. If the proposed archaeological dating is accepted, Ceawlin would be reigning from 495 to 528, well before Ethelbert began ruling in Kent. The genealogy of the house of Wessex as given by the Chronicle, however, is contradicted in the genealogy of Aethelwulf in the preface of some manuscripts,[2] where Creoda and not Cynric is cited as the son of Cerdic, i.e. the line is given as Cerdic—Creoda—Cynric—Ceawlin, so that even the succession is doubtful. The commands of Aelle, Ceawlin and Ethelbert were held during a period of 167 years (449–616 on archaeological reckoning) or a minimum of 139 years if the Chronicle dates of 477–616 are accepted, so that at some time there must have been one period, or perhaps two, when there was no *imperium*. The most likely explanation of a hiatus is that this should have happened immediately after the Battle of *Mons Badonicus*, when Gildas says the Saxons were quiet for some time. It must certainly have happened after the *imperium* of Aelle on either method of calculation. If Ceawlin was in power 495–528, as suggested, this envelops all the period during which the battle must be dated, i.e. 490–516, but still one more puzzle of the Chronicle will be solved if we adhere to these dates. According to the Chronicle, nine years before his death (584), Ceawlin, in company with Cutha, fought the Britons at *Fethanleag*. Although it is reported that Ceawlin took many townships and countless spoils, it is also said that Cutha was killed, followed by the curious phrase that Ceawlin 'returned in anger to his own'. The taking of many townships and countless spoils must have been Ceawlin's prosecution of the traditional family feud for his son Cutha, but the fact of his death, and the implied retreat of Ceawlin to safely defended and settled territory, suggest that this event might be equated with a smashing defeat such as happened at *Mons Badonicus*. This is fully supported by the ensuing entries in the Chronicle which records a great slaughter at *Wodnesbeorg* when Ceawlin was 'driven out',[3] to be followed in the next year by the deaths of Ceawlin, Cwichelm and Crida. Ceolwulf began to reign in Wessex in 597, apparently succeeding Ceol(ric) whose reign started two years before Ceawlin's death, so that it is obvious that Ceawlin lost his power long before he died, and as the opponents at *Wodnesbeorg* are not named, it was no doubt a revolt of his own people he had to face at that time. In this system of reckoning the Ethelbert mentioned in 568 could not have been the famous king of Kent. The date of the battle of *Fethanleag* when Cutha was killed would fall in 519

---

[1] 560 may be the date of Ethelbert's birth rather than the beginning of his reign: G. H. Wheeler, 'Gildas de Excidio Britanniae, Chapter 26', *English Historical Review*, XLI (1926), pp. 501–2.

[2] D. Whitelock, *The Anglo-Saxon Chronicle* (1961), p. 4, note 7.

[3] A phrase which the entries in the years 645 and 658 show means 'was deprived of his kingdom'.

if calculated nine years before the death of Ceawlin by the suggested method, and here is a date which fits as well as can be expected with that of *Mons Badonicus*. The hiatus when there was no *imperium* and the peace of Gildas spread throughout the land would then fall between Ceawlin and Ethelbert. His kingdom of Kent had, by the time of his accession in ?560, become the richest in the country, much of this affluence being dependent on continued good relations with the Frankish kingdom.

As the early entries of the Chronicle referring to the three separate districts are set down in a processional order of self-contained units, and the entries within these units are spaced at regular intervals, this suggests, of its own accord, that the relative arrangement of items is mechanically arbitrary, and the possibility that two or even three of the sets of events may have been contemporary seems to be a reasonable conjecture. The physical traces of the invaders, as brought forward by archaeological study of grave goods, insist that there was no appreciable difference in the date of the first landings in Kent, Sussex and Hampshire, and so a simultaneous beginning for the three sets of Chronicle events seems unavoidable. Amongst other possible conjectural reconstructions is the suggestion that the Chronicle records the history of selected tribes only, that this is correct, and that the invasion by the other people noticed here was not recorded. This theory, however, leaves the problem of the dates of the battles of *Mons Badonicus* and Bedford still unsolved.

The archaeological traces of Frankish culture in the invasion goods of people in the upper Thames area, Hampshire, the Isle of Wight and Sussex are indisputable, but there seems to be comparatively little later trace of them. It is otherwise in Kent, where the continued presence of Frankish goods throughout the sixth century testifies to unbroken contact with the continent. Historical records, too, are plentiful on this score. Ethelbert issued laws inspired by the *Lex Salica* which were the laws of the Salian Franks made by Clovis, and Ethelbert himself married Bertha, daughter of Charibert, king of Paris, an alliance which suggests the possibility that he held the position of under-king.[1] His son Eadbald also married Bertha, and then later a second Frankish wife. Two of his great-grandchildren bore Frankish names, Hlothere and Eorcengota.

Perhaps this attack of A.D. 449 represents the first successful attack recorded by Gildas, and it was followed by a long period of peace without further invasions. This should coincide with a break in the grave goods. They certainly change after about A.D. 500, for few of the objects shown in the distribution maps occur in sixth-century contexts, and the Quoit Brooch animal style disappears, leaving little or no trace of itself in the subsequent Style I of the early sixth century. It will require a detailed study of the cemeteries to establish whether or not there was anywhere a period of non-occupation. In Kent, the Isle of Wight and the upper Thames area, most ceme-

---

[1] Stenton 1943, p. 59.

teries must have been in continuous use, but in Wiltshire, where grave clusters are often small, there certainly seems to be a gap in date between, say, Bassett Down and the late burials of Rodmead Down, Roundway, Purton, Alvediston, etc.

The archaeology shows that the whole of this area south of the Thames was settled at the same time, and by people who came from northern France and Belgium in the middle of the fifth century. By comparison with graves of their contemporaries in the areas they left and by studying the metal-working techniques and the animal ornament they favoured, we may say that they must have been members of the Frankish cultural group, but with an admixture of other tribes.

These Frankish ex-*laeti*, or settlers in northern Gaul, were soldiers who had the advantage of the training and the accoutrement of the Roman army. When a large-scale invasion of Romanized Britain was about to be launched, they were the men with the best qualifications to lead, organize and discipline the horde of attackers. Archaeological evidence suggests that this, in fact, is what they did, and when they died, a few well-furnished graves remained at Petersfinger, Abingdon, Brighthampton, Chatham Lines, Long Wittenham, and elsewhere to prove that this first settlement included not only commanders, but their wives and children as well.

Appendix

EXCERPTS FROM THE ANGLO-SAXON CHRONICLE[1]
RELATING TO THE INVASIONS SOUTH OF THE THAMES

449   In this year Mauritius and Valentinus succeeded to the throne and ruled for seven years.

    In their days Hengest and Horsa, invited by Vortigern, king of the Britons, came to Britain at the place which is called Ebbsfleet, first to the help of the Britons, but afterwards fought against them.

455   In this year Hengest and Horsa fought against King Vortigern at the place which is called *Ægelesthrep*, and his brother Horsa was killed there; and after that Hengest and his son Æsc succeeded to the kingdom.

456 (457 A)   In this year Hengest and his son Æsc fought against the Britons in the place which is called *Creacanford* and killed 4000 men; and the Britons then deserted Kent and fled with great fear to London.

465 (461 B, C; 466 F)   In this year Hengest and Æsc fought against the Britons near *Wippedesfleot*, and there slew twelve British chiefs, and a thegn of theirs was slain there whose name was Wipped.

473   In this year Hengest and Æsc fought against the Britons and captured countless spoils and the Britons fled from the English as from fire.

477   In this year Ælle and his three sons, Cymen, Wlencing, and Cissa, came into Britain with three ships at the place which is called *Cymenesora*, and there they killed many Britons and drove some into flight into the wood which is called *Andredeslea*.

485   In this year Ælle fought against the Britons near the bank of *Mearcredesburna*.

488   In this year Æsc succeeded to the kingdom and was king of the people of Kent for twenty-four years.

491 (490 F)   In this year Ælle and Cissa besieged *Andredesceaster*, and killed all who were inside, and there was not even a single Briton left alive.

495   In this year two chieftains, Cerdic and his son Cynric, came with five ships to Britain at the place which is called *Cerdicesora*, and they fought against the Britons on the same day.

501   In this year Port and his two sons Bieda and Mægla came to Britain with two ships at the place which is called Portsmouth; and there they killed a [young] British man of very high rank.

---

[1] *The Anglo-Saxon Chronicle*, ed. D. Whitelock (Eyre and Spottiswoode Ltd. and Rutgers University Press, 1961). The figures and letters in brackets refer to alternative dates given in different manuscripts of the Chronicle.

508   In this year Cerdic and Cynric killed a British king, whose name was Natanleod, and 5000 men with him; and the land right up to Charford was called Netley after him.

514   In this year the West Saxons came into Britain with three ships at the place which is called *Cerdicesora*; and Stuf and Wihtgar fought against the Britons and put them to flight.

519   In this year Cerdic and Cynric succeeded to the kingdom; and in the same year they fought against the Britons at a place called Charford.

527   In this year Cerdic and Cynric fought against the Britons in the place which is called *Cerdicesleag*.

530   In this year Cerdic and Cynric captured the Isle of Wight and killed a few men in *Wihtgarabyrig*.

534   In this year Cerdic died; and his son Cynric ruled for twenty-seven years. And they gave the Isle of Wight to their two kinsmen, Stuf and Wihtgar.

544   In this year Wihtgar died and he was buried in *Wihtgarabyrig*.

552   In this year Cynric fought against the Britons in the place which is called Salisbury, and put the Britons to flight. Cerdic was Cynric's father. Cerdic was the son of Elesa, the son of Esla, the son of Gewis, the son of Wig, the son of Freawine, the son of Freothogar, the son of Brand, the son of Bældæg, the son of Woden.

556   In this year Cynric and Ceawlin fought against the Britons at Barbury.

560 (**559** F)   In this year Ceawlin succeeded to the kingdom in Wessex.

565   In this year Ethelbert succeeded to the kingdom of the people of Kent and held it for fifty-three years.

568   In this year Ceawlin and Cutha fought against Ethelbert, and drove him in flight into Kent, and killed two ealdormen, Oslaf and Cnebba, at *Wibbandun*.

571   In this year Cuthwulf fought against the Britons at *Biedcanford*, and captured four towns, Limbury, Aylesbury, Bensington, and Eynsham; and in the same year he died.

577   In this year Cuthwine and Ceawlin fought against the Britons and killed three kings, Conmail, Condidan, and Farinmail, at the place which is called Dyrham; and they captured three of their cities, Gloucester, Cirencester, and Bath.

584   In this year Ceawlin and Cutha fought against the Britons at the place which is called *Fethanleag*, and Cutha was killed there; and Ceawlin captured many villages and countless spoils, and in anger returned to his own land.

591   In this year Ceol reigned for five years.

592   In this year there occurred a great slaughter at 'Woden's barrow' and Ceawlin was driven out.

593   In this year Ceawlin, Cwichelm, and Crida perished.

List of Maps

Inlaid loops

21. Chessell Down, I.o.W.; no. 1, pl. III, a.
22. Chessell Down, I.o.W.; no. 2, pl. III, b.
23. Chessell Down, I.o.W.; no. 3, pl. III, d.
24. Long Wittenham, Berks., grave 111; no. 4, pl. III, e.
25. Prittlewell, Essex; no. 12.
26. Alfriston, Sussex, grave 52; no. 17, pl. V, d.
27. High Down, Sussex; no. 25.
28. High Down, Sussex; no. 26.
29. High Down, Sussex; no. 27.
30. Guildown, Surrey, grave 130; no. 28.
31. Guildown, Surrey, grave 135; no. 29.
32. Petersfinger, Wilts, grave LXIII; Leeds and Shortt 1953, pl. VII.
33. Mitcham, Surrey, grave 29; Evison 1958, pl. XXVI, a.
34. Winterbourne Gunner, Wilts., grave VI; to be published in *Wilts. Arch. Mag.*, 1964.

Inlaid iron buckle loops with semicircular plates

35. High Down, Sussex, grave IX; no. 18, pl. V, e.
36. Petersfinger, Wilts., grave 29; no. 30. Leeds and Shortt, 1953, pl. VI.

Iron purse mounts[1]

37. High Down, Sussex, grave XIV; no. 19, pl. VI, a.
38. High Down, Sussex; no. 24, pl. VI, f.
39. Alfriston, Sussex, grave 91 (Fig. 23, *b*); previously unpublished except for mention *Sussex Arch. Coll.* LVII, 205.
40. Alfriston, Sussex, grave ?B (Pl. 6, *e*);[2] previously unpublished.

MAP 3
Metal-inlaid work of the fifth century on the continent[3]

Inlaid iron buckle loops with repoussé plates

1. Éprave, Belgium; Dasnoy 1954, pl. I, 1.
2. Envermeu, Seine Inf., France; Dasnoy, pl. I, 4.
3. Lavoye, Meuse, grave 189, Chenet 1941, p. 116, note 3.
4. Normée, Marne, Épernay Museum.
5. St. Pierre du Vauvray, France; L. Coutil, *Archéologie gauloise, gallo-romaine, franque et carolingienne*, II, opp. p. 98, no. 50.
6. Kärlich, Rhineland, Germany; Dasnoy 1954, pl. I, 3.

---

[1] The purse mount from Brighthampton, Oxon. grave 5 (*Arch.* 37, p. 394; Holmqvist 1951, p. 49, Dasnoy 1954, p. 282) has been X-rayed, but does not show inlay.

[2] The label on this object has become illegible, but the length, 3 in., agrees with the description under grave B of 'An iron object, 3 in. long (possibly the top of a purse, or a strike-a-light)'.

[3] A few of these occur in early sixth-century contexts.

Inlaid iron buckle loops with inlaid iron plates

   Inlaid circles

7. Pry, Belgium; Dasnoy 1954, pl. II.
8. Éprave, Belgium; *ibid.*, pl. III, 3.
9. Spontin, Belgium; Namur museum.
10. Reuden, grave 8, Thuringia, Germany; Holmqvist 1951, Abb. 16, 3.
11. Weimar, grave 83; Holmqvist 1951, p. 40.
12. Weimar, grave 84; *ibid.* Abb. 16, 1.
13. Herten, Lörrach, grave 57; Garscha 1962, 135 ff., Abb. 1–4, Taf. 44, 1–4.
14. Saint-Prex, Vaud, Switzerland; Salin 1952 II, fig. 153 bis.
15. Unknown provenance, Sammlung Diergardt; Holmqvist 1951, Abb. 16, 2.

   Complicated inlaid patterns

16. Fère-Champenoise, Marne, France; Salin 1957, III, p. 182, fig. 73 bis.
17. Oberlörick, Rhineland, Germany; Böhner 1951, Taf. 27, c.
18. Unknown provenance, Sammlung Diergardt; Holmqvist 1951, Abb. 25, 2.
19. Unknown provenance, Sammlung Diergardt; Werner 1953, Taf. 6, 4.

Inlaid buckles with oval plates

20. Lézeville, Meurthe et Moselle, France; Salin 1922, pl. II, 3.
21. Caranda, France; Salin 1943, pl. XX, 1.
22. Niederbreisig, Rhineland; S. de Ricci, *Catalogue of Germanic Antiquities belonging to J. Pierpont Morgan* (1910), pl. II, 49.
23. Basel-Kleinhüningen, grave 37; unpublished.[1]
24. Basel-Kleinhüningen, grave 67; Holmqvist 1951, Abb. 17, 3.
25. Basel-Kleinhüningen, grave 105; unpublished.
26. Basel-Kleinhüningen, grave 112; unpublished.
27. Basel-Gotterbarmweg, grave 19; Holmqvist 1951, Abb. 17, 1.
28. Basel-Gotterbarmweg, grave 32; *ibid.*, p. 43.

Inlaid buckles with semicircular plates

29. Basel-Kleinhüningen, grave 18; unpublished.
30. Basel-Kleinhüningen, grave 82; unpublished.

Inlaid loops

31. Samson, Belgium; Dasnoy 1954, pl. V, 1.
32. Samson, Belgium; *ibid.*, pl. V, 2.
33. Caranda, France; Salin 1957, III, fig. 68.
34. Nettersheim, grave 2, Schleiden, Germany; *Bonner Jahrbücher*, 142 (1937), 344, Taf. 78, below, left.
35. Grosskarben, Oberhessen; *Germania*, 15 (1931), 258 ff., Abb. 4.
36. Straubing, grave 2, Niederbayern; Holmqvist 1951, p. 42.

---

[1] For information on unpublished buckles in Switzerland, I am very much indebted to Dr. Moosbrugger-Leu. Since the map was completed, Herr R. Wiesendanger has advised me of four other inlaid loops and one inlaid buckle with oval plate at St. Prex.

37. Elstertrebnitz, Borna; *ibid.*, p. 42.
38. Elxleben, Thuringia; B. Schmidt, *Die späte Völkerwanderungszeit in Mitteldeutschland* (1961), Abb. 17, a.
39. Bodman, Stockach, grave 20; Garscha 1962, 145, Taf. 45, 13.
40. Bodman, Stockach, grave 3; *ibid.*, 148, Taf. 46, 5.
41. Bodman, Stockach, grave 29; *ibid.*, 153–4, Abb. 2, 9.
42. Basel-Kleinhüningen, grave 139, Switzerland; unpublished.
43. Basel-Kleinhüningen, grave 229; Garscha 1962, 152–3, Taf. 44, 5–6.
44. Basel-Gotterbarmweg, grave 17; *ibid.*, 151–2, Taf. 44, 6–7.
45. Basel-Bernerring, grave 31; unpublished.
46. Bülach, grave 4; Werner 1953, 85, Taf. 1, 16.
47. Bülach, grave 14; *ibid.*, 86, Taf. 1, 5.
48. Elgg, grave 130; unpublished.
49. Lausanne, Bel-Air, grave 174; unpublished.

Purse mounts

50. Éprave, Belgium, grave 245; Dasnoy 1954, pl. v, 3.
51. Krefeld-Gellep, grave 43, Germany; Pirling 1960 b, Taf. 59.
52. Carnuntum; Holmqvist 1951, Abb. 21, 1.
53. Unknown provenance, Leiden Museum; Evison 1955, pl. VII, a.
54. Unknown provenance, Sammlung Diergardt; Holmqvist 1951, Abb. 21, 2.

Strap-slides with close trellis-work inlay

55. Oberlörick, Germany; Werner 1953, Taf. 6, 1.
56. Andernach-Kirchberg; *ibid.*, Taf. 6, 5.
57. Unknown provenance, Sammlung Diergardt; *ibid.*, Taf. 6, 6.

MAP 4
Frankish fifth-century animal ornament and Quoit Brooch Style

Frankish fifth-century animal ornament in England

1. Winterbourne Gunner, Wilts., grave VI; strap-end (Fig. 20, *b*, p. 60).
2. Howletts, Kent; plate on francisca (Fig. 27, *l*, p. 60).
3. Brighthampton, Oxon., grave 31; sword scabbard (Fig. 11, *c*, pp. 60–1).
4. Bidford-on-Avon, Warwicks.; bronze-bound bucket (Fig. 24, *f–j*, p. 61).

Quoit Brooch Style—animal

(for descriptions, etc., see pp. 101 ff., 119 ff.)

5. Bowcombe Down, I.o.W., grave 13; roundel (Fig. 28, *a*).
6. Lyminge, Kent; penannular brooch (Fig. 28, *g*).
7. Howletts, Kent, grave 5; rectangular plate (Pl. 13, *b*).
8. Alfriston, Sussex, grave 17; buckle loop, plate and counter-plate (Pl. 14, *c*).
9. Croydon, Surrey; tubular strap distributor (Pl. 13, *a*).
10. Bifrons, Kent; pendants (Pl. 12, *a*).
11. Bishopstone, Bucks.; rectangular plate (Pl. 12, *b*).

12. Bifrons, Kent; strap-end (Pl. 11, *a*).
13. Faversham, Kent; disc used as brooch. (Pl. 10, *a*).
14. Howletts, Kent; quoit brooch (Pl. 11, *b*).
15. Howletts, Kent, grave 13; quoit brooch (fragment) (Pl. 10, *c*).
16. Sarre, Kent; quoit brooch (Pl. 12, *c*).

Quoit Brooch Style—horses' heads and human masks

17. High Down, Sussex, grave xii; strap-slide (Pl. 13, *c*).
18. Chessell Down, I.o.W.; strap-end (Pl. 14, *a*).
19. Croydon, Surrey; strap-end (Pl. 14, *b*).
20. Alfriston, Sussex, grave 43; penannular brooch (Pl. 15, *a*).
21. Riseley, Kent, grave xxii; penannular brooch (Fig. 28, *i*).
22. High Down, Sussex, grave 34; rectangular buckle loop and heart-shaped plate (Pl. 14, *d*).
23. Higham, Kent; disc brooch (Pl. 15, *b*).

Quoit Brooch Style—non-zoomorphic

24. Howletts, Kent, grave 28; square plate used as brooch (Pl. 16, *a*).
25. High Down, Sussex, grave 60; square quoit brooch (Pl. 16, *b*).
26. Alfriston, Sussex, graves A and 17; rectangular plate (Fig. 28, *j*).

MAP 5

Roman glasses in Anglo-Saxon graves

(This, and map 6, are after Harden 1956 with additions and omissions. The plate and figure references, unless otherwise stated, are to Harden 1956.)

a. *Cone-beakers*

1. Chessell Down, I.o.W.; Carisbrooke Castle Museum, I.o.W. (*J.B.A.A.* ii, 52, fig.).
2. Chessell Down, I.o.W.; B.M. 69 10–11 2.
3. East Shefford, Berks.; B.M. 93 7–16 2.
4. High Down, Sussex (grave 32); Worthing Museum (Harden 1951, fig. 2).
5. Alfriston, Sussex (grave 60); Lewes Museum (pl. xv, a).
6. Faversham, Kent; B.M. 1320 '70 (pl. xv, b).
7. Westbere, Kent; Canterbury Museum (Jessup 1946, pl. iii, 15).
8. Selmeston, Sussex, Lewes Museum.

b. *Mould-blown beaker*

9. Newport Pagnell, Bucks.; B.M., Cooke loan (pl. xv, c).

c. *Inscribed goblet*

10. High Down, Sussex (grave 49); Worthing Museum (pl. xv, d).

d. *Bowls*

  i. *With indents*

11. High Down, Sussex; Worthing Museum (Harden 1951, fig. 5).
12. Bifrons, Kent; Maidstone Museum (pl. xv, f).

13. Eastry, Kent; Brook House, Eastry (*P.S.A.* (2) xxii, 365, fig. 2).
14. Milton-next-Sittingbourne, Kent; B.M. 1905 4–18 13.

ii. *With pushed-in base*
15. High Down, Sussex (grave 53); Worthing Museum (Harden 1951, fig. 5).

iii. *With concave or straight sides; rounded rim*
16. East Shefford, Berks.; B.M. 93 7–16 4.
17. Holme Pierrepont, Notts.; B.M. 1931 3–31 2 (pl. xv, g).
18. Faversham Kent; Pitt-Rivers Museum, Farnham, Dorset.

iv. *With concave or straight sides; knocked-off rim*
19. Bifrons, Kent; Maidstone Museum (pl. xv, e).
20. Great Chesterford, Essex. M.o.W. excavation.
21. Selmeston, Sussex, Lewes Museum.

e. *Flasks*
i. *Bulbous, plain*
22. Bifrons, Kent; Maidstone Museum (pl. xv, i).
23. High Down, Sussex; Worthing Museum (Harden 1951, fig. 7).

ii. *Bulbous, with cut circles on body*
24. Westbere, Kent; Canterbury Museum (pl. xv, j).

f. *Amphora*
25. Mitcham, Surrey; Museum of Arch. and Ethnology, Cambridge, Bidder loan (pl. xv, k).

g. *Square-based bottle*
26. Howletts, Kent; B.M. 1925 7–7 2 (missing).

MAP 6
Fifth-century glasses

Stemmed beakers
a. *With short stem*
1. Croydon, Surrey; Croydon Public Library, fig. 25.
2. Howletts, Kent; B.M. 1925 7–7 2 (pl. xvi, a).

b. *With tall stem*
3. High Down, Sussex (grave 24), Worthing Museum (fig. 25).

Claw-beakers
a. *Experimental types*
4. Finglesham, Kent; private possession (fig. 25).
5. Eastry, Kent; Brook House, Eastry (*P.S.A.* (2) xxii, 365, fig. 2).
6. Broadstairs, Kent; Council Offices, Broadstairs (Thorpe 1935, pl. x, a).
7. Howletts, Kent (grave 7); B.M. 1936 5–11 30.

8. Howletts, Kent (grave 14); B.M. 1936 5–11 48.
9. Sarre, Kent (grave 60); Maidstone Museum (pl. xvi, b).
10. Lyminge, Kent (grave 41); *Arch. Cant.* lxix, pl. xi.

b. *Fine types*

11. Castle Eden, Durham; B.M. 1947 10–9 1 (fig. 25).
12. Gilton, Kent (grave 82); Liverpool Museum 6073 (Thorpe 1935, pl. xii, c).
13. Faversham, Kent; B.M. 1336 a '70.
14. Faversham, Kent; B.M. 1336 b '70.
15. Reculver, Kent; Canterbury Museum 955 (pl. xvi, c).

Cone-beakers

a. *With horizontal trails at neck and vertical loops on body*

i. *Tall and slender*

16. Kempston, Beds.; B.M. 91 6–24 1 (pl. xvi, d, fig. 25).
17. Alfriston, Sussex (grave 39), Fig. 16, e, present work; Lewes Museum (*Sussex Arch. Coll.* lvi, pl. xiv, 1).
18. Alfriston, Sussex (grave 43); Lewes Museum (*idem*, lvii, pl. xxvi, 2).
19. Alfriston, Sussex (grave uncertain); Lewes Museum (*ibid.*, pl. xxvi, 3).
20. High Down, Sussex (grave 27); Worthing Museum (Thorpe 1935, pl. xiii, a).
21. 22. Guildown, Surrey (graves 56 and 109); Guildford Museum (*Surrey Arch. Coll.* xxxix, 10).
23. Mitcham, Surrey (grave 201); London Museum A 19747 (*Surrey Arch. Coll.* lvi, pl. xx).
24. Ozingell, Kent; Liverpool Museum 6643 (Roach Smith iii, pl. iii, 8).
25. Westbere, Kent; Canterbury Museum (Jessup 1946, pl. iii, 5).
26. Howletts, Kent (grave 18); B.M. 1936 5–11 71.
27. Howletts, Kent (grave 30); B.M. 1936 5–11 103.
28. Chessell Down, I.o.W.; Carisbrooke Castle Museum (*J.B.A.A.* ii, 52, fig. 1).
29. Cassington, Oxon.; Ashmolean Museum 1940.220 (*Oxoniensia*, vii, pl. v, a).
30. East Shefford, Berks. (grave 24); Newbury Museum, Berks. (*Journ. Roy. Anthrop. Inst.* xlv, pl. iii).
31. East Shefford, Berks.; B.M. 93 7–16 1.
32. Longbridge, Warwicks.; B.M. 80 2–14 22.
33. Dover, Kent; M.o.W. excavation (Fig. 12, g present work.)
    Also one without provenance in Canterbury Museum.

b. *White festoons on body, with or without trails at neck*

34. Bifrons, Kent (grave 1); Maidstone Museum 269 (pl. xvi, f, fig. 25).
35. Dinton, Bucks.; Aylesbury Museum, Bucks. (Douglas 1793, pl. xvi 5).
36. High Down, Sussex (grave 33); Worthing Museum (Thorpe 1935, pl. ix, c).
37. Great Chesterford, Essex (grave 128); M.o.W. excavation.

Bell-beakers, pointed, with knob on base, without constriction in body

38. Howletts, Kent; B.M. 1918 7–8 32 (fig. 25).
39. Bifrons, Kent; Maidstone Museum 268 (*Arch. Cant.* xix, pl. I, 5).
40. Sarre, Kent (grave 4); Maidstone Museum 261 (pl. xvi, j.).

Bottles

41. Bifrons, Kent; Maidstone Museum 270 (pl. XVI, i, fig. 25).
42. Lyminge, Kent (grave 13); Maidstone Museum, (*Arch. Cant.* LXIX, pl. V, 1).

Bowls

    a. *'York' type, with neck-spiral and vertical loops*

43. Islip, Northants; Northampton Museum (fig. 25).
44. York (The Mount); Yorkshire Museum (pl. XVI, g).
45. Lackford, Suffolk; Museum of Arch. and Ethnology, Cambridge (Lethbridge 1951, fig. 23).
46. Faversham, Kent; B.M. 1314 '70.

    b. *'Westbere' type with various trailed or mould-blown decoration*

47. High Down, Sussex (grave 14); Worthing Museum (pl. XVI, h, fig. 25).
48. High Down, Sussex (grave 22); Worthing Museum (*Arch.* LIV, 376, fig. 6).
49. Westbere, Kent; Canterbury Museum (Jessup 1946, pl. III, 28).
50. Westbere, Kent; lost (Jessup 1946, pl. III, 27).
51. Westbere, Kent; lost (Jessup 1946, pl. III, 29).

    c. *With constricted neck*

52. Alfriston, Sussex (grave 28); Lewes Museum (Harden 1951, fig. 6).
53. Howletts, Kent (grave 27); B.M. 1836 5–11 106 (pl. XV, h).

MAP 7
Fifth-century imports

Glass armlets

1. Chessell Down, I.o.W. (Fig. 9, *a*); Carisbrooke Castle Museum, unpublished.
2. Malling Hill, Sussex; British Museum (not traceable); Brown 1915, IV, pl. CLVI, 8.
3. and 4. Milton Regis, Kent (Fig. 9, *b, c*); *Arch. Cant.* LXXIV (1960), pp. 181–2, pl. III.
5. Chatham Lines, Kent (Fig. 15, *b*); Douglas 1793, pl. 14.

Bow brooches with upturned foot

6. Howletts, Kent, grave 4 (Fig. 10, *f*); *Ant. Journ.* XXVIII, p. 170, pl. XXIV, c and d.
7. Glaston, Rutland (Fig. 10, *d*); *ibid.*, pp. 169–73, fig. 1.
8. West Stow, Suffolk (Fig. 10, *a*); C. Fox, *Archaeology of the Cambridge Region* (1948), p. 281, pl. XXXV, 4.
9. West Stow or Icklingham, Suffolk (Fig. 10, *c*); Smith 1852, II, 167, pl. XLI, B, fig. 3.

Bronze cauldrons with triangular lugs

10. Long Wittenham, Berks.; F. H. Thompson, 'Anglo-Saxon sites in Lincolnshire', *Ant. Journ.* XXXVI (1956), p. 197.
11. Sawston, Cambs.; *ibid.*, p. 197.
12. Ixworth Thorpe, Suffolk; *ibid.*, p. 197.

H

Zoomorphic buckles with fixed plate

(For continental distribution cf. Werner 1958, 391, fig. 14)

13. Sarre, Kent; Hawkes and Dunning 1963, fig. 20, h.
14. Unknown provenance, Royal Museum, Canterbury; *ibid.* fig. 19 bis.
15. Long Wittenham, Berks. (Fig. 12, *a*); *ibid.*, fig. 20, g.
16. Alfriston, Sussex, grave 14 (Fig. 24, *d*); *Sussex Arch. Coll.*, pl. x, 4.

Imported pottery

17. Chessell Down, I.o.W. (Fig. 9, *f*); British Museum Reg. no. 67 7–29 141

Bow and arrows

18. Chessell Down, I.o.W. Bow, Hillier, p. 30; Brown 1910, III, 242. Arrows; Hillier, p. 37.
19. Bowcombe Down, I.o.W.; *J.B.A.A.* XVI (1860), 258.
20. Buttsole, Kent; Brown 1915, III, pl. XXXII, 1.
21. Chatham Lines, Kent; Douglas 1793, p. 77, pl. XIX, 2, 3, 6 and 8.
22. Bifrons, Kent, grave 37; Brown 1915, III, 242.

MAP 8

Bronze-bound wooden vessels with repoussé decoration
in arcade-and-dot and Christian motifs

England

1. Bidford-on-Avon, Warwicks.; Brown 1915, IV, pl. CXIII, 5 and 6.
2. Faversham, Kent; unpublished, British Museum Reg. No. 1278 '70.
3. Howletts, Kent, grave 23; unpublished, British Museum Reg. No. 1936 5–11 88 and 89 (two bronze bands).
4. Fetcham, Surrey; *Ant. Journ.* XIII, 50, fig. 2.
5. Chessell Down, I.o.W.; unpublished, British Museum Reg. No. 69 10–11 11.
6. Brockbridge, between Soberton and Droxford, Hants.; Brown 1915, IV, pl. CXIII, 2, p. 464.
7. Petersfinger, grave LX; Leeds and Shortt 1953, 38–9, pl. x.
8. Long Wittenham, Berks.; *B.M. Guide*, 1923, pp. 69–70.

Continent

9. Marchélepot, Somme; Boulanger 1909, p. 118, pl. 17.
10. Buire sur l'Ancre, Somme; *ibid.*, p. 119, fig. 127.
11. Beauvais, Oise; *ibid.*, p. 120, fig. 129.
12. Koblenz, Germany; G. Behrens, *Merowingerzeit* (1947), Abb. 159.
13. Marouil, Pas de Calais; Boulanger 1909, p. 122, fig. 130.
14. Escames, Oise; A. Houlé, 'Notice-étude sur une petite seille provenant des fouilles du cimetière franc d'Escames (Oise)', *Mémoires de la Soc. Acad. d'archéologie, sciences et arts du département de l'Oise*, XIX (1904), 556–64.
15. Haillot, Belgium, grave III; Breuer and Roosens 1957, pp. 200–2, fig. 4, 12.
16. Lavoye, Meuse; Chenet 1935, 60 ff., pl. I.
17. Weissoppenheim, Germany; Chenet 1935, pp. 94–7, figs. 26 and 27.

18. Miannay, Somme; Chenet 1935, pp. 97–9, fig. 28, Boulanger 1909, p. 122, fig. 129.
19. Roussent, Pas de Calais; Chenet 1935, p. 99, fig. 29.

MAP 9

Bronze objects manufactured in the pre-invasion period
and found in Anglo-Saxon graves

Disc or oval brooches with cabochon stone centres[1]

1. East Shefford, Berks.; *V.C.H. Berks.* I, 240, fig. 11.
2. Long Wittenham, Berks, grave 129; *Arch.* XXXIX, pl. XI. 1.
3. Gilton, Kent, grave 87; Faussett 1856, p. 28, pl. X, 15.
4. Cestersover, near Bensford Bridge, Warwicks.; *V.C.H. Warwicks.* I, 254.
5. Woodstone, Hunts.; *V.C.H. Hunts.* I, 276, fig. 15.

Continental Roman bronze belt mounts

6. Croydon, Surrey: three objects—rosette attachment, diamond-shaped strap-end
   (Hawkes and Dunning 1963, figs. 24, *e*, 23, *c*) and buckle with triangular open plate.
7. Cassington, Oxon: diamond-shaped strap-end (*ibid.*, fig. 23, *f*).

Buckles made in Britain, fourth–fifth centuries

(After Hawkes and Dunning 1963; the fig. numbers refer to that article)

   a. *Horses' head buckle loops*

8. Bifrons, Kent, fig. 15, k.
9. Stratford-on-Avon, Warwicks., fig. 16, a.

   b. *Dolphin-head loops*

10. Ash, Kent, fig. 13, o.
11. Beddingham Hill, Sussex, fig. 13, n.
12. Blewburton Hill, Berks., fig. 14, a.
13. Broadway, Worcs., fig. 13, k.
14. Reading, Berks., fig. 14, b.
15. Dover, Kent (Fig. 9, *e* of this book).
16. Mitcham, Surrey, fig. 18, f.
17. Sarre, Kent, fig. 18, i.
18. Sleaford, Lincs., fig. 19, b.

MAP 10

Bronze tubular mounts

1. Droxford, Hants.; Brown 1915, IV, pl. XCIX, 5.
2. Bifrons, Kent; *ibid.*, pl. CV, 5 (three).
3. Barrington, Cambs.; *ibid.*, pl. CV, 4; *Camb. Ant. Soc. Comm.* V, ii, p. 15, pl. V, fig. 2.

---

[1] Another brooch, from Emscote, Warwick, probably came from an Anglo-Saxon cemetery; *Ant. Journ.* V, 269, pl. XXIX, 2.

4. East Shefford, Berks.; British Museum.
5. Willsborough, near Ashford, Kent; Pitt-Rivers Museum, Farnham, Dorset.
6. High Down, Sussex, grave XXIX; *Arch.* LIV, pp. 377–8.
7. Petersfinger, Wilts., grave XLVIII; Leeds and Shortt 1953, pp. 30–2, fig. 12, pls. IV, VII and IX.
8. Reading, Berks., grave 13; Hawkes and Dunning 1963, fig. 14, b.
9. Chatham Lines, Kent, tumulus VI; Douglas 1793, pl. 6, pp. 23–4.
10. Riseley, Horton Kirby, Kent, grave XCVII; *Trans. Dartford District Ant. Soc.* VIII, 27.
11. Alfriston, Sussex, grave 91 (Fig. 23, *e*); *Surrey Arch. Coll.* LVII, p. 205, pls. XXVIII, XXIV, 9: grave 103 (Fig. 23,*f*), *ibid.* LVII, p. 207, pls. XXII, 3; XXIV, 8; XXV, 1; grave 14 (Fig. 24, *e*), *ibid.* LVI, p. 32, pls. IV, 6; X, 3 and 4; XI, 8.
12. Croydon, Surrey; *P.S.A.* 2nd ser. XV, fig. on p. 333 (Pl. 13, *a*).
13. Orange Terrace, Rochester, Kent; Rochester Museum.
14. Horton Kirby, Kent; Maidstone Museum.
15. Stowting, Kent; Maidstone Museum.

MAP II

Germanic two-dimensional animal ornament on bronze buckles, and silver-inlaid bronze buckles, of c. 400 A.D.

Germanic two-dimensional animal ornament

1. Landifay (Guise) (Fig. 27 *a*, *c*); Fleury 1877–82, II, 250.
2. Misèry, near Neslé, Somme (Frontispiece, Fig. 2, 2–3, Fig. 3, 8); Rigollot 1850, pp. 216–223, pls. X and XI.
3. Vermand, Aisne (Fig. 26, *c–e*); Pilloy 1895, II, pl. 14, 1a, 2a and 3a.
4. Vermand, Aisne (Fig. 26, *a*, *b*); Pilloy 1895, II, pl. 15, 8 and 9.
5. Sédan (Pl. 9, *c*); Forssander 1937, Abb. 24, 1.
6. Hungary; Forssander 1937, Abb. 24, 2.
7. Unknown provenance; Oldenburg Museum (Pl. 18, *a*); Behrens 1953, Abb. 19, 5.
8. Colombier-sur-Seulles, Calvados (Pl. 9, *b*); Pilloy 1912, III, 251–3.

Silver-inlaid bronze buckles[1]

9. Herbergen, Oldenburg (Pl. 9, *a*); Behrens 1953, Abb. 19, 4.
10. Mainz; Lindenschmit 1864–91, IV, Taf. 12, 1.
11. Vermand, Aisne; Pilloy 1895, II, pl. 15, 6.
12. Abbeville (Homblières); Pilloy 1880, I, p. 190, pl. 5, 1.

[1] Nos. 3, 4, 5, 7 and 8 above are also inlaid with silver.

Description of Figures

FIGURE I

Vermand, Aisne, grave of military leader (see also Plate 1)

a. Silver-gilt *strap-end*, split end attached by two rivets, scroll decoration. L. 4·3 cm.
b. Silver-gilt *buckle*, L. 3·8 cm; loop with zoomorphic terminals and triangle niello inlay; shield-shaped plate with niello triangle border and heart-shaped chip-carved gilt panel.
c. One of ten *darts* or *spearheads*. L. 20–25 cm.
d. *Francisca*. L. of blade 12 cm.
e. Oval silver *plate* with three rivets and four other rivet holes. L. 4·9 cm.
f. *Spearhead*, inlaid with silver on the blade, and with bronze binding and projecting animal head on the socket. L. 50 cm.[1]

Vermand, Aisne, grave 24

g. Silver-gilt applied *disc brooch* with repoussé star pattern; separate silver collar 3 mm wide.
h. Silver-gilt applied *disc brooch* with repoussé lion mask and zigzag border.
i. Gold *finger ring* with oval imitation chalcedony stone.
j. Silver-gilt *bow brooch* with disc foot.
k. Silver-gilt *bow brooch* with spatulate foot.
l. Silver *tutulus brooch* with amber top.
m. Silver *tutulus brooch*.

The grave also contained gold spindle-shaped beads and a gold medallion of Valentinian I. A photograph published B. Brown 1915, IV, pl. XCLVIII is said to show the contents of a lady's tomb at Vermand. Two of the tutulus brooches, a bow brooch with spreading foot and the two repoussé discs are obviously from grave 24, but there are no gold beads or gold ring shown, and the other objects no doubt belong to other graves, particularly the man's type cross-bow brooch and belt mounts. The grave was quoted by Werner 1950, pp. 25–6, without mention of the two discs. Åberg 1956, p. 138, figs. 153–7 omits the tall tutulus and includes the gold finger ring and one disc brooch. According to Eck 1891, pp. 25–6 and 229–31 the woman in grave 24 had six brooches arranged in three pairs, the tutulus (Fig. 1, *l*), the bow with spatulate foot and the bow with disc foot. There was also a gold ring with oval imitation chalcedony stone, two small brooches in silver, a necklace of gold spindle-shaped beads and a gold medallion of Valentinian I (364–75) in the mouth. Pilloy (II, p. 273) adds the information that his pl. 19, 4a (Fig. 1, *i*) is the finger ring in question, but says that at the top of the breast were one bow with disc foot (Fig. 1, *j*) and a tall tutulus (Fig. 1, *m*), then there was a pair of the large tutulus (Fig. 1, *l*) and a pair

[1] Remains of this spear are in the Römisch-Germanisches Museum, Köln.

of the bow with spatulate foot (Fig. 1, *k*). On pp. 276–7 he adds that the two disc brooches (Fig. 1, *g* and *h*) were also found in this grave. Pilloy states that he was present at the uncovering of this grave, and as he was particularly interested in the tutulus brooches (for previous discoveries of the type in fragments had mystified him) it seems he is hardly likely to have made a mistake here. Nevertheless, he does not enlarge on the subject of the tall tutulus, and both the journal of MM. Lelaurain and Wargny (Eck 1891, pp. 25–6) and the list given in Eck's discussion (pp. 229–31) assume that there were three identical pairs of Figs. 1, *j*, *k* and *l*.

FIGURE 2

Misèry, Somme

(Rigollot 1850, pp. 216–23, pls. x and xi)

1–3. *Belt mount* as Frontispiece.
4–5. Iron *shield-boss* covered with silver-gilt sheet, ht. 12 cm, diam. 15 cm; stamp on rim of human figure and letters MAR; shield said to have been covered with plaques of copper.

FIGURE 3

Misèry (continued)

5. Gilt-bronze *pommel* and guards of double-edged sword, L. 87 cm.
6. *Knife*, L. 10 cm, with silver collar and inlaid silver spiked circles on the blade.
7. *Spearhead* with pronounced mid-rib.
8. *Buckle* as Frontispiece.

The buckle and plates, as Frontispiece, are preserved at the Musée Danicourt, Péronne, but the other objects seem to be lost.

FIGURE 4

Haillot, grave xi

(Breuer and Roosens 1957, fig. 12)

1. *Bowl*, red ware, rouletted decoration.
2. *Bowl* with wide rim, red ware.
3. *Jug*, light brown.
4. *Bowl*, rouletted decoration.
5. *Glass cone beaker*, colourless, diagonal ribbing with self-colour trails at mouth.
6. *Plate*, red ware.
7. *Plate*, light brown.
8. Bronze *buckle* with fixed plate; zoomorphic terminals to the loop, two rivets on the plate.

FIGURE 5

Haillot, grave xi (continued)

9. Iron *strike-a-light*.
10. Bronze *rivet* with disc head decorated with stamps and ornamental perforations, with a bronze *strip* near by.

11. Bronze *tweezers*.
12. Five bronze *coins*, of which two illegible: Delmatius, 335–7; Gratian, 367–83; Valentinian I, 364–75.
13. Bronze *strap-end*, split at one end with rivet, decoration by double-ring stamps; also bronze *penannular ring*.
14. Two *stones* for strike-a-light.
15–16, 18–21. Iron *arrowheads*.
17. *Francisca*.

FIGURE 6

Haillot, grave XIII

1. *Sword* with bronze chape.
2–3. Two bronze *strap-slides* from scabbard.
4. Bronze *buckle*.
5. Fragments of purse and *bronze balance*: including a worn coin, ornamented disc weight and coin of Severus II (305–7).
6. *Knife*.
7. Bronze *buckle* with oval plate.
8. *Axe*.

With various iron fragments, nail and sherd.

FIGURE 7

Haillot, grave XVI

1. *Sword* with bronze band scabbard edging.
2. Two bronze *strap-slides* from scabbard, with birds' head terminals.
3. Large *bead*.
4. Iron *buckle* plated with silver gilt and inset with garnets; rectangular loop, rectangular base to gilt bronze tongue, kidney-shaped plate.
5. *Flint*.
6. Iron *strike-a-light*.
7. Iron *pin*.
8. *Knife*.
9. *Spearhead*.
10. *Shield-boss* with silver-covered disc-headed rivets and extended grip.
11. Greenish *glass bowl*, applied white threads in zone round mouth and as quatrefoil on base.
12. *Bowl*, brown ware.

FIGURE 8

Gold, garnet-inset jewellery from the grave of Childeric I, Tournai, Belgium
(J. J. Chiflet, *Anastasis Childerici I* (1655), p. 226)

The two birds' head terminals, top centre, are from opposite ends of a purse mount; the plaque immediately below is a later development of the tubular mounts at Belleray (Pls. 2, *d* and 3, *d*) and Misèry (Frontispiece); the two mounts outside lowest row are from the edges of the sword scabbard; the rest are various studs and appliqués.

FIGURE 9

a.　Chessell Down, I.o.W.; *glass armlet*, diam. 9·2 cm, brown, bubbly metal, decorated by sets of three sloping, notched lines with an impressed oval with raised centre between each; Carisbrooke Castle Museum, 53.5.

b.　Milton Regis, Kent; *glass armlet*, diam. 9 cm, light olive bubbly glass, outer surface corrugated by diagonal comb-like impressions.

c.　Milton Regis, Kent; *glass armlet*, diam. 9·2 cm, amber bubbly glass, outer surface corrugated by diagonal impressions as *b*, but shallower; *b* and *c*, Canterbury Museum.

d.　Broadstairs, Kent; iron *buckle plate*, 4·5 × 3 cm, covered with repoussé silver sheet, bearing stylized design of two facing peacocks, with border of triangles with circular apices; Evison 1958, pp. 240–1, fig. 1; Broadstairs Museum.

e.　Dover, Kent, grave 48; bronze dolphin *buckle loop* with iron tongue, diam. 3·6 cm; British Museum.

f.　Chessell Down, I.o.W.; wheel-turned *bowl* with foot, light brown ware; girth groove below rim and on shoulder, rouletting decoration, diam. 12·5 cm; British Museum, Reg. No. 67 7–29 141.

FIGURE 10

Bow brooches with up-turned foot

a.　West Stow, Suffolk; a projecting ring at the head is cast in one with the brooch; the bronze cross-bar with some of the iron spring remains; the bow is triangular in section except in the middle where it is flattened and decorated with transverse lines; the foot, with a rounded terminal, turns up slightly; L. 7·3 cm; Museum of Archaeology and Ethnology, Cambridge.

b and c.　Icklingham or West Stow, Suffolk; *b*. bronze *buckle* with shield-on-tongue, diam. 2·9 cm; *c*. bronze *brooch* with half of bronze cross-bar remaining; perforation at head for fixture of ring; faceted bow with raised square in middle; up-curved foot with spherical terminal; L. 7·5 cm; Ashmolean Museum, Oxford.

d and e.　Glaston, Rutland; *d*. bronze *brooch*, spring missing; looped staple inserted in head with a loose ring; to this was attached a tab (now lost) for holding a strap; the bow is flattened at both ends and in the middle, where it is decorated with circles within squares; the motif appears also on the foot which is further scored in chevrons and turns up to a flattened disc terminal with ring-and-dot stamp on the upper surface; L. 6·6 cm.

e.　Bronze *penannular brooch*, diam. 3·5 cm; turned back and flattened terminals with geometric pattern reminiscent of animal heads; transverse scoring near terminals and at three other points where the ring narrows; bronze pin; Oakham School Museum, Rutland.

f. Howletts, Kent, grave 4; bronze *brooch* with fixed ring at head; bow flattened in middle and decorated with square; transverse lines on foot which turns up to end in knob; L. 7·6 cm; British Museum Reg. No. 1935 5–11 17.

FIGURE 11

Brighthampton, Oxon., grave 31

a c. *Sword*, L. 96·2 cm, and *scabbard mounts*: pommel; pyramid cone with flat top and concave sides; perforation at top for tang, one projecting lug each side for rivet. Front side only remains of scabbard mouth edging; panel of chip-carved S-spirals, two at the end lying on their sides, the rest upright; border beaded along top, reserved zigzag along other sides, moulding at each edge. A pair of metal U-sectioned edges to scabbard 8·5 cm from scabbard top and each 9·2 cm long; moulding at each end and a small rivet; a pair of disc-headed rivets in the middle. The chape is 16·2 cm. long, fixed with a pair of rivets at top and a pair of disc-headed rivets lower down. At the back a bronze sheet fills the space inside the frame for a length of 5·6 cm. On the front, a row of nicks appears along the top edges, with transverse moulding below extending into triangular shapes with antennae-like extensions. A pair of backward-glancing animals, one following the other, both with two front legs and one hind leg, the front creature with a knob-like scut, and the second with a long tail held over its back. The types of tail suggest an origin in the Roman hare-and-hounds motif even if, in this instance, the dog as well as the hare is looking back. The scut has previously been interpreted as a curly tail like a pig's, but this impression is caused by the survival of the gilding only in the impressed contour line. Two pairs of birds' heads face the tip which is finished with a semicircular shape. The area of moulding at the top, the triangles and antennae, the animals, birds' heads and semicircle are all heavily gilded. The material of all the scabbard mounts, and probably the pommel, too, is silver.[1] It is probable that the zigzag ornament on the mouth plate and the circles on the pommel were inlaid with niello, but these details will become clearer if the sword is cleaned.

d. *Spearhead*, L. 15 cm, angular blade, tip broken.

e. Bronze *stud* with Maltese cross head covered with silver, diam. 1·2 cm, probably from scabbard.

f. Amber *bead*, diam. 2·2 cm, 'sword knot'.

g. Bronze *strip* 4 × 1·5 cm, perforated.

h. Bronze *strip* 1·5 × 1·5 cm.

i. Four bronze disc-headed *rivets* with silver-plated tops; diam. 8·5 mm, i.e. larger than disc rivets on scabbard mount which are 7 mm; these must have fastened a strap across the scabbard, cf. Pl. 4, *a*, Krefeld-Gellep.

j. Bronze *strap-end*, rounded at tip with two rivet holes at the other end; L. 4 cm; a row of triangular stamps along one edge.

k. Two *bronze strips* 3·4 × 1·4 cm fastened together by four rivets; decoration by impressed dots. These were broken and mended by two other plates placed over them (the top one decorated by transverse lines) and fastened together by two rivets.

[1] Not bronze as Hawkes 1961, pp. 39–40. Gold inlay on bronze as there described is extremely rare, but heavy gilding on silver is more common, cf. Frontispiece.

l.   *Knife*, L. 9·6 cm.
m.   Bronze mounts of a wooden *bucket*; ht. 12 cm, diam. at top 12·5 cm; three horizontal
      hoops, the lower edge of the top one cut into triangles and decorated with repoussé
      dots; a U-section mount binds the top; four vertical bands with repoussé dots are fixed
      with dome-headed rivets; the escutcheons fixing the handle are bifurcated and have
      degenerate animal-head terminals (*n* shows an animal head on the opposite side where
      the ear and tongue are clear); the strip handle and the escutcheons are decorated with
      stamps, crescents and zigzags. Ashmolean Museum, Oxford.

FIGURE 12

Long Wittenham, Berks., grave 57

a.   Bronze *buckle*, width of loop 5·3 cm, zoomorphic terminals to loop; rectangular plate
      with beaded border and two rivets.
b.   Black burnished *bowl*, ht. 12 cm, spherical body, narrowing at neck; horizontal line
      decoration round neck and shoulder with two rows of crescent stamps in groups, and a
      row of larger triangular stamps with lattice-work; five longitudinal bosses on the body
      are decorated with a vertical row of crescent stamps and bordered with groups of
      vertical lines.
c.   *Knife*, L. 12 cm.

Dover, Kent, grave 22

d.   *Spearhead socket*, L. 8·8 cm; gripped by iron band inlaid with bronze strip; ribbing or
      iron wire binding below.
e.   *Spear ferrule*, L. 9·5 cm, with riveted-on bronze disc.
f.   *Knife*, L. 13·7 cm.
g.   *Glass cone beaker*, L. 30·5 cm, diam. mouth 9·4 cm; light green, zone of self-coloured
      horizontal trails at rim, vertical loops below; flattened tip.
h.   *Sword*, L. 87·7 cm × 4·8 cm.
i.   *Bronze ring*, oval, max. diam. 1·5 cm. British Museum.

FIGURE 13

Chessell Down, I.o.W.

a.   Bronze *bracelet*; only this drawing remains, but it appears to represent the side view of
      the penannular bracelet and a full-face view of one of the ends. Decoration is by stamps,
      and the outer ring looks as though it may have been carried out by the same sort of
      stamp as on the Chatham Lines bracelet (Fig. 15, *c*), i.e. arc and semicircle. After
      R. Walker, *Phoenicia in Freshwater*, pl. 4.

Long Wittenham, Berks., grave 93

b.   Bronze *cauldron* with triangular lugs.
c.   Bronze-bound wooden *stoup*, ht. 15·2 cm, bearing repoussé designs of alpha and omega
      and various Christian scenes. After B.M. Guide 1923, figs. 77–8. British Museum.

FIGURE 14

Strood, Kent

(Smith 1852, II, p. 158 and pl. XXXVI)

1. Cylindrical bronze *mount* with repoussé design of vine-scroll border and a repetition of a scene consisting of three figures, the central one with a nimbus.
2. *Sword*, L. 2 ft 11½ in.
3. *Spearhead*, L. 10½ in.
4. *Knife*, L. 6½ in.
5. *Shield boss*, ht. 3 in, diam. 6 in.
6. *Shield grip*.
7. Bronze shoe-shaped *stud*.
8. Iron *strip*, possibly on shield, L. 5 in.
9. Bronze *buckle* with shield on tongue.

No. 1 is at Liverpool Museum, the rest of the objects are presumably lost.

FIGURE 15

Chatham Lines, Kent, grave XVII

(Douglas 1793, pp. 58–62, pl. XIV)

a, a′. Bronze bracelet: a band 0·45 cm wide, max. diam. 6·3 cm with hinge fastening; decoration by transverse lines, some of which contain traces of silvering.
b. *Glass bracelet*, diam. 10 cm, light blue-green bubbly glass.
c. Bronze penannular *bracelet*, one end missing; the loop swells to a D-section in the middle where it is decorated with transverse moulding and semicircle-within-crescent stamps; at the end the narrowed band is decorated, possibly by an animal head, and then thrusts as a triangular shape into a thin flat disc which bears traces of tendril decoration.
d. 20 blue *glass beads*.
e. Fragment of plain band silver *finger ring*.
f. Bronze *finger ring* fragment, loop expanding to 9 mm; blank bezel, band divided into panels by transverse incised line decorated by chevron incisions and dot stamps. (Douglas thought these two rings belonged together—'the ring is of mixed metal'.)
g. *Iron ring*, max. diam. 5·8 cm.
h, h′. Bronze bracelet, max. diam. 7 cm; D-section, hinge fastening; much worn, but in seven places the face is flattened and carries a design bordered by transverse lines; 1, 4 and 7 are a guilloche with central pellet, 3 and 6 rectangle and line within, 2 cross in cruciform frame, 5 step pattern. Ashmolean Museum, Oxford.

FIGURE 16

Alfriston, Sussex

Grave 24

a. *Hammer-axe*, spreading blade on one side of the socket, hammer the other, L. 19 cm.

b. Crescent-shaped silvered bronze *mount* with rivet at back; width 1·1 cm; fits hook of *c*.

c. Bronze *disc*, pierced with six holes of equal width, and one smaller, extending at one point into a hook and with a rivet through the centre; a border of tooled triangles at intervals and three crescent stamps between each perforation; diam. 1·7 cm.

d. Iron *buckle*; loop, width 5 cm, kidney-shaped, with transverse strips inlaid in groups of three, each inner strip being twisted and of a different metal from the two outer ones; base of tongue rectangular with grid of broader strips; rectangular repoussé silver plate 4·3 × 2·8 cm, originally riveted to an iron base; rectangular central field of trellis design surrounded by a border of running tendrils with heart-shaped leaves and pairs of birds pecking at rosettes of grapes (Pl. 5, *b* and *c*).

Also in this grave: 'an iron object, probably a knife, but of unusual character, 4½ in. long', not identifiable.

Grave 39

e. Green *glass cone beaker*, ht. 29 cm, diam. mouth 10 cm; slightly everted mouth, zone of horizontal trails below rim with looped vertical trails below; punty mark on base.

f. Iron *buckle*, width 4·4 cm.

g. *Francisca*, L. 13·5 cm, remains of shaft in iron sleeve.

Also in this grave a knife (not identifiable).

Grave 20

h. Iron *buckle*; loop, width 4·6 cm, inlaid with transverse strips, and chequered pattern on rectangular tongue base; double rectangular iron plates covered with remains of repoussé bronze plate with central rectangular panel and running tendril border.

i. Square bronze *plaque*, 3·1 cm × 3·1 cm, rivet hole in each corner from which emanates a double wavy line; beaded outer border, and beaded border to circle of design in middle of quadrilateral chip-carved pelta pattern.

Two other objects in the grave are not now identifiable: 'A bronze split tang, 2 in. long, split at the one end to take a leather thong, where the rivet still remains *in situ*. No ornament except three lines across in front of rivet hole. Knife 4½ in. long.'

Grave 52

j. Iron *instrument* (chisel ?), L. 6·8 cm.

k. Kidney-shaped iron *buckle loop*, width 4·7 cm, transverse inlaid wires; remains of tongue.

l. Horned *pedestal urn*, ht. 15·7 cm, diam. mouth 12·8 cm; black, burnished; three longitudinal bosses project most at the shoulder where a ring stamp on each side gives the impression of an eye; longitudinal lines along the spine and herring-bone lines each side further suggest a fish; the intervening spaces are decorated by vertical grooving alternating with lines and rows of stamps placed zigzag fashion; double grooves round the neck border a row of stamps probably modelled on the classical ovolo. (J. N. L. Myres, 'Romano-Saxon Pottery', in *Dark Age Britain*, ed. D. B. Harden, p. 16.)

Also in this grave: 'knife L. 6⅜ in.' and a 'small fragment', not identifiable.
Barbican House Museum, Lewes.

FIGURE 17

Alfriston, Sussex

Grave 26

a. *Sword*, L. 86·8 cm; bronze pommel, a pyramid with incurved sides and hole at the top for tang.

b. *Francisca*, L. 17·2 cm, now missing, drawing from *Sussex Arch. Coll.* LVI, p.. XIX, 3.

c, d. Pair of iron *strap-slides* from sword scabbard, L. 5·5 cm.

Grave 17

e. Triangular bronze *mount*, L. 2·8 cm, triangular perforation in middle, rivet in each corner; the front is decorated with roughly-tooled beaded edges and three ball-in-triangle stamps. An incised and stamped pattern on the back shows that this is a re-used piece (see pp. 65–6 and Figs. 17, *i*, 28, *j*).

f. Bronze *buckle* with rectangular plate and duplicate counter-plate. The loop is kidney-shaped and grooved at intervals, with two lines and cross-hatching between along each of the ridges. The plates, 3·8 × 2·9 cm, are divided into three longitudinal panels, a row of four circular cavities occupying the middle row, with one cell on each plate still retaining green glass inlay. In the outer zones are pairs of backward-glancing animals with double contours, hatched, an ear, round eye, fore and back leg and long tail over the back; a circle-and-dot roundel is placed behind the hind-quarters. A row of dotting follows the outline of each rump, the shoulders of the animals on the plate attached to the loop are indicated by a lenticular shape, and those on the other plate by rows of crescent stamps. On two animals silver sheet inlay remains between the inner contours. (Pl. 14, *c*.)

g. Bronze *strap-end*, L. 3·7 cm, duplicate strips, round at one end, square at the other where they were joined by two rivets; decorated by transverse lines.

Grave A

h. *Knife*, L. 10 cm.

i. Bronze triangular *mount*, L. 2·7 cm, corner broken, otherwise as *e* above with identical decoration on each side (see pp. 65–6, Fig. 28, *j*).

j. Fragment of *ivory ring*, L. 3·8 cm.

k. Iron *purse mount* with birds' heads terminals and remains of buckle in middle, L. 9·2 cm (X-rayed, no inlay).

l. Iron *buckle*, width 3·4 cm.

m, n, o. Iron *fragments*.

p. Iron *buckle plate*, 5·8 × 3·6 cm; the drawing is taken from a radiograph which seems to show a rectangular repoussé bronze or silver plate, a rivet hole in each corner, and a tendril border.

q. Bronze *buckle plate* with hole in each corner and one in middle, 3 × 1·3 cm, with bronze ? washers adhering to back.

r. Bronze *buckle tongue*. q and r must have formed parts of a buckle of which the loop was of iron; together with *i* they were embedded in an iron lump described in *Sussex Arch. Coll.* LVI, p. 48 as 'another fragment of wood preserved in rust 2⅜ in. long'. This has recently been X-rayed and disentangled at the Institute of Archaeology.

Barbican House Museum, Lewes.

FIGURE 18

Petersfinger, Wilts., grave xxi

a.   *Sword*, L. 92 cm.

b, c. Bronze *pommel*, a straight-sided pyramid with lenticular depressions along each corner; the front decorated with horizontal lines along the base and ring-and-dot stamp in the middle. At one end the projecting lug for the rivet is in the form of a curling bird's head *c*. At the other end an indentation at the edge and a worn groove in the side of the pommel show that a movable ring was once fastened here.

d.   Bronze *mounting* to scabbard mouth; moulding at each outer edge and three horizontal rows of decoration, tongue, wave and ring-and-dot motifs. A separate bronze rectangle, decorated by a diagonal cross, was soldered to the back of the mount.

e.   *Buckle*, L. 5 cm. Iron loop and tongue; rectangular bronze plate set in an iron plate and frame; copper rivet in each corner, the bronze frame extending as a collar to contain these rivets at the farther corners, while the pair near the tongue are in a line with the frame. A square bone inset with garnet disc centre is set diamond-wise in a square with colourless glass triangular insets in the corners, three rectangular glass-filled cloisons for a border each side.

f.   *Axe*, L. 14 cm, symmetrical spreading blade.

g.   Bronze *tweezers* on wire suspension loop, L. 8·5 cm, decoration by transverse and crossed lines near top, and borders of triangular stamps.

FIGURE 19

Petersfinger, Wilts., grave xxi (continued)

a.   Iron *hoop* to bucket, diam. 17 cm.

b.   Iron *handle* to bucket. As the span of the grip is 14 cm the bucket must have been narrower at the top than the bottom.

c.   Bronze *ear-scoop*, L. 5·6 cm; square-sectioned shaft and loop terminal.

d.   *Knife*, L. 13 cm.

e.   *Spearhead*, split socket, L. 17·5 cm.

f.   Amber *bead*, flat disc, diam. 2·2 cm (with sword).

g.   *Shield boss*, diam. 16·6, cm, ht. 8·4 cm; low, straight-sided dome, button top, wide flange with disc-headed rivets.

h.   Iron *disc*, diam. 2·1 cm.

i.   *Shield grip*, upturned sides and leather binding, L. 8·5 cm; iron *bar*, L. 12 cm, extension to grip.

Salisbury, South Wilts. and Blackmore Museum, Salisbury, Wilts.

FIGURE 20

Winterbourne Gunner, Wilts., grave vi

a.   *Francisca*, L. 31·5 cm.

b.   Bronze *strap-end*, L. 6·5 cm; lozenge shape at one end tapering to point at the other, rivet at each end; separate back plate. On the front is a drawing of an animal with ear and fore-leg, undulating body with fins projecting alternately from back and belly, bifoliate tail; arc stamps are used to decorate the body and indicate the mane, this last ending in a scroll; the joint of the fore-leg to the body is represented by an oval shape.

c. Bronze *tweezers* with suspension ring, L. 6·2 cm.
d. Fragmentary *iron plate* with rivet, L. 3·2 cm.
e. Iron *rivet*.
f. Rectangular *iron plate*, 3·8 × 2·3 cm.
g. Kidney-shaped iron loop and tongue of *buckle*, inlaid with transverse strips, width originally c. 5·4 cm.
h. *Sherd* with pendant triangle and stamps, found in grave fill.

Salisbury, South Wilts. and Blackmore Museum, Salisbury, Wilts.

FIGURE 21

West Overton, Wilts., skeleton IV

a. Bronze *key*, L. 6·8 cm, hollow shaft, ring head with knob at top.
b. Bronze *penannular brooch*, diam. 3 cm; returned terminals, flattened sideways and with tool impressions; iron pin.
c. One of ten *amber beads*.
d. Bronze *ring*, diam. 1·5 cm; consisting of bent wire with one end doubled back.
e. Fragment of *sheet bronze*, L. 1·7 cm, with double row of repoussé dots, one boss and one perforation.
f. Bronze *semi-spherical disc* with scored edges and perforation.
g. Bronze *strip*, L. 2·8 cm, three perforations.
h. Two small *iron plates*, L. 2·8 cm, riveted together with transverse wood grain between.
i. Fragments of *iron keys* on a ring; one shaft with looped end, L. 7·6 cm; another shaft L. 6·6 cm, bending towards one end, ring fragment, diam. 4 cm.[1]
j. *Knife*, L. 15·5 cm.
k. Circular *iron buckle*, diam. 3·5 cm.

There were also fragments of a blue translucent glass bead. *d* and *f* were at the neck, presumably on the necklace with the beads.

Loose find in the same barrow:

l. Triangular *lug of bronze cauldron* with perforation.

FIGURE 22

Abingdon, Berks., grave 42

a. Curving *bone strip*, L. 24·5, cm, one side convex, the other flat; fifteen perforations, five of which show traces of iron and must have held iron rivets. The large size and number of the perforations make it unlikely that this was a comb—perhaps a type of lyre?
b. *Knife*, L. 10·5 cm.

[1] These drawings are taken from sketches on my index cards, as the objects themselves did not survive the preserving process in the laboratory.

c. Bronze *mount* for scabbard mouth; moulded side edge; one row each of tongue and wave decoration; lower edge serrated.

d. Three of four bronze *studs* from scabbard.

e, f. Bronze *strap divider*, ring, diam. 1·3 cm, into which were linked three bronze tabs.

g. Iron *buckle*, width 2·7 cm.

h. Iron *buckle* with bronze plate, L. 3·2 cm.

i. *Flint.*

j. Bronze *chape* to scabbard; U-sectioned edging with motif of man's head and bird's head on each side.

k. *Sword*, L. 89 cm.

Abingdon Museum, Berks.

FIGURE 23

Unknown provenance

a. Bronze *annular brooch*; flat ring with ring-and-dot ornament and slot for passage of pin; two pairs of projecting animal heads (one broken) spring from the outer edge of the ring each side of the pin slot. Laon Museum, northern France.

Alfriston, Sussex, grave 91

b. Iron *purse mount*, L. 10 cm; bird's head terminals and remains of inlaid strips along the edges.

c. *Horse's bit*; two rings, diam. 6 cm; two bars, L. 7 cm.

d. *Francisca*, L. 12·5 cm.

e. Bronze *tube*, L. 3·4 cm, made from sheet riveted at back.

Also in the grave 'three fragments iron handle; spearhead, haft broken. L. 5$\frac{5}{8}$ in.; three iron fragments' not identifiable.

Alfriston, Sussex, grave 103

f. Bronze *tube*, L. 2·7 cm; one end of the front projecting, the other flush with back; transverse line decoration.

g. *Openwork bronze mount*, L. 6·2 cm; square with triangular projection from one side; rivet hole in each corner and one in the triangle; a curvilinear cross occupies the centre of a lozenge shape on the square, and one pair of projecting animal heads remains on the triangle; three hinge loops on one side of the back, and the remains of two iron rings rusted on.

h. *Iron tool*, L. 6 cm; this object bears no number, but may be the item described as 'an iron punch (?) 2$\frac{3}{8}$ in. long'. Also in this grave were 'an iron buckle 1$\frac{5}{16}$ in. across, iron tongue' and 'six beads, one a small flint with natural perforation. One barrel-shaped, black glass with white lines, 1$\frac{1}{2}$ in. long. One pale bluish white porcelain, with blue spiral line. Three plain glass, two azure, one black.' *Sussex Arch. Coll.* LVIII, pl. XXII, fig. 3, not identifiable.

Barbican House Museum, Lewes.

FIGURE 24

Alfriston, Sussex, grave 14

a. *Bronze disc brooch*, diam. 3·8 cm; central punched circle with perforation, border of six circles with depressed centres sometimes perforated.

b. Bronze *buckle loop*, diam. 2·5 cm, with remains of iron tongue. (This is the buckle illustrated *Sussex Arch. Coll.* LVI, pl. X, 3 as from grave 14, but it now bears a label '29'. There is no bronze buckle recorded from grave 29, but its measurements are not as given, *Sussex Arch. Coll.* LVI, p. 32 for the buckle in grave 14.)

c. Perforated *coin* of Vespasian.

d. Bronze *buckle* with zoomorphic terminals to loop and fixed trapezoid plate with two rivets in the corners; a row of beading each side of tongue hole; L. 2·7 cm.

e. Bronze flattened *tube*, L. 3·9 cm, with extension on the front at each end, and transverse beaded band decoration. Also in the grave but not identified: 'Knife L. 4⅝ in. long; spearhead, two fragments of an iron ring, two fragments of an iron rim.'

Barbican House Museum, Lewes.

Bidford-on-Avon, Warwicks.; *bronze-bound wooden bucket*

f. Remains of stave, L. 13·1 cm; horizontal bronze band in the middle still fixed, and the position of the other appliqués ensured by bronze marks on the wood and the position of rivet holes. The horizontal band is decorated by repoussé dotted rings, and a bronze ring swings from a staple which passed through this band and the wood. Below is a pendant triangle with border of stamped arcs and repoussé motifs of boss and dotted ring and arc-and-dot. The bottom of this triangle was crossed by a horizontal band 1·6 cm wide. Above the middle band is an appliqué of an animal with head turned backward to bite its own tail; there are outer borders of stamped arcs and repoussé dots; a lenticular shoulder compartment contains a boss and ring of dots, a hip compartment contains a curving line and dots in threes.

g. *Band*, 1·6 cm wide, with arc and dot decoration, probably mounted round the top of the bucket.

h. *Strip*, 4·4 × 1·5 cm; border of stamped arcs and repoussé dots, and two rows of intersecting arcs and dots; four rivet holes. The lack of curvature shows this must have been in an upright position. There is a similar less complete strip.

i. *Animal appliqué* facing opposite way, hip compartment, ring-and-dot and arc-and-dot motifs and longitudinal lines on the neck.

j. *Animal appliqué* still attached to a piece of wood; hip compartment, decoration by arcs and dots, and the shoulder is indicated by a spiral.

Worcester Museum.

FIGURE 25

Engraved *bronze plate*; outer border of triangles; stylized figures of five shield-bearing soldiers each side facing centre, with standards above, figure of boar and sea-lion and inscriptions LEG(IO) XX V(ALENS) V(ICTRIX) LEG(IO) SECVNDA AVGVS(TA). Centre eagle with inscription below AVRELIVS CERVIANVS. Hunting scene of stylized animals below,

I

including lion, stag, two dogs and hare; there are also two peacocks and a flower. Inscription VTEREFELIX. The foot of the plate is decorated in an entirely different design of floral type, and is inlaid with red and white metals. After Rigollot 1850, pl. XII.

FIGURE 26

Vermand, Aisne

a. Bronze *buckle and plate*; loop has outer border of tendril scroll, inner row of zigzags with ? silver sheet inlay; animal head at each end of loop; the tongue has a trapezoidal base inlaid with blue glass stones and a sea-lion each side. The plate has a zigzag border with silver sheet inlay and an inner border of stamped arc-and-semicircle motif with dashes between. In the middle panel a backward-glancing animal is outlined with silver wire or strip inlay; its body is decorated with chevrons, rings and dots, and rows of crescents indicate a furry mane and tail.

b. Double *counter-plate* with folded edge tubular and moulded; decoration as for a, except that the animal faces the other way.

Vermand, Aisne, grave 32

c. Bronze *buckle and plate*; outer border of loop scalloped with inner row of inlaid silver triangles; the tongue has animal head tip, square base and sea-lion each side of base. The plate has a border of inlaid silver wave motif; the inner panel is bordered with connected rings; in the middle a human head with band round the forehead and flowing locks, below which is a racing dog, its body decorated with dashes and dots.

d. Bronze *counter-plate*; silver inlaid border; animal with head to ground in inner panel, its body ornamented with dashes and dots, and dashes indicating fur on the spine.

e. Opposite side of d; silver inlaid border of 'fir-tree' motif; lion on inner panel with two front legs and one hind leg, full-face, with outline of whiskers.

Pilloy 1895 II, pls. 14, 1a, 2a and 3a and 15, 8 and 9.

FIGURE 27

Landifay, Guise

a. *Buckle and plate*; the loop has scalloped edge and zoomorphic terminals; the tongue has an animal head tip, and square base between a pair of backward-glancing sea-lions. On the plate, left, a portrait of a woman with long hair, on the right a soldier with helmet and spear, both stylized, with rows of dots following the contours.

b. Part of a *buckle loop* with zoomorphic terminals.

c. *Counter-plate* to a; scroll border on three sides; the inner panel divided into two parts, each containing a sitting animal with one paw raised; the one on the right belongs to the lion family and may be intended to be a lioness, while the one on the left, which is confused about the head, may be the lion with its heavy mane.

d, e. *Two plates*, one ornamented with a bird. (Described as 'petites boucles' by Fleury.)

f. *Chape* of knife sheath.

g. *Arrows*.

h. *Knife* with curved blade inlaid with yellow metal, handle ivory, with silver collar and four-pointed pommel.

i. This item is not mentioned by Fleury, but possibly represents the moulded tubular edge of *c.*

a–f are said to be plated with precious metals and inlaid with black enamel, i.e. ? niello. Fleury 1877–82, p. 250.

Wor Barrow, Dorset

j. Bronze *toilet implement*, L. 14·3 cm; ring terminal, moulded shaft becoming flat, with nick at end; the flat part is decorated with border of arc stamps, in the middle a human face bordered by arc stamps to represent whiskers.

Richborough, Kent

k. Bronze *strap-end*, L. 7·3 cm; one end split with rivet for attachment to strap; the outline swells in the middle, then tapers to a notched terminal; ornamented by an undulating serpent with one horn or ear, dotted neck band, arc stamps to represent scales, and a furry outline indicated by dashes; from the mouth issues a flower-like arrangement of lines and rings. Richborough Museum.

Howletts, Kent

l. *Francisca* and oval plate riveted to the top of the shaft ornamented with a racing hare, the body covered with dashes to represent fur and the shoulder compartment bordered by dots. Lost. (See p. 50.)

FIGURE 28

Bowcombe Down, Isle of Wight, grave 13

a. *Bronze disc*, max. diam. 5·7 cm; centre occupied by openwork cross with bifurcating cross-hatched scroll terminals, beaded border; the surrounding zone is plain and raised, sinking to a flat openwork border originally in three sections of two animals each, back to back, with snouts touching a curving triangle shape. One pair is almost completely preserved, a second complete except for the head of one animal, and only one animal preserved of the third; a very smooth edge at this point indicates long wear. The animals are of greyhound type with long down-curving tail; an inner contour line is visible on the limbs, with hatching along the top of the feet; on the shoulder of one of the best-preserved pair is a crescent shape, and an S-line on the haunch of its partner.
b. Bronze *disc brooch*, diam. 3·1 cm, central perforation.
c. *Lead spindle whorl*, diam. 2·5 cm.
d. Iron penannular *ring*, diam. 4·7 cm.
e. Type of shield-on-tongue *buckle.*
f. Three bronze kite-shaped belt *rivets.*

These objects in Carisbrooke Museum, I.o.W., were identified with those described in *J.B.A.A.* xvi (1860), pp. 255–6, pl. xx, 4 by G. A. Sherwin in his manuscript on Anglo-Saxon antiquities in the Isle of Wight, Society of Antiquaries MS. No. 767. Not identified are 'knife, 4¾ in. long', 'pieces of bronze with rivet holes', apparently belonging to the sheath of the knife, one of the 'two iron rings' and 'pieces of pottery and glass'.

Lyminge, Kent, grave 10

g. Bronze *penannular brooch*, diam. 4·25 cm, hole for pin; flat, turned-back terminals, one broken, the other a profile animal head; the band is divided into panels, of which one is cross-hatched, two have a diagonal cross, and two have a double ring-and-dot with triangle combination reminiscent of an animal head. The two largest panels each contain an animal with head to ground, lenticular ear, body divided into segments with hatching and dotting, the tail a single line with terminal dot cluster.

h. Bronze *applied disc brooch*, diam. 3·5 cm, star design. Maidstone Museum.

Riseley, Horton Kirby, Kent, grave XXII

i. Bronze *penannular brooch*, diam. 4·1 cm, iron pin; beaded borders with a row of double circles and annulet stamps in between; the terminals are returned, one is broken off, but the other is a flat animal head full-face, ears indicated by vertical modelling and two hollows, the nostrils by circular depressions, and the eyes by incised spirals. Also in this grave was a knife and beads; *Trans. Dartford District Antiquarian Soc.* VIII (1938), p. 17. Dartford Museum.

Alfriston, Sussex, graves A and 17

j. Two triangles cut from an original bronze *rectangular* plate c. 3·7 × 3·3 cm; incised running scrolls in the outer zone, with intervening dot-in-triangle stamps; the next zone is plain except for three ring stamps at each corner; the inner rectangle contains a cross with curling terminals and a diagonal cross of small triangular cuts; chip-carved triangles occupy the spaces. Barbican House Museum, Lewes.

FIGURE 29

Continental animals

a. Rhenen, Holland, grave 846; detail of human mask flanked by two animals chip-carved on edge of bronze strap-slide (Pl. 4, *c*).

b–d. Development of classical sea-lion (after Werner):
> *b.* Sea-lion on Roman bronze bucket from Heddernheim.
> *c.* Sea-lion on a late Roman chip-carved buckle.
> *d.* Sea-lion brooch from Brochon, France.

e. Animal on Vermand spear mount: backward-glancing quadruped; body divided in half by diagonal beading and moulding, the front half decorated by arc-and-semi-circle stamps, the back by dashes (Pl. 1, *a*).

f. Animal on Vermand spear mount; backward-glancing sea-lion; the last coil has become separated from the body, so showing clearly how the later type with single coil arose (cf. Fig. 29, *h* and *i* and Fig. 30, *b–e*). Decorative stamps as for *e*.

g. East Shefford, Berks., grave 24; sea-lion on repoussé sheet of applied brooch; it retains the trefoil tail which has become a trident shape, while the convolutions of the body are now represented by a hind leg and pellets; it has a curling tongue and lappet at the back of the head (cf. Pl. 17, *b*).

h. Gilt bronze pin from Faversham, Kent (B.M. Guide, fig. 40); the sea-lion at the head has a single curl to the body, a crescent-shaped ear, out-curving jaws, tongue and one fore-paw. British Museum.

i. Alveston, Warwicks., Frankish brooch; sea-lion with single convolution to body. Stratford-on-Avon Museum.

j. Animal appliqué, probably from Northfleet, Kent. Although of the same family as *h* and *i*, this specimen is fully developed as a quadruped with hind and fore leg and long tail. Gravesend Museum.

FIGURE 30

Quoit Brooch animals

Sea-lions, forward-looking
a. Howletts quoit brooch (No. 10) inner zone; with developed hind-leg. *b.* Bifrons pendants (No. 6). *c.* Faversham disc (No. 9).

Sea-lions, backward-glancing
d. Howletts quoit brooch (No. 10), outer zone. *e.* Croydon strap-distributor (No. 5), pair of sea-lions, back to back, single coil to body and one fore-paw.

Quadrupeds, crouching
f. Bowcombe roundel (No. 1); *g.* Howletts plate (No. 3) pair of animals back to back. *h.* Bifrons strap-end (No. 8). *i.* Sarre quoit brooch, outer zone (No. 12); longitudinal lines on neck to indicate mane.

Quadruped, running
j. Howletts fragmentary quoit brooch, outer zone (No. 11).

Quadrupeds, backward-glancing
k. Bishopstone plate (No. 7). *l.* Sarre quoit brooch, inner zone (No. 12). *m.* Howletts fragmentary quoit brooch (No. 11). *n.* Alfriston buckle (No. 4).

Quadrupeds, head to ground
o. Croydon strap-distributor (No. 5). *p.* Lyminge penannular brooch (No. 2).

Description of Plates

FRONTISPIECE

Misèry, France

Parcel-gilt *silver buckle*, 7 cm long, plate 4·35 cm wide; loop flat on top, both edges sloping; the top is divided into triangles, within each of which are two wave motifs and a small triangle; on the outer rim ring-and-dot stamps with tangents emulate cable pattern; ring-and-dot stamps on inner rim; the loop has animal head terminals, open jaws rendered by deep ring-and-dot stamp; small ring-and-dot stamps in front of the jaw give the impression of bubbles issuing from it; the tongue has a wide, rectangular base divided into six square recessed segments by lines inlaid with niello; a pair of griffin heads with arc stamps project from each side of the base; the tip terminates in an animal head, the middle is beaded at the sides with ring-and-dot stamps on top.

The plate is doubled, fastened by two rivets and moulded in tubular fashion at the fold. A central rectangular panel is surrounded on three sides by two decorative nielloed bands, each separated by a row of beading; the outer one is a running wave motif, the inner one quatrefoils, separated by a roughly-executed row of three triangles; the central panel contains a sea-lion with beak, one fore-paw and tri-lobed tail. The nielloed silver surfaces on the plate and the loop contrast with the gilded parts which are, on the plate, the rectangular panel and the beaded borders, on the loop, all the tongue, except the nielloed parts of the base, the inner and outer surfaces of the loop and the terminal animal heads. There is no ornament on the back of the plate.

The *counter-plate*, 3·9 × 3·9 cm, is folded back on itself and decorated on both sides, the curved edge being covered with a separate piece of moulded gilt silver. On one side the central rectangular panel and beaded border are gilt, and the outer band of decoration on three sides is a nielloed wave pattern. The edge of the central panel has a border of zigzag lines with ring-and-dot stamps. The backward-glancing animal has one hind and one fore-leg, a string-like tongue issues from a closed mouth, lenticular ears are tipped with a ring-and-dot stamp; the body is divided into segments with vertical divisions on the neck, double contour along the spine, hachuring and dots; the long tail ends in a bifoliate tip.

On the other side of the counter-plate are two nielloed borders, the outer one wave motifs, the inner one triangles; the outer gilt border is moulded lengthwise, and the gilt border separating the two decorative zones is beaded. In the central rectangular panel, the border is an incised line with parallel row of dots; the lion is shown full-face, with two front legs and one hind; the body is segmented by lines and dots, the backbone marked by dashes within a double contour; there are ring-and-dot eyes and arc-stamp whiskers round the face.

Musée Danicourt, Péronne.

PLATE 1

Vermand, Aisne, grave of military leader

a. Silver-gilt *plaque* for spear-shaft, L. 12·5 cm; from top to bottom the motifs on the plaque are: animal head, quatrefoil, six-pointed interlaced star, trefoil, spirals and a rosette; the reserved surfaces are decorated with niello; two rings attached the plaque to the shaft, and these are ornamented with two pairs of backward-glancing creatures, the top pair each having fore-leg, hind-leg and tail, the body divided diagonally and ornamented with dashes and arc-and-semicircle stamps; the bodies of the lower pair end in double convolutions and are decorated with the same dashes and stamps (Fig. 28, *e* and *f*).

b. Silver-gilt *buckle*, L. 5·9 cm; loop with niello triangles and zoomorphic terminals; a griffin head projecting from each side of the tongue base. A six-pointed marigold motif on the shield-shaped plate has niello scroll patterns between the leaves and the border consists of niello triangles; three rivets fasten the back plate.

c. Rectangular silver-gilt *plaque*, 9·4 × 1·6 cm, a rivet hole at each end and one in the middle; chip-carved pattern of double row of running spirals, the crests inlaid with niello; arc-and-semicircle stamps along the border.

d. Silver-gilt *cylindrical mount*, ht. 3 cm, diam. 2·3 cm, with a rectangular extension at one point. This part is perforated by a rivet hole, and it was suggested by de Ricci that one end of a thong was fastened to the spear-shaft in this extension, and the other end was fastened under the plaque *c* above. The cylindrical mount has three main bands of decoration, gilt triangular panels in the middle chip-carved with niello-crested spirals, and two outer bands of thin running spirals of reserved silver in niello; one border is slightly recessed and decorated with arc-and-semicircle stamps, the other has a beaded border or row of bosses, each stamped with a rosette of dots.

e. Iron *shield-boss* covered with silver-gilt sheet, ht. 16 cm, diam. 20 cm; conical shape with carination, becoming slightly concave near the point, wide flange; four groups of three conical-headed rivets round the rim are equally spaced with four imitation chalcedony flat studs in between.

f. Iron *shield-grip*, covered with silver sheet; L. 36·4 cm; each end of the grip proper was fastened by three rivets at a point where there are outward curved projections, the shape of these, and the placing of two of the rivets, suggest the form of birds' heads, the rivets representing the eyes; the grip extends further in a bar to be fastened by a quadripartite dome-headed rivet at each end. See Fig. 1 for more objects from this grave. S. de Ricci, *Catalogue of a Collection of Merovingian Antiquities belonging to J. Pierrepont Morgan* (1910), pls. x and xi. The above objects are preserved in the Metropolitan Museum of Art, New York.

PLATE 2

Belleray, Meuse

a. Bronze *bar*, with beaded border and two rows of double ring stamps, swivels on a ring, to which is also attached a disc decorated with concentric circles, a row of double ring stamps and scalloped border. Total L. 10 cm.

b. Bronze *bar*, L. 4·3 cm, bifurcating into two birds' heads; the middle bar, broken at each end, is decorated by panels of chevrons, tongue motif and double ring-and-dot stamps; these stamps and dots also ornament the necks of the birds, and there is a rivet hole in each head.

c. Bronze *bar* with double ring stamp swivelling on a ring to which is attached another bar; L. 6·8 cm; the rosette, Pl. 2, *e*, may have been attached to this.

d. One of a pair of *tubular attachments*, L. 11·8 cm; the tubes are transversely moulded, and the flat plates, fastened by three rivets, are decorated by a row of double ring stamps and dots or dashes.

e. Bronze *rosette*, diam. 2·8 cm, possibly once attached to *c* above.

f. Bronze *suspension loop*, L. 3·9 cm; beaded middle line, with zigzag motif each side and ring-and-dot stamps on the angles.

PLATE 3
Belleray, Meuse

a. Bronze *bar* looped on a ring, the top end of the bar shaped into a disc and two points and carrying a rivet; a second rivet further down attaches the back; decoration by beading and a ring stamp. The rosette also attached to the ring is decorated by concentric circles, ring-and-dot stamps and nicked border. L. 8·6 cm.

b. Bronze *attachment*, the top bar being identical to *a*; this loops on to a bar with a washer at the back, the bar bends at right angles horizontally, bearing a rivet, and then at right angles again downwards where it extends into curving animal heads at each side, and a bar with disc and points terminal in the middle; there is a rivet hole in each terminal and decoration by ring stamps. L. 9·1 cm.

c. Bronze *bar* swivelling on a ring, beading along middle with zigzag and ring-and-dot stamps on the angles each side; suspended rosette with ring-and-dot stamps. L. 9·3 cm.

d. One of a pair of *tubular attachments*, L. 12·1 cm and 11·8 cm; transverse moulding and beading on the tubular part, zigzag line with ring-and-dot stamps in the angles on the flat part.

e. Bronze *buckle* with fixed trapezoidal plate; zoomorphic terminals to the loop; beaded borders on the plate and zigzag motif with ring-and-dot stamps; these stamps placed near the mouths of the animal heads give the impression of issuing bubbles, cf. the Misèry buckle, Frontispiece. Width of plate, 4·7 cm.

f. Bronze *strap-end*, diamond shape with split end and two rivets for attachment; beaded border with ring-and-dot stamps. L. 6·6 cm.

Liénard 1881–5, II, pp. 121–3, pl. XXXI. Musée de la Princerie, Verdun.

PLATE 4
Krefeld-Gellep, grave 43, *sword scabbard*

a. Bronze *fitting* at scabbard mouth, moulded edges and tongue motif along top; strap attached lower on scabbard by disc-headed bronze rivets.

b. Bronze *fitting* on scabbard tip; U-sectioned chape with terminal mount knobbed at end and decorated with human mask between birds' heads. Steeger 1937.

Landschaftsmuseum des Niederrheins, Krefeld-Linn.

Rhenen, Holland, grave 846

c. Chip-carved bronze *belt slide*, still fixed to its wide leather belt; L. 10·8 cm; the two triangular end pieces which were fastened by four rivets to the belt are decorated by a scroll in the middle and two pairs of border animals, with a human mask between the pair on the end (Fig. 29, *a*); the raised inner bar is decorated by two outward-facing animal heads and a pair of backward-glancing border lions each side. Oudheidkundig Bodemonderzoek in Nederland, Amersfoort.

Tournai, Belgium

d. Plaster cast of a bronze ring made from the impression in sealing wax of *Childeric's finger ring*, max. diam. 2.1 cm. Ashmolean Museum, Oxford.

PLATE 5

Inlaid iron *buckles*

a. Bifrons, Kent. Iron buckle loop, tongue, rectangular plate and duplicate counter-plate; kidney-shaped loop, width 5·9 cm, with trellis-work silver inlay and transverse strips at intervals; transverse strips on tongue. The plate and counter-plate, 4·3 × 2·8 cm, are covered with sheets of repoussé silver, divided into three longitudinal panels; one outer panel contains the inscription VIVAT QVI FECIT, and the other coiled spirals; in the centre and extending into the outer panels is a full-face bust of a man with shoulder-length hair and decorated robe, and on each side a bird, a lion and a backward-glancing quadruped. Maidstone Museum.

b and c. Alfriston, Sussex, grave 24. Kidney-shaped loop, and repoussé silver plate. See Fig. 16, *d*. Barbican House Museum, Lewes.

d. Unknown provenance, Canterbury Museum. Iron buckle, oval loop and rectangular plate, total L. 5 cm. The plate is inlaid with a quincunx of concentric circles in red metal, each group surrounding a cavity.

e. Kempston, Beds. Kidney-shaped and undulating loop, width 4·8 cm, with traces of sheet and strip inlay. Rectangular plate with inlaid border of ring-and-dot; three large disc cavities in the middle, each with an inner ring, contain remains of other inlaid material — ?bone or glass. British Museum, Reg. No. 91 6–24 118.

f. Howletts, Kent, grave 28. Kidney-shaped loop, width 5·5 cm, with undulating surface, the valleys inlaid with silver gilt sheet, and the ridges with silver strip; the tongue is likewise inlaid and has transverse strips on the base. The rectangular plate has a border of formal cable motif inlaid in silver framing three double rings of gilding metal which hold, in the centre, the remains of colourless glass inlay, and, in the outer zone, bone or ivory. Found with square bronze brooch, Pl. 16, *a*, etc. British Museum, Reg. No. 1935 10–29 13.

PLATE 6

a. Howletts, Kent, grave 25. Inlaid iron *buckle*; loop, width 5 cm, kidney-shaped with convex surface inlaid with silver net-work and occasional transverse strips; strips also on the tongue. The rectangular plate is divided into a central field and border filled with closely coiled spirals; the framing lines consist of small triangles, point to apex; a bronze rivet in each corner. Also in the grave, shield-boss and disc rivets, sword fragments and three shoe-shaped rivets. British Museum, Reg. No. 1935 10–29 12.

b. Howletts, Kent, *Francisa*. L. 19 cm along the curved top; remains of inlaid silver wire on the butt end and bronze wire on one side; on the top adjoining the shaft-hole is a triangular repoussé sheet of bronze. Cf. p. 50, Fig. 27, *l*. British Museum, Reg. No. 1938 10–6 1.

c. Droxford, Hants. Iron *buckle and plate*, total L. 4·6 cm. Oval loop inlaid with silver strips on the outer surface only; strips across the base of the tongue. Rectangular plate fastened by red metal rivet in each corner to a back plate; decoration by silver inlay, framing lines consisting of small triangles, base to apex; borders on the long sides are in stylised cable design, each side border containing an S-shaped scroll; two S-scrolls placed side by side and embellished with further lines and tendrils fill each side panel; in the middle, two ladder-like borders enclose a four-petalled shape formed by triangular insets. Winchester Museum.

d. Alfriston, Sussex, grave 10. Inlaid iron *buckle*; loop, width 4·7 cm, with convex surface; trellis pattern of strips with occasional transverse strips. Rectangular plate has a toothed frame, and is divided into three longitudinal bands, the inner one containing diamond-shapes with dots inside, and the outer ones a wavy line and rings with tangents. Also in the grave: a knife and 'many small metal fittings (? silver) with glass settings loose' (not now traceable). Barbican House Museum, Lewes.

e. Alfriston, Sussex, ? grave B. Inlaid iron *purse mount*; L. 7·9 cm; remains of birds' head terminals; one spiked framing line, the others small triangles base-to-apex, surround a stylized cable. Barbican House Museum, Lewes.

PLATE 7

Chessell Down, Isle of Wight

a. Grave 12: Four *knives*, bronze *tweezers*, rectangular *iron plate*, *bronze plate*, part of iron kidney-shaped *loop*, probably originally with the iron plate above; other fragments of wood and iron.

b. Grave 13: three *knives* and remains of a fourth; two mask *button brooches*; *bronze fitting*; bronze *buckle* with oval plate.

Reproduced from Dennett MS. 1, Carisbrooke Castle Museum.

PLATE 8

a. Enns, Austria. Bronze *annular brooch*, diam. 7·7 cm; an inner penannular ring is surrounded by an openwork border of twelve pelta shapes, each joined to the inner ring by a bar, except for three on the side opposite the opening; this space would have allowed the pin (missing) to slide on the ring.

b. Linz, Austria. Bronze *annular brooch*, diam. 7·2 cm; an inner penannular ring is joined at the pin-slot and three other quarter points to an openwork frame; wave motifs spring from each side alternately, with triangular shapes in between; the outer edge is nicked, and there is a small projection by the pin-slot; part of the pin remains on the inner ring. Landesmuseum, Linz/Donau, inv. Nos. B242 and B636.

c. Unknown provenance, Louvre, Paris. Bronze *plaque*, 18·7 × 15 cm, with hunting scene, the figures of which are inlaid with silver and copper sheet fixed by contour lines and stamping.

PLATE 9

a. Herbergen, Oldenburg. Bronze chip-carved *buckle and plate*; width of loop 13 cm; the loop has zoomorphic terminals, chip-carved triangles on its outer rim and inlaid silver sheet with running scroll on its flat upper surface; the tongue is double with animal head tips, rectangular base flanked by a pair of creatures with one fore-paw and body ending in an animal head; the two plates are ornamented by step-pattern chip-carving. Oldenburg, Landesmuseum für Kunst u. Kulturgeschichte, inv. No. 2858.

b. Colombier-sur-Seulles, France. Bronze *buckle and plate*, L. 7 cm; loop with zoomorphic terminals and row of inlaid triangles; one animal remains flanking the base of the tongue. On the plate within a border of triangular shapes is a griffin with fore and hind leg and animal-headed tail.

c. Sédan, France. Bronze *buckle*, plate and counter-plate. Loop c. 8 cm wide, with zoomorphic terminals and stamped and inlaid ornament; tongue with zoomorphic tip, square base overlaid with silver plate and a coiled animal each side decorated with an inlaid stone. The plate has moulded outer borders, with inner borders of running scroll and stamped arc and semicircle; in each of the two panels is a backward-glancing animal. The counter-plate is similar, except that the animals are running forwards, the border dividing the panels is a fir-tree motif, and both this border and the outline of the animals show traces of inlaid silver. b, c, Musée des Antiquités Nationales St. Germain-en-Laye.

PLATE 10

a and b. Faversham, Kent. Bronze *disc brooch*, diam. 5·8 cm; divided by concentric circles into two main zones of decoration with a plain zone between; in the outer one a row of sea-lion creatures, all facing one way; each has an ear and fore-leg, its body curled underneath with a roundel as a relic of more convolutions (Fig. 30, c); the inner border consists of wave motifs springing from opposite sides of the frame alternately; pellet-in-triangle stamps ornament the rim. Traces of silver sheet inlay suggest that the two decorated zones were so covered, contrasting with the intervening bands of bronze. A blue glass cabochon in the centre is held by a silver collar with repoussé dots; this, and the clumsy fixture of pin and catch at the back b, contrast strongly with the adroitness of the rest of the work, and suggest that the disc was not intended as a brooch in the first place but was refurbished for this purpose by an inferior craftsman. B.M. Guide, 1923, fig. 38; British Museum Reg. No. 1060 '70.

c. Howletts, Kent, grave 13. Fragment of silver *quoit brooch*, original diam. 6·8 cm; the brooch is broken at the pin-slot; the rim is raised and milled; remains of separate pin ring with moulded top, a pin stop and a dove in the round riveted to the plate; there are two gilt decorated zones: in the outer one a pair of racing animals each face a human mask; the animals have feathered fore-paws and tail, flattened ears, double contour, a shoulder compartment of curving shape, and fur markings; the inner zone has backward-glancing animals with a straight ribbon body and only one hind-leg. British Museum Reg. No. 1935 10–29 11. In the same grave there was said to be a wheel-turned bottle, neck broken, red ware, decorated by a continuous scored zigzag line in four rows, ht. 28 cm.

PLATE 11

a. Bifrons, Kent. Bronze strap-end, L. 4 cm, two strips, rounded at one end and squared at the other, with two rivet holes at the square end; a rectangular panel at this end contains a quadruped with curled fore-paw, feathered hind-leg and a scut, the whole being covered with silver sheet (Fig. 30, *h*); the other half is stamped with a row of double concentric rings and curved tangents in imitation of a plait; the underside is decorated by two scored lines along the edges. Evison 1955, pl. viii, *b*. Maidstone Museum.

b. Howletts, Kent. Silver *quoit brooch*, diam. 6·2 cm; upturned, milled edge, oblong hole for fixture of pin opposite a pin-slot flanked by a pair of pin stops and two further perforations, probably for attachment of free-standing birds as Pl. 12, *c*. Two gilt zones of decoration are separated by a plain silver zone; in the outer one stylized round human masks alternate with backward-glancing, eared sea-lions with under-curled body decorated with hatched double contours, dotting and lenticular shoulder compartment; the inner zone bears two pairs of eared sea-lions facing each other; although they have developed hind-legs, they still have a curling tail and roundel on the haunch; two have spiraliform eyes (Fig. 30, *a*, *d*). This brooch was said to have been found with a spiral silver finger ring and a loose sliced garnet. *P.S.A.* xxx, pp. 104–5. British Museum Reg. No. 1918 7–8 35.

The division by Hawkes 1961 (pp. 30–2) of these quoit brooches, Pls. 10, *c*, 11, *b* and 12, *c* into 'chasing technique' and 'carving technique' is not comprehensible to me. The meaning of the terms used is not clear since 'chasing' is now a loose term used to mean little more than decorating from the front. Perhaps a distinction between the excisory method of engraving and the pushing, displacement method of tracing was intended?[1] As far as I can see, there is no difference at all in the techniques used in these three brooches, the only difference being in the level of competence of the craftsmen who produced ragged work on the Howletts complete brooch, and an almost mechanical smoothness on the other two.[2]

[1] H. Hodges, *Artifacts*, 1964, p. 79, fig. 14.

[2] Mr. H. Hodges, of the Institute of Archaeology, kindly examined the Sarre quoit and the Howletts complete quoit brooch, and reports as follows: 'The fundamental process of decoration in both cases would seem to be identical. The areas to be decorated were lightly delimited with a scorper, following which a wide variety of punches and tracers was used to execute the design. In the case of the Sarre brooch, it seems likely that some of the deeper impressions were later cleaned up with a graver. The whole feeling of the Howletts brooch is that the design is softer, and that no graver was used as in the Sarre brooch. This observation, however, fails to take into account the condition of the Howletts brooch. The whole state of preservation—whether due to corrosion, wear in use or even recent cleaning—is far worse than that of the Sarre brooch. In some areas shallow decoration has been completely removed. In view of this it would be exceptionally rash to suggest that in its original condition the decoration was not much sharper, and that it, like the Sarre brooch, was not cleaned up with a graver after the first punching of the design'.

PLATE 12

a. Bifrons, Kent. Two pear-shaped silver *pendants*. L. 3·25 cm and 3 cm; loop at top; a flat frame surrounding an oval blue-glass cabochon; the frame is divided into three panels each side with a diamond-shaped panel by the loop; each side panel is occupied by a simple sea-lion with square jaws, round eyes and tail curled under belly (Fig. 30, *b*). Brown 1915, IV, pl. CII, 1. Maidstone Museum.

b. Bishopstone, Bucks. *Rectangular bronze plate*, 3·5 × 3·2 cm; a rivet hole in each corner; a central rectangular panel divided by diagonal cross into segments containing opposing scrolls and triangles is framed by a plain panel and an outer border of pairs of backward-glancing quadrupeds. The deep inner contour line may indicate that the animals were once inlaid with silver sheet[1] (Fig. 30, *k*). Leeds 1936, pl. III, c. Aylesbury Museum.

c. Sarre, Kent. Silver *quoit brooch*, diam. 7·8 cm; see p. 127, note 2; upturned, milled edge, separate moulded inner ring attached to the brooch by the pin-slot and at two other points; a bird sits on the base of the pin and two more are riveted to the plate by the pin tip; two decorated zones are gilt, the plain zone between remaining silver; in the outer zone a series of quadrupeds regularly face alternate ways, and the inner zone of backward-glancing quadrupeds are similarly arranged; the inner zone animals and about half in the outer zone have hip compartments and fur markings; the rest in the outer zone have longitudinal markings on the neck (Fig. 30, *i*, *l*). B.M. Guide, 1923, p. 54, fig. 59. British Museum Reg. No. 1893 6–1 219.32.

PLATE 13

a. Croydon, Surrey. Bronze tubular *strap distributor*; tube, flat at back, convex at front, 8·6 cm long with a tubular off-shoot at right-angles in the middle; three loops of a hinge on the opposite side to this projection; a larger loop on each side near one end, in one of which swivels a double bronze tag; the convex surface is divided into three panels, the centre panel framing a horse-like quadruped and the end section a pair of backward-glancing sea-lions back to back with one fore-paw, body curled under, and double hatched contours. The animals all bear remains of silver sheet inlay (fig. 30, *e*, *o*).[2] *P.S.A.* 2nd ser. IV, 333. British Museum Reg. No. 95 3–13 40.

b. Howletts, Kent, grave 5. Rectangular bronze re-used plate, 4·1 × 3·1 cm, rivet hole in each corner; rectangular panel chip-carved in cruciform pattern; border cut off at one end shows lower part of two animals, back to back; feathered hind feet, double contour and decorative markings on the body are visible (Fig. 30, *g*). Also in the grave were a buckle with rectangular plate in Style I animal ornament, button brooch and a gilt bronze fragment. *B.M.Q.* x, pl. XXXIX. British Museum Reg. No. 1935 10–29 10.

c. High Down, Sussex, grave XII. Bronze *strap-slide*. L. 4·6 cm; the raised middle square has a diamond shape filled with a chip-carved cross with curling terminals, a scroll filling each remaining corner of the square; the ends, on a lower plane, consist of pairs

[1] Hawkes 1961 states (p. 41) that this plate was once inlaid, and (p. 37) that it was not.

[2] According to Hawkes 1961, p. 36, this was found with a bronze-bound wooden bucket, but I am unable to find any evidence of this. The B.M. register records 'Brought in with a bucket in the possession of Mr. Rigby', but does not state that the two objects were found together.

of horses' heads curving outwards; the necks and space between are inlaid with silver sheet, and a copper rivet remains in one eye. Found with a small-long brooch with horned head and lozenge foot, and iron rust. *Arch.* LIV, pl. XXVII, 8. Worthing Museum.

PLATE 14

a. Chessell Down, Isle of Wight. Bronze *strap-end*. L. 5·1 cm; long rectangle of double strip, solid at one end which has three projections, and split at the other where it narrows into two out-curving horses' heads, surmounted by a diamond shape and disc with rivet. The rectangle is divided into diamonds and triangles inlaid with silver sheet, keyed with cross-hatching and dots. Also in the grave, a mounted crystal ball, two silver square-headed brooches, a duck brooch, a buckle and beads. Hillier, p. 30, figs. 23, 26, 65, 83. British Museum 67 7–29 117.

b. Croydon, Surrey. Bronze *strap-end*. L. 5·3 cm; similar shape to a, except that the diamond shape has developed lateral lobes and central perforation, and a pair of perforations appear under the horses' heads and at the other end; traces of incised tendril design. Evison 1958, pl. XXVI, e. Croydon Public Library.

c. Alfriston, Sussex, grave 17. Bronze *buckle* loop, plate and duplicate counter-plate. See Fig. 30, n. Also in the grave, bronze *strap-end*, bronze triangular *mount*, Fig. 17, e–g. *Sussex Arch. Coll.* LVI, p. 33, pl. IX, 1. Barbican House Museum, Lewes.

d. High Down, Sussex, grave 34. Bronze *buckle*; rectangular loop, width 3·8 cm with two attachment tabs; three oval shapes along each short side and five along the long side, each with hatched border; the corners occupied by concentric circles, one with cross centre; traces of silver sheet inlay. The plate is gilt and heart-shaped, with three rivet holes, central dark amber glass[1] cabochon, and ball-in-triangle stamped border. Also in the grave, spearhead, knife and purse mount. *Arch.* LV, p. 211, pl. IX, 2. Worthing Museum.

PLATE 15

a. Alfriston, Sussex, grave 43. Silver *penannular brooch*, diam. 4·1 cm; both ends returned and decorated with full-face animal heads; the pin rides on a separate penannular ring fixed to the quoit; an outer openwork border of pairs of animal heads surrounds a zone of running tendrils with dotted following lines and a motif in the middle of human mask with pointed chin flanked by four semi-masks. Also in the grave: glass cone beaker, square-headed brooch, pair of small square-headed brooches, a pair of equal-armed brooches, silver rings with beads attached, two Roman coins, cowrie shell, spiral finger ring, bronze rings and other fragments: *Sussex Arch. Coll.* LVI, pls. I, 9; III, 1; IV, 10; IV, 5 and 5a; V, 5 and 5a; X, 8; XI, 1a–e, 2 and 3; *Sussex Arch. Coll.* LVII, pls. XXIV, 1; XXVI, 2. Barbican House Museum, Lewes.

b. Higham, Kent. Bronze *disc brooch*, max. diam. 5·2 cm; outer border of oval shapes (? faces) retaining traces of silver strip inlay;[2] an inner zone is plain except for traces of

---

[1] Not red glass, as stated Hawkes 1961, p. 36. Red glass was not made at this period.

[2] Unlike Hawkes 1961, p. 34 n. 3, I am unable, even with the aid of a microscope, to detect any ragged edges which would indicate that this was the remains of silver sheet inlay rather than silver strips or wires.

ball-in-triangle stamps; remains of a central bronze plate with impressed dot decoration; this plate was fastened to the brooch by four rivets, and may originally have held a stone as on the Faversham brooch; as on the Faversham brooch, too, the pin and catch were riveted on in a primitive fashion. Brown 1915, III, pl. LXI, 3. Rochester Museum.

PLATE 16

a. Howletts, Kent, grave 28; Bronze *square plate* converted to use as a brooch, 3·8 cm wide; the central square panel contains four spirals, the surrounding plain zone has a ring stamp in each corner; the next zone is depressed and faintly hatched, the next plain zone holds a rivet in each corner, and the outer border a running tendril; each zone is separated by an inlaid silver strip. The contents of this grave were no doubt mixed, for it is said to have contained a sword, the inlaid buckle (Pl. 5, *f*) and a bronze disc and annular brooch. *Ant. Journ.* XXXV, pl. VII, f. British Museum Reg. No. 1935 10–29 9.

b. High Down, Sussex, grave 60. Bronze *square quoit brooch*, 4·6 × 4·7 cm; this is basically a circular quoit brooch with extensions to form a square; it has a pin and two pin stops; the main inner zone of decoration consists of a row of wave motifs with tendrils and dotting; this is surrounded by beading and a plain zone containing a row of arc stamps; in the corners a diagonal line of small triangles base to apex with tendrils each side. Also, in the grave two bronze disc brooches, one with stamped rings, a knife, iron buckle and ? nail. *Arch.* LV, p. 213, pl. IX, 4. Worthing Museum.

c. High Down, Sussex, grave 26. Bronze *buckle*, width 3·8 cm; the loop curls inwards near the base of the tongue which widens in similar pointed shapes; a second bar for attachment to the belt is joined to the loop by means of two rings each with a pair of confronted animal heads; decoration by beading, and by tendrils on the loop terminals and tongue base. Also in the grave, a pair of radiate brooches, a small quoit brooch and an iron ring. *Arch.* LIV, p. 377, pl. XXXVII, 5, 6 and 9. Worthing Museum.

PLATE 17

a. Waben, Pas-de-Calais. Repoussé *silver disc*, diam. 4 cm; egg-and-tongue border; centre (missing) surrounded by four lion masks interspersed with rosette motifs. *Arch.* 63, p. 174, fig. 12.

b. East Shefford, Berks., grave XXIV. *Disc brooch*, diam. 3·5 cm; one of a pair, with gilt bronze repoussé sheet and separate, upstanding rim; beaded outer border and boss in the centre; pattern of three identical animals as on *c* below, but stamped with less detail; the same are the backward-glancing position, curling lappet and tongue, one hind-leg and trident tail; the roundels lack the central dot, the body lacks hachuring, and the roundel in the haunch has become elongated (Fig. 29, *g*). Also in the grave, a glass bead and glass cone beaker. *Journ. Royal Anthrop. Inst.* XLV (1915), 92. Newbury Museum, Berks.

c. Sigy, Northern France. *Disc brooch* with applied repoussé plate of gilt bronze; diam. 5·5 cm; simplified egg-and-tongue border; the damaged plate shows the remains of a design of three identical animals: backward-glancing, with curling lappet at back of head and curling tongue; hind leg, haunch with roundel, and trident-shaped tail;

two more roundels below the hind-leg emphasize its evolution from the sea-lion with coiled body. Musée départemental des antiquités de la Seine-maritime, Rouen.

PLATE 18

a. Unknown provenance. Square bronze double *belt plate*, 4·5 × 4·5 cm, fastened by two rivets at one side and with moulded tubular edging at other; border on three sides of row of triangles with double arc motifs sprouting from their tops inlaid in silver strips; the inner panel has an arc-and-dot border round a backward-glancing animal; the creature has a square nose, pair of lenticular ears, a long tail, parallel lines following the neck and decoration by hachuring, arc-and-dot stamps; the outlines are emphasized by silver strip inlay. Oldenburg, Landesmuseum für Kunst u. Kulturgeschichte, inv. No. 3141.

b. The Meuse, Heerenwaarde, Holland. Bronze *mount* in the form of two identical animals fastened by a rivet in the middle, L. 2 cm; the animal has a small ear and tail, feathered paws, pear-shaped haunch compartment and the rest of the body decorated with longitudinal markings. Museum van Oudheiden, Leiden.

c. Unknown provenance, Ashmolean Museum; Bronze *mount*, L. 4·4 cm; broken at both ends; in the middle an animal head with long, projecting ear and the middle of the open jaws indicated by a perforation; ornamentation by concentric ring stamps, one of which indicates the eye of the animal.

d. Staxton, Yorks. Bronze *appliqué* in the form of an animal, with applied silver sheet. L. 2·5 cm; two short studs project at the back, probably for fixing on to leather. *Hull Museum Publications No. 195*, 'second skeleton', pp. 8–10, pls. II and III. Hull Museum, Yorks.

e. Parfondeval, Northern France. Bronze *strip*. L. 5 cm; perforation near one end and loop at the back of the other; ornamented by a backward-glancing animal, geometrically expressed. L'Abbé Cochet, *La Normandie Souterrain* (1854), pl. xv, 2. Musée départemental des antiquités de la Seine-maritime, Rouen.

Abbreviations

Åberg 1956   N. Åberg, *Den historiska relationen mellan senromersk tid och nordisk folk-vandringstid* (1956).

Acta Arch.   *Acta Archaeologica.*

Akerman 1855   J. Y. Akerman, *Remains of Pagan Saxondom* (1855).

Ant. Journ.   *Antiquaries Journal.*

Arch.   *Archaeologia.*

Arch. Cant.   *Archaeologia Cantiana.*

Bakka 1959   E. Bakka, 'On the beginning of Salin's Style I in England', *Universitetet i Bergen Årbok*, 1958, *Historisk-Antikvarisk rekke Nr. 3*, 1–83.

Behmer 1939   E. Behmer, *Das Zweischneidige Schwert der Germanischen Völkerwanderungszeit* (1939).

Behrens 1930   G. Behrens, 'Spätrömische Kerbschnittschnallen', *Schumacher-Festschrift* (1930), 285–94.

Behrens 1950   G. Behrens, *Das frühchristliche und merovingische Mainz* (1950).

Behrens 1952   G. Behrens, 'Das rückblickende Tier in der vor- und frühgeschichtlichen Kunst Mitteleuropas', *Festschrift des Römisch-Germanischen Zentralmuseums in Mainz*, 1 (1952), 26–43.

Bidder and   H. F. Bidder and J. Morris, 'The Anglo-Saxon cemetery at Mit-
   Morris 1959   cham', *Surrey Archaeological Collections*, LVI (1959), 51–131.

Bjørn 1929   A. Bjørn, 'Bronsekar og glas begre fra Folkevandringstiden', *Det Kongelige Norske Videnskabers Selskabs Skrifter*, Nr. 6 (1929).

B.M. Guide 1923   *British Museum Guide to Anglo-Saxon Antiquities* (1923).

B.M.Q.   *British Museum Quarterly.*

Boeles 1951   P. C. J. A. Boeles, *Friesland tot de elfde eeuw* (1951).

Böhner 1948   K. Böhner, 'Das Langschwert des Frankenkönigs Childerich', *Bonner Jahrbücher*, 148 (1948), 218–48.

Böhner 1950   K. Böhner, 'Zum Langschwert Childerichs', *Bonner Jahrbücher*, 150 (1950), 104–6.

Böhner 1951   K. Böhner, 'Fränkische Gräber von Oberlörick im Stadtkreis Düsseldorf', *Bonner Jahrbücher*, 151 (1951), 312–19.

Böhner 1958   K. Böhner, *Die fränkischen Altertümer des Trierer Landes* (1958).

Boulanger   G. Boulanger, *Le cimetière franco-mérovingien de Marchélepot* (1909).

Breuer and   J. Breuer et H. Roosens, 'Le Cimetière franc de Haillot', *Archaeologia
   Roosens 1957   Belgica*, 34 (1957).

Brown 1915, III   G. Baldwin Brown, *The Arts in Early England* (1915), III.

Brown 1915, IV   G. Baldwin Brown, *The Arts in Early England* (1915), IV.

Bushe-Fox 1926, II   J. P. Bushe-Fox, *Second Report on the excavation of the Roman fort at Richborough, Kent* (1926).

Bushe-Fox 1932, III   J. P. Bushe-Fox, *Third Report on the excavation of the Roman fort at Richborough, Kent* (1932).

Bushe-Fox 1949, IV   J. P. Bushe-Fox, *Fourth Report on the excavation of the Roman fort at Richborough, Kent* (1949).

Cabrol Leclercq, *Dict.*   F. Cabrol and H. M. Leclercq, *Dictionnaire d'archéologie chrétienne et de liturgie* (1920–53).

Chenet 1935   G. Chenet, 'La tombe 319 du cimetière mérovingien de Lavoye (Meuse)', *Préhistoire*, IV (1935), 34–118.

Chenet 1941   G. Chenet, *La céramique gallo-romaine d'Argonne au IVe siècle* (1941).

Collingwood and Myres 1937   R. G. Collingwood and J. N. L. Myres, *Roman Britain and the English Settlements* (1937).

Dasnoy 1954   A. Dasnoy, 'Les premières damasquinures mérovingiennes de la région namuroise', *Annales de la Société archéologique de Namur*, XLVII (1953–4), 267–86.

Dasnoy 1955   A. Dasnoy, 'Quelques tombes de la région Namuroise datées par des monnaies', *Annales de la Société archéologique de Namur*, XLVIII (1955) 5–40.

De Laet, Dhondt and Nenquin 1952   S. J. De Laet, J. Dhondt and J. Nenquin, 'Les Laeti du Namurois et l'origine de la civilisation mérovingienne', *Études d'histoire et d'archéologie dediées a Ferdinand Courtoy* (1952), 149.

Douglas 1793   J. Douglas, *Nenia Britannica* (1793).

Eck 1891   T. Eck, *Les deux cimetières gallo-romains de Vermand et de Saint-Quentin* (1891).

E.H.R.   *English Historical Review.*

Evison 1955   V. I. Evison, 'Early Anglo-Saxon inlaid metalwork', *Antiquaries Journal*, XXXV (1955), 20–45.

Evison 1958   V. I. Evison, 'Further Anglo-Saxon inlay', *Antiquaries Journal*, XXXVIII (1958), 240–4.

Faider-Feytmans 1951   G. Faider-Feytmans, 'Sépultures du IVe siècle a Tournai', *Latomus*, X (1951), 29 ff.

Faussett 1856   B. Faussett, *Inventorium Sepulchrale* (1856).

Fleury 1877–82   E. Fleury, *Antiquités et Monuments du Département de l'Aisne* (1877–82).

Forssander 1937   J. E. Forssander, 'Provinzialrömisches und Germanisches', *Meddelanden från Lunds Universitets Historiska Museum* (1937), 183–272.

Fowler 1960   E. Fowler, 'The origins and development of the penannular brooch in Europe', *Proceedings of the Prehistoric Society*, XXVI (1960), 149–77.

Garscha 1962   F. Garscha, 'Fränkische Tauschierarbeiten aus frühen Reihengräbern am Oberrhein', *Badische Fundberichte*, 22 (1962), 133–63.

Glazema and Ypey 1956	P. Glazema and J. Ypey, *Merovingische Ambachtskunst* (1956).
Gricourt 1958	J. Gricourt, G. Fabre et M. Mainjonet, J. Lafaurie, *Trésors monétaires et plaques-boucles de la Gaule romaine, XIIe supplément à Gallia* (1958).
Grohne 1953	E. Grohne, *Mahndorf* (1953).
Harden 1951	D. B. Harden, 'Saxon glass from Sussex', *Sussex County Magazine*, XXV (1951), 260 ff.
Harden 1956	D. B. Harden, 'Glass vessels in Britain and Ireland, A.D. 400–1000', *Dark Age Britain*, ed. D. B. Harden, 1956.
Hawkes 1961	S. Hawkes, 'The Jutish Style A', *Archaeologia*, XCVIII (1961), 29–74.
Hawkes and Dunning 1963	S. Hawkes and G. C. Dunning, 'Soldiers and Settlers in Britain, fourth to fifth century', *Medieval Archaeology*, V (1961) (1962), 1–70.
Hillier	G. Hillier, *History and Antiquities of the Isle of Wight*.
Holmqvist 1951	W. Holmqvist, *Tauschierte Metallarbeiten des Nordens* (1951).
Holmqvist 1955	W. Holmqvist, *Germanic Art* (1955).
Hougen 1936	B. Hougen, *The Migration Style of ornament in Norway* (1936).
J.B.A.A.	*Journal of the British Archaeological Association*.
Jessup 1946	R. F. Jessup, 'An Anglo-Saxon cemetery at Westbere, Kent', *Antiquaries Journal*, XXVI (1946), 11 ff.
Journ. Royal Anthrop. Inst.	*Journal of the Royal Anthropological Institute*.
Kilbride-Jones 1937	H. E. Kilbride-Jones, 'The evolution of penannular brooches with zoomorphic terminals in Great Britain and Ireland', *Proc. Roy. Irish Acad.*, Sect. C, XLIII (1937), no. 13.
Kirk and Leeds 1952–3	J. R. Kirk and E. T. Leeds, 'Three early Saxon graves from Dorchester, Oxon.', *Oxoniensia*, XVII–XVIII (1952–3), 63–76.
Lantier 1948	R. Lantier, 'Un cimetière du IVe siècle au "Mont-Augé" (Vert-la-Gravelle, Marne)', *L'Antiquité Classique*, XVII (1948), 373.
Leeds 1912	E. T. Leeds, 'The distribution of the Anglo-Saxon saucer brooch in relation to the Battle of Bedford, A.D. 571', *Archaeologia*, LXIII (1912), 159–202.
Leeds 1913	E. T. Leeds, *The Archaeology of the Anglo-Saxon Settlements* (1913).
Leeds 1936	E. T. Leeds, *Early Anglo-Saxon Art and Archaeology* (1936).
Leeds 1945	E. T. Leeds, 'The distribution of the Angles and Saxons archaeologically considered', *Archaeologia*, XCI (1945), 1–106.
Leeds 1954	E. T. Leeds, 'The Growth of Wessex', *Oxoniensia*, XIX (1954).
Leeds and Harden 1936	E. T. Leeds and D. B. Harden, *The Anglo-Saxon cemetery at Abingdon, Berks.* (1936).
Leeds and Shortt 1953	E. T. Leeds and H. de S. Shortt, *An Anglo-Saxon cemetery at Petersfinger, near Salisbury, Wilts.* (1953).
Lethbridge 1951	T. C. Lethbridge, *A cemetery at Lackford, Suffolk* (1951).

Liénard 1881–5   F. Liénard, *Archéologie de la Meuse* (1881–5).

Lindenschmit   L. Lindenschmit, *Die Alterthümer unserer heidnischen Vorzeit* (1864–
  1864–1911, IV   1911).

Mainz. Zeitschr.   *Mainzer Zeitschrift.*

Nenquin 1953   J. A. E. Nenquin, *La nécropole de Furfooz* (1953).

Pilloy 1880 I   J. Pilloy, *Études sur d'anciens lieux de sépultures dans l'Aisne* (1880), I.

Pilloy 1895 II   J. Pilloy, *Études sur d'anciens lieux de sépultures dans l'Aisne* (1895), II.

Pilloy 1912 III   J. Pilloy, *Études sur d'anciens lieux de sépultures dans l'Aisne* (1912), III.

Pirling 1959   R. Pirling, 'Gräber des frühen 5. Jahrhunderts aus Krefeld-Gellep',
                      Bonner Jahrbücher, 159 (1959), 215–42.

Pirling 1960a   R. Pirling, 'Neue Grabfunde des 4. und 5. Jahrhunderts aus Krefeld-
                      Gellep', *Germania*, 38 (1960), 80–9.

Pirling 1960b   R. Pirling, 'Ein silber und messingtauschierter Feuerstahl aus
                      Krefeld-Gellep', *Jahrbuch des Römisch-Germanischen Zentralmuseums,
                      Mainz*, 7 (1960), 311–14.

Plettke 1921   A. Plettke, *Ursprung und Ausbreitung der Angeln in Sachsen* (*Die Urnen-
                      friedhöfe in Niedersachsen*, Bd. III, H.1, 1921.)

Proc. Brit. Acad.   *Proceedings of the British Academy.*

Proc. Roy. Irish Acad. *Proceedings of the Royal Irish Academy.*

P.S.A.   *Proceedings of the Society of Antiquaries.*

Riegl 1927   A. Riegl, *Spätrömische Kunstindustrie* (1927).

Rigollot 1850   Rigollot, 'Recherches historiques sur les peuples de la race teutonique
                      qui envahirent les Gaules au Ve siècle', *Mémoires de la Société des
                      Antiquaires de Picardie*, X (1850), 121–227.

Roeder 1927   F. Roeder, *Die Sächsische Schalenfibel der Völkerwanderungszeit* (1927).

Roes 1953   A. Roes, 'Une garniture de ceinturon à décor entaillé, provenant de
                      Rhenen (Utrecht)', *Berichten van de Rijksdienst voor het outheidkundig
                      bodemonderzoek in Nederland*, IV (1953), 32–7.

Roosens 1962   H. Roosens, 'Quelques mobiliers funéraires de la fin de l'époque
                      romaine dans le nord de la France', *Dissertationes Archaeologicae
                      Gandenses*, VII (1962).

Salin 1922   *Le cimetière barbare de Lézeville (Haute-Marne)* (1922).

Salin 1952 II   E. Salin, *La civilisation mérovingienne* (1952), II.

Salin 1957 III   E. Salin, *La civilisation mérovingienne* (1957), III.

Salin and   E. Salin et A. France-Lanord, *Rhin et Orient: Le fer à l'époque
France-Lanord 1943   mérovingienne* (1943).

Savory 1956   H. N. Savory, 'Some Sub-Romano-British brooches from South
                      Wales', *Dark Age Britain* (1956), ed. D. B. Harden, pp. 40–58.

Schmidt 1961   B. Schmidt, *Die späte Völkerwanderungszeit in Mitteldeutschland* (1961).

Sjövold 1962   T. Sjövold, *The Iron Age settlement of Arctic Norway* (1962).

Smith 1852, II   C. R. Smith, *Collectanea Antiqua* (1852), II.

Steeger 1937a   A. Steeger, *Germanische Funde der Völkerwanderungszeit aus Krefeld* (1937).

Steeger 1937b   A. Steeger, 'Ein frühfränkisches Kriegergrab von Krefeld-Gellep', *Germania*, 21 (1937), 182–8.

Stenton 1943   F. M. Stenton, *Anglo-Saxon England* (1943).

Surrey Arch. Coll.   *Surrey Archaeological Collections.*

Sussex Arch. Coll.   *Sussex Archaeological Collections.*

Thorpe 1935   W. A. Thorpe, *English Glass* (1935).

V.C.H. Berks. 1   *Victoria County History, Berkshire* (1906), 1.

V.C.H. Hunts. 1   *Victoria County History, Huntingdonshire* (1926), 1.

V.C.H. Warwicks. 1   *Victoria County History, Warwickshire* (1904), 1.

Verlinden 1954   C. Verlinden, 'Frankish colonizations: a new approach', *Trans. Royal Historical Society*, 5th ser., vol. 4, 1–17.

Werner 1941   J. Werner, *Die beiden Zierscheiben des Thorsberger Moorfundes* (1941).

Werner 1949   J. Werner, 'Eine nordfranzösische Tierfibel von Basel (Bernerring)', *Ur-Schweiz*, XX, XIIIe année, 60–8.

Werner 1950   J. Werner, 'Zur Entstehung der Reihengräberzivilisation', *Archaeologia Geographica*, Bd. 1, 1950–1, 23–32.

Werner 1953a   J. Werner, 'Zu fränkischen Schwertern des 5. Jahrhunderts', *Germania*, 31 (1953), 38–44.

Werner 1953b   J. Werner, *Das Alamannische Gräberfeld von Bülach* (*Monographien zur Ur- und Frühgeschichte der Schweiz*), Bd. IX (1953).

Werner 1956   J. Werner, 'Fränkische Schwerter des 5. Jahrhunderts aus Samson und Petersfinger', *Germania*, 34 (1956), 156–8.

Werner 1958   J. Werner, 'Kriegergräber aus der ersten Hälfte des 5. Jahrhunderts zwischen Schelde und Weser', *Bonner Jahrbücher*, 158 (1958), 372–413.

Werner 1961   J. Werner, *Katalog der Sammlung Diergardt*, 1 (1961).

Werner 1962   J. Werner, 'Ein reiches Laetengrab der Zeit um 400 n. Chr. aus Fécamp (Seine-maritime)', *Archaeologia Belgica*, 61 (1962), *Miscellanea Archaeologica in honorem J. Breuer*, 145–54.

Wilts. Arch. Mag.   *Wiltshire Archaeological Magazine.*

Index

Maps

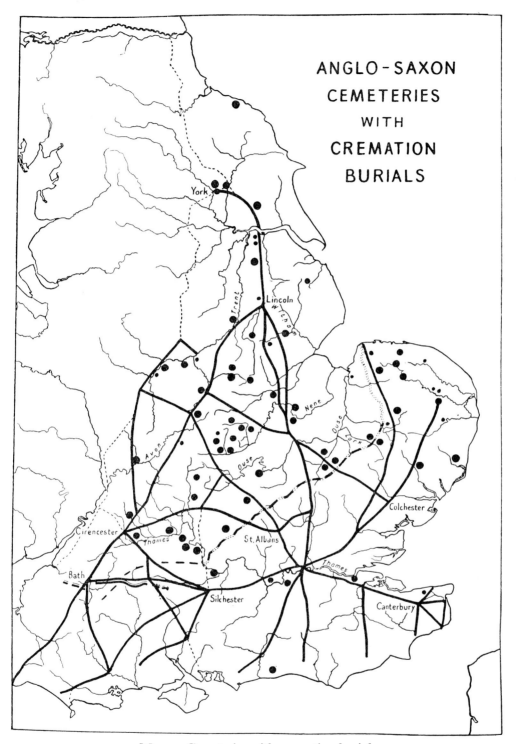

MAP 1. Cemeteries with cremation-burials.

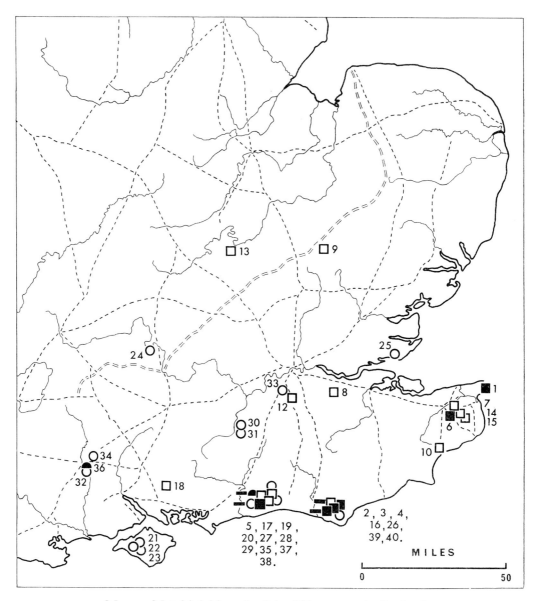

MAP 2. Metal-inlaid work of the fifth century in England.

■   Inlaid iron buckle loops with repoussé plates.

☐   Inlaid iron buckle loops with inlaid iron plates.

○   Inlaid loops.

◖   Inlaid iron buckle loops with semicircular plates.

▬   Inlaid iron purse mounts.

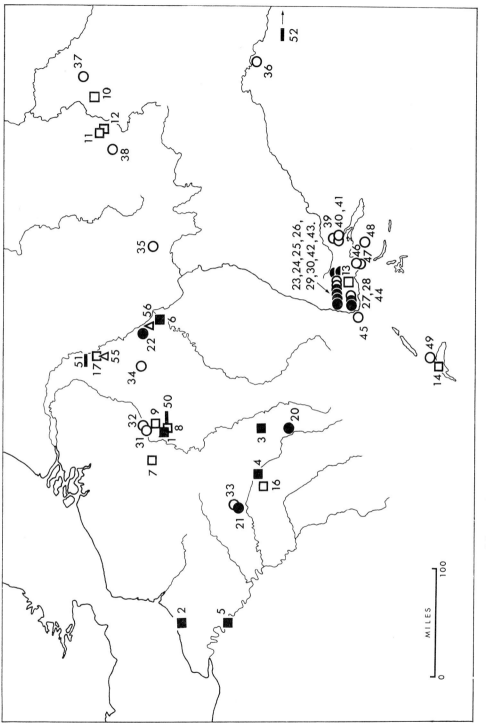

MAP 3. Metal-inlaid work of the fifth century on the continent.

▪ Inlaid iron buckle loops with repoussé plates.   ◖ Inlaid buckles with semicircular plates.

☐ Inlaid iron buckle loops with inlaid iron   ○ Inlaid loops.
   plates.
                                                      ▮ Inlaid purse mounts.
● Inlaid buckles with oval plates.
                                                      ◁ Strap-slides with close trellis-work inlay.

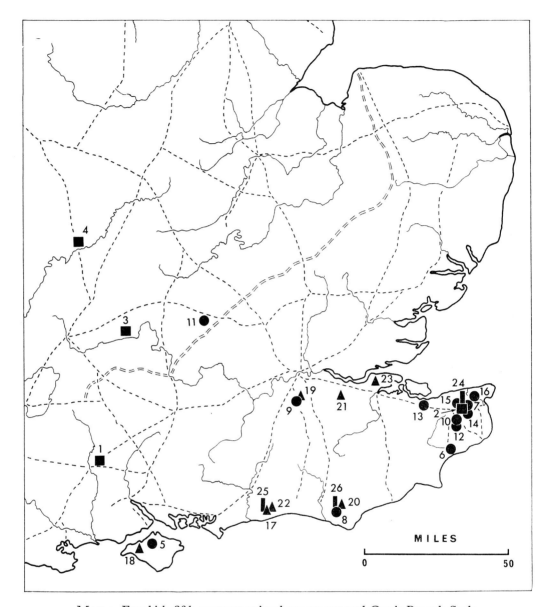

MAP 4. Frankish fifth-century animal ornament and Quoit Brooch Style.

■ Frankish fifth-century animal ornament.

● Quoit Brooch ornament – animal.

▲ Quoit Brooch ornament – horses' heads and human masks.

▌ Quoit Brooch ornament – non-zoomorphic.

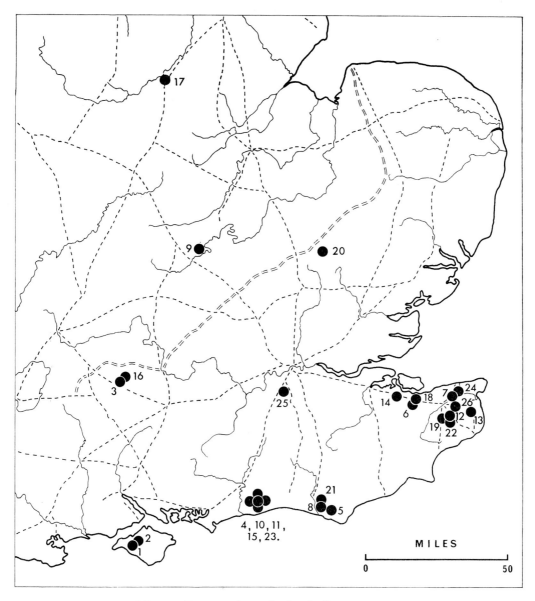

MAP 5. Roman glasses in Anglo-Saxon graves.

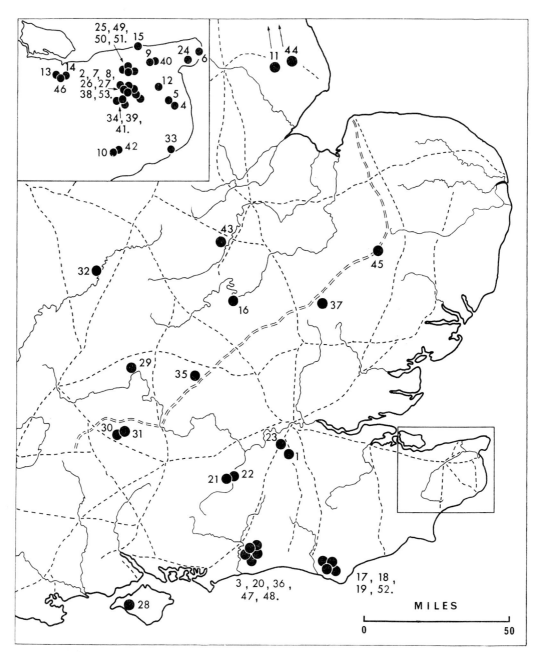

MAP 6. Fifth-century glasses.

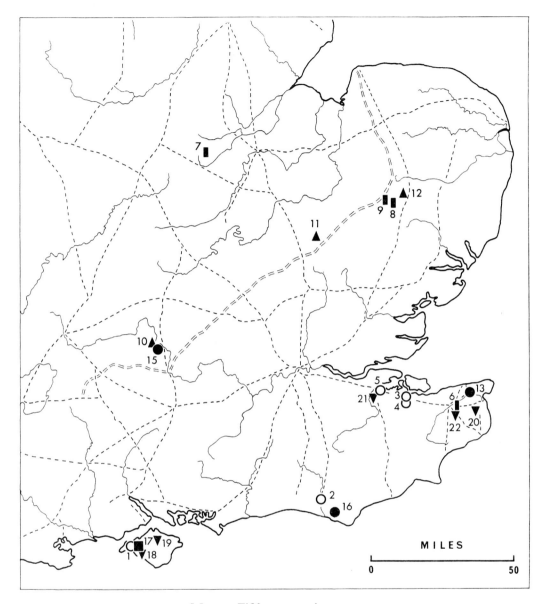

MAP 7. Fifth-century imports.

○	Glass armlets.	●	Zoomorphic buckles with fixed plate.
▮	Brooches with upturned foot.	◼	Imported pottery.
▲	Bronze cauldrons with triangular lugs.	▼	Bows or arrows.

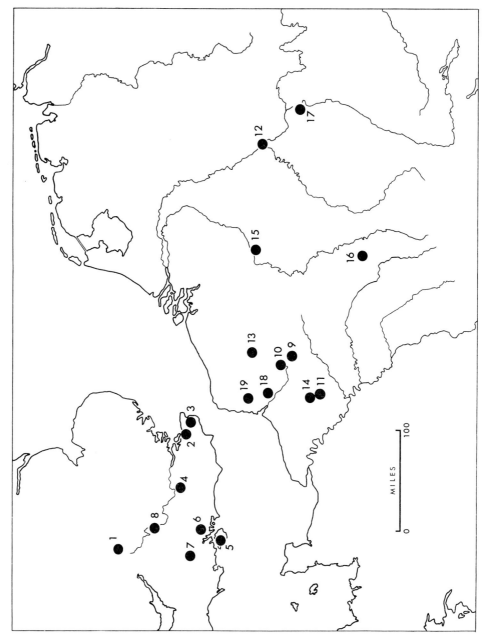

MAP 8. Bronze-und bowooden vessels with repoussé decoration in arcade-and-dot and/or Christian motifs.

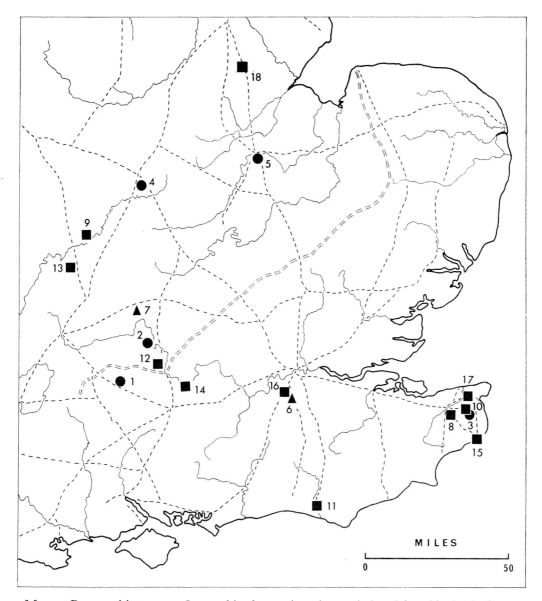

MAP 9. Bronze objects manufactured in the pre-invasion period and found in Anglo-Saxon graves.

● Disc or oval brooches with cabochon stone centres.

▲ Continental Roman bronze belt mounts.

■ Buckles made in Britain.

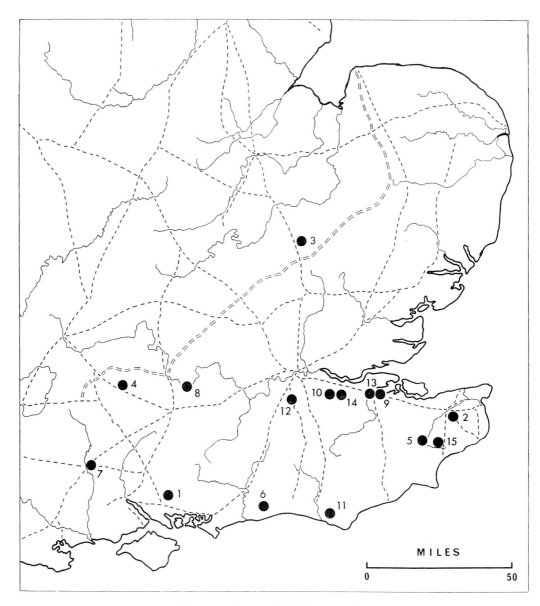

MAP 10. Bronze tubular mounts.

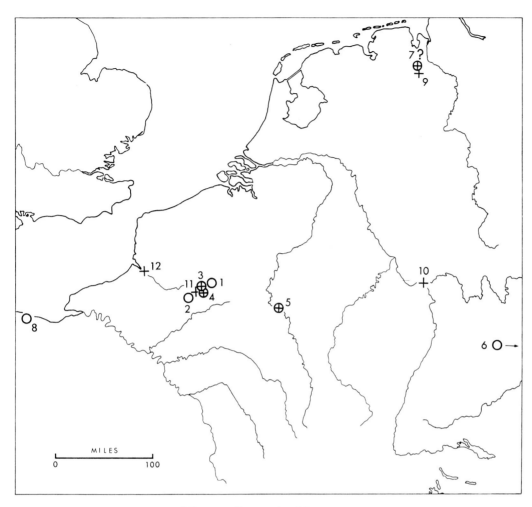

MAP 11. Bronze buckles c. 400 A.D.

○ Germanic two-dimensional animal orna-   + Silver-inlaid bronze buckles.
   ment on bronze buckle plates.

Figures

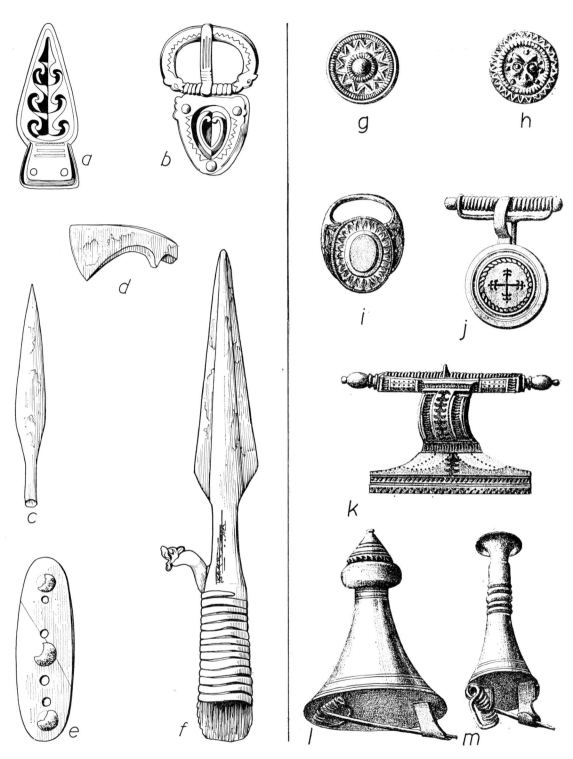

Fig. 1. *a–f*, Vermand (Aisne), tomb of military leader; *g–l* and ?*m*, Vermand (Aisne), grave 24 (all after Pilloy).

Scale: 1/1 except *c*, *d*, and *f*, about 1/4.

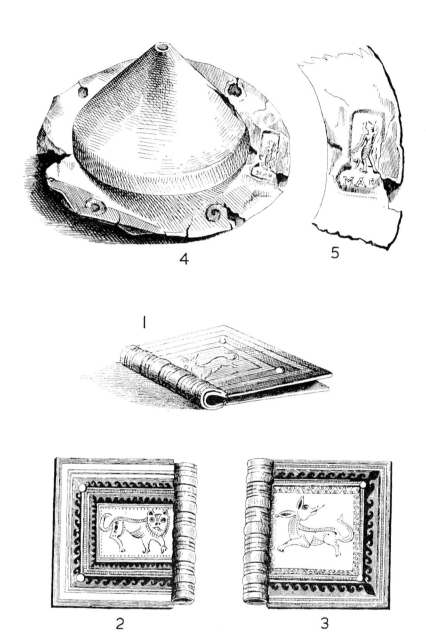

FIG. 2. Misèry (Somme) (after Rigollot).
Scale 1–3 and 5, 1/1, 4, c, 1/2.

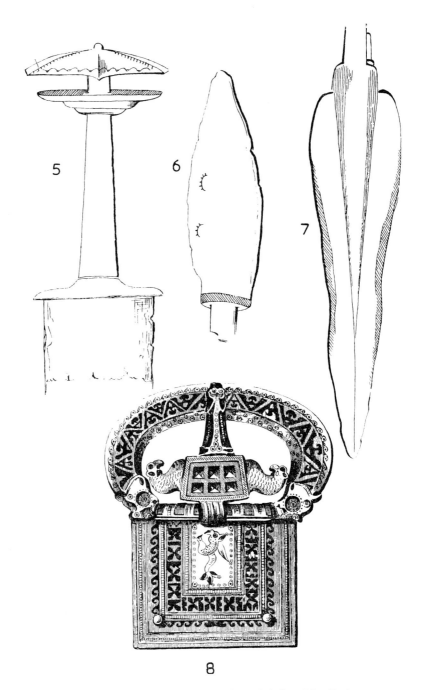

FIG. 3. Misèry (Somme), continued (after Rigollot).
Scale: 5, c. 1/2; 6, c. 1/1; 7, ?c. 1/2; 8, 1/1.

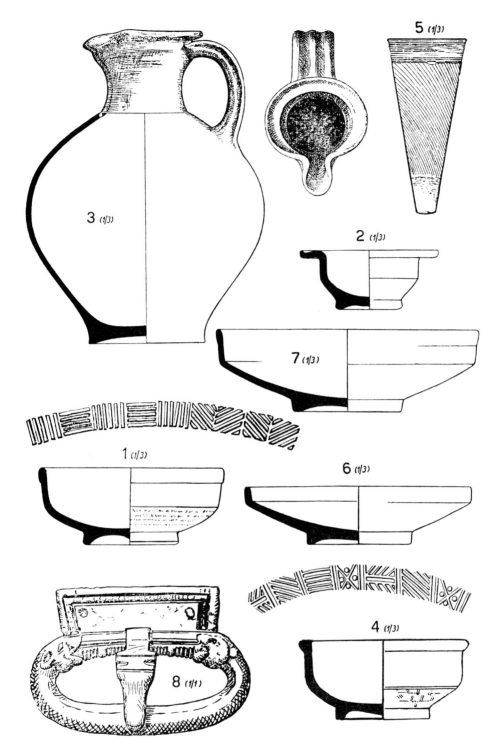

FIG. 4. Haillot, grave XI (after Breuer and Roosens).

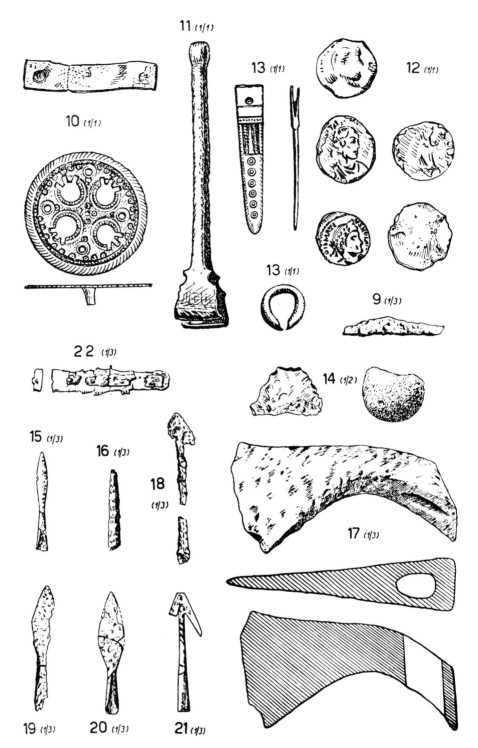

FIG. 5. Haillot, grave XI continued (after Breuer and Roosens).

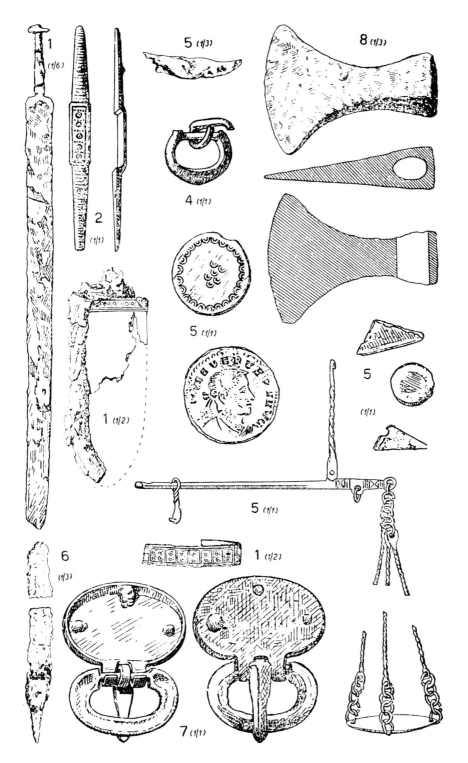

FIG. 6. Haillot, grave XIII (after Breuer and Roosens).

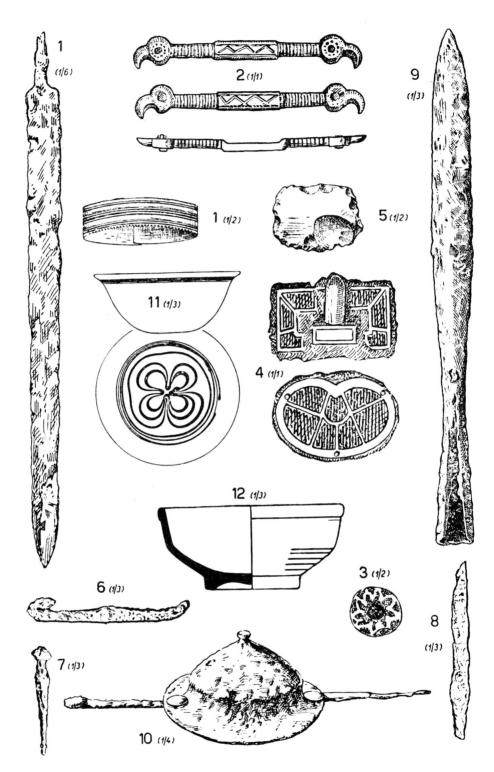

FIG. 7. Haillot, grave XVI (after Breuer and Roosens).

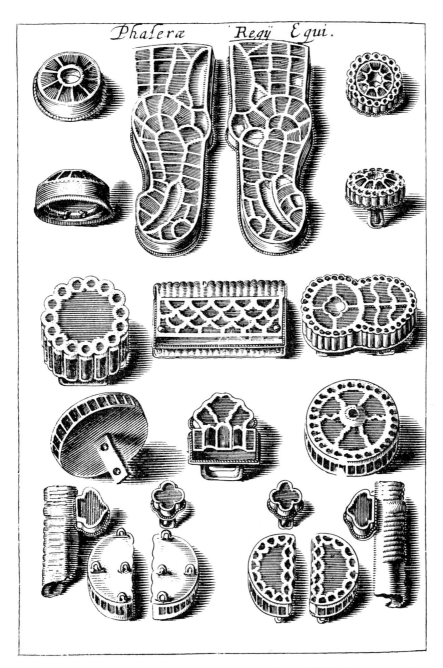

Fig. 8. Gold jewellery decorated with garnets from Childeric's grave (after Chiflet).

Scale: 1/1.

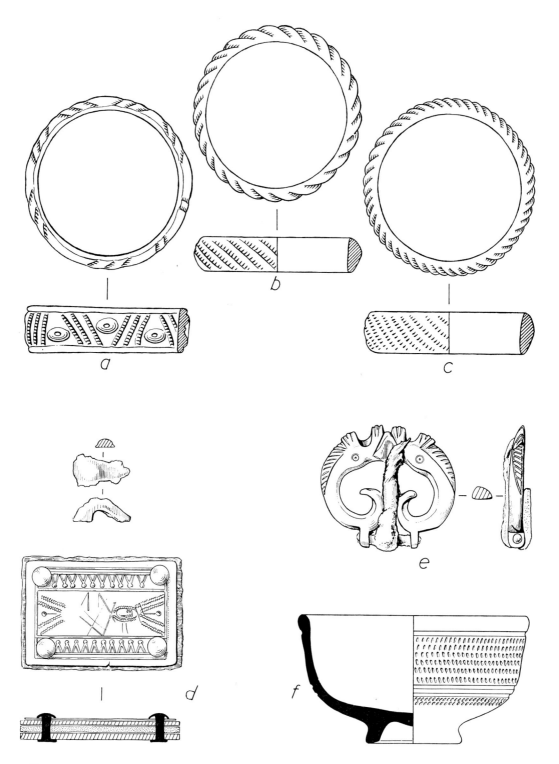

FIG. 9. *a*, Chessell Down, I.o.W.; *b* and *c*, Milton Regis, Kent; *d*, Broadstairs, Kent;
e, Dover, Kent, grave 48; *f*, Chessell Down, I.o.W.
Scale: *a*, *b*, *c*, *f*, 1/2; *d*, *e*, 1/1.

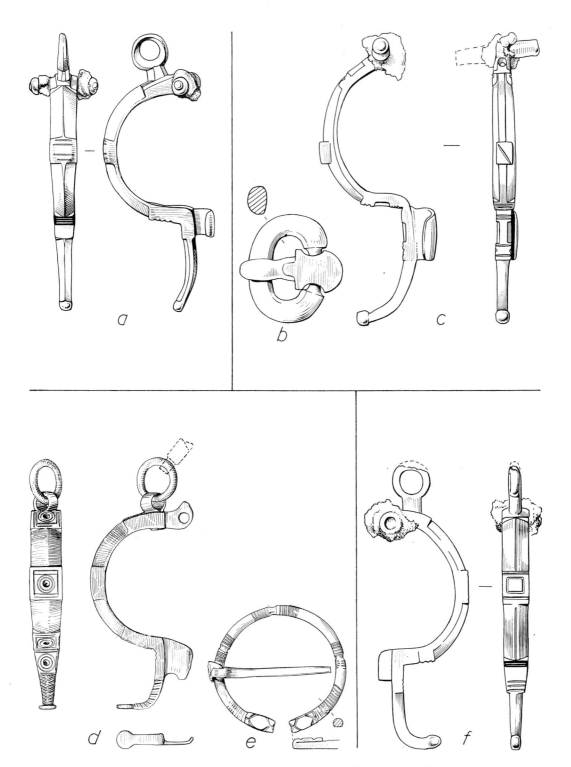

FIG. 10. *a*, West Stow, Suffolk; *b*, *c*, West Stow or Icklingham, Suffolk; *d*, *e*, Glaston, Rutland; *f*, Howletts, Kent, grave 4.
Scale: 1/1.

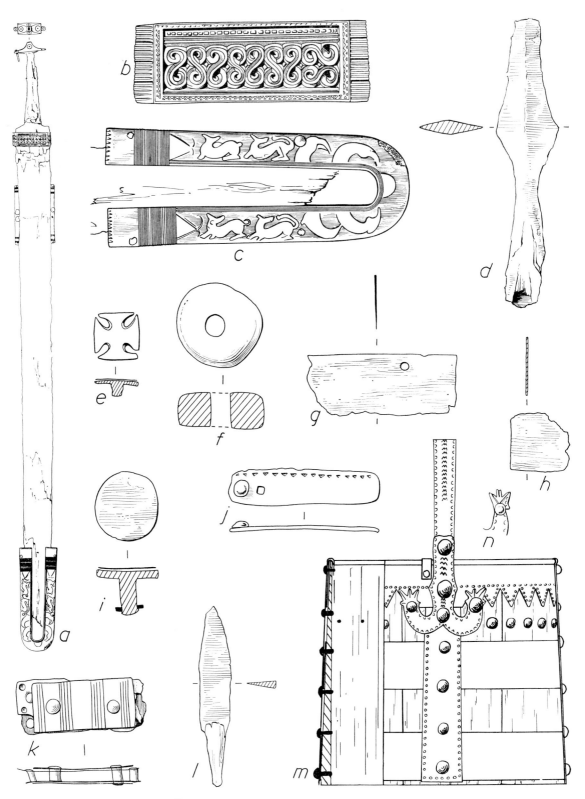

FIG. 11. Brighthampton, Oxon, grave 31.
Scale: all 1/1, except *a*, c. 1/6; *d, l, m, n*, 1/2.

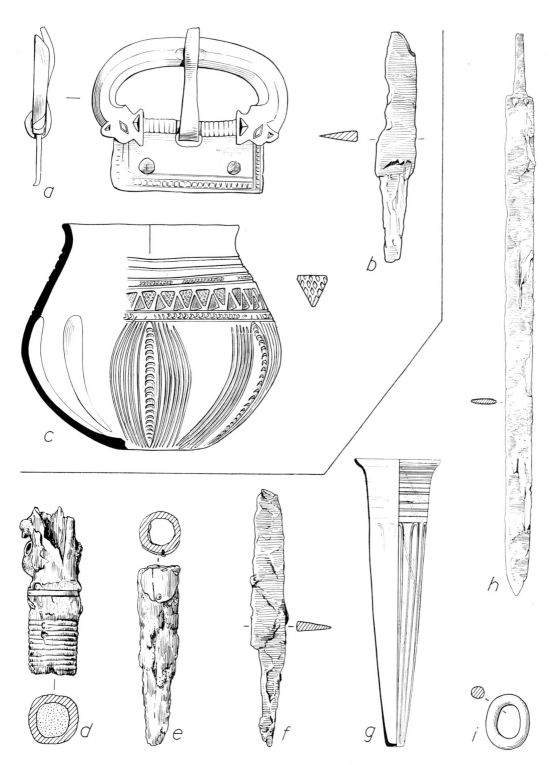

Fɪɢ. 12. *a–c*, Long Wittenham, Berks., grave 57; *d–i*, Dover, Kent, grave 22.
Scale: *a, i*, 1/1; *b–f*, 1/2; *g*, 1/4; *h*, approx. 1/6.

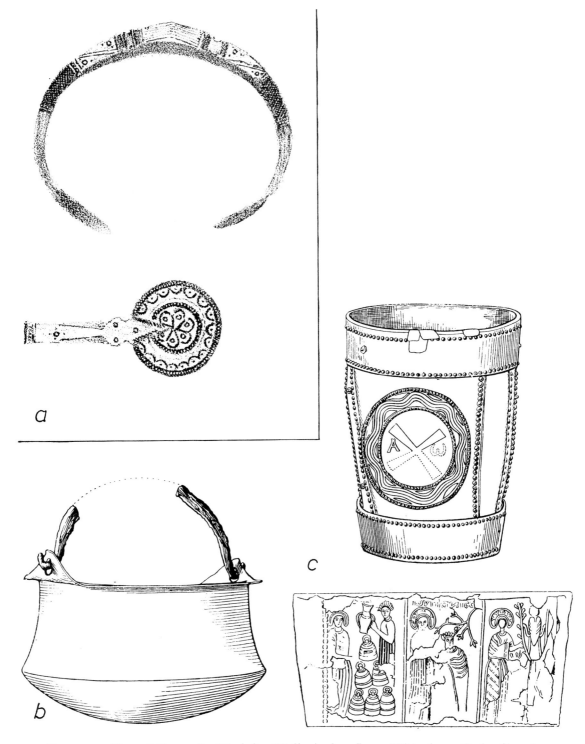

FIG. 13. *a*, Chessell Down, I.o.W. (after Walker); *b, c*, Long Wittenham, Berks. (*b and c by courtesy of the Trustees of the British Museum*).
Scale: *a*, 1/1; *b*, 1/4; c, 1/2.

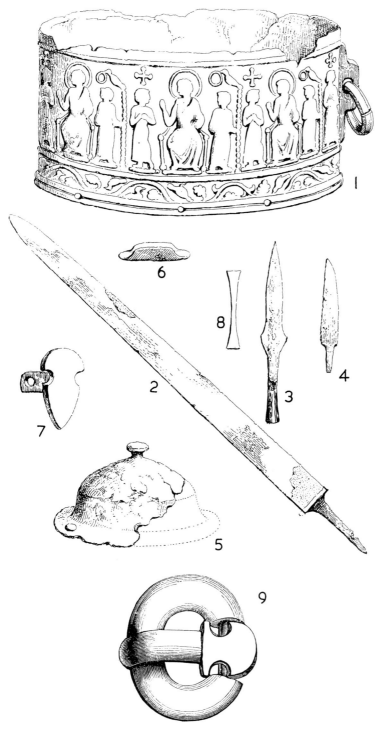

FIG. 14. Strood, Kent, grave group (after C. R. Smith).
Scale: 1, 7, 9, 1/1; 2–6, 8, scales various—see p. 107 for measurements.

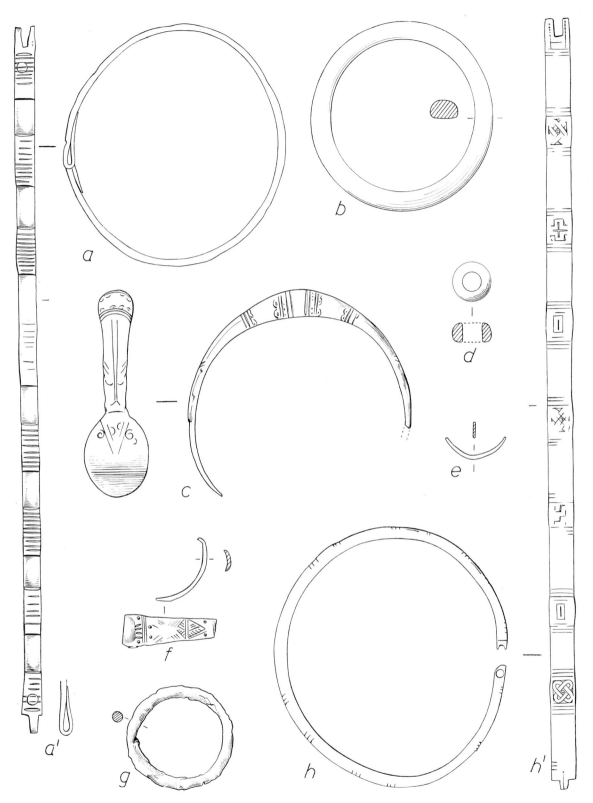

FIG. 15. Chatham Lines, Kent, grave XVII.
Scale: all 1/1 except *b*, *g*, 1/2.

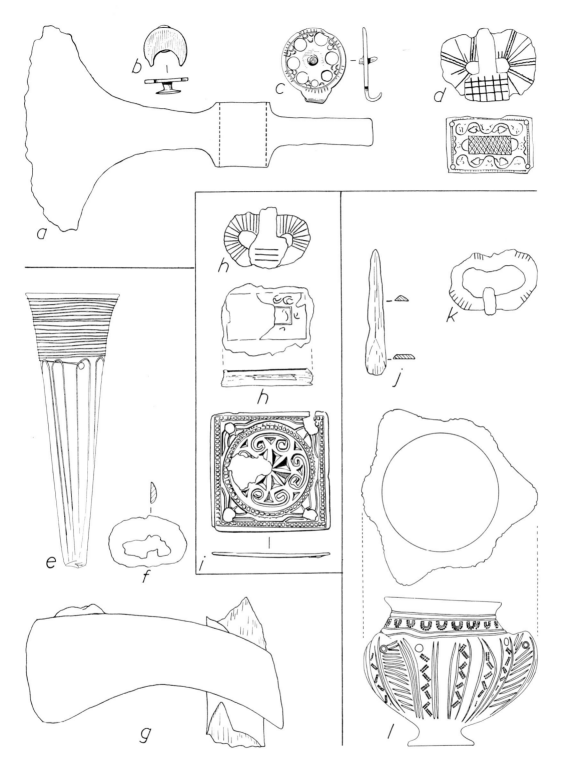

Fig. 16. Alfriston, Sussex. *a–d*, grave 24; *e–g*, grave 39; *h, i*, grave 20; *j–l*, grave 52. Scale: all 1/2, except *b, c, i*, 1/1; *e, l*, 1/4.

Fig. 17. Alfriston, Sussex. *a–d*, grave 26; *e–g*, grave 17; *h–r*, grave A.
Scale: *a*, approx. 1/6; *b*, 1/4; *c, d, f, h, j, k–p*, 1/2; *e, g, i, q, r*, 1/1.

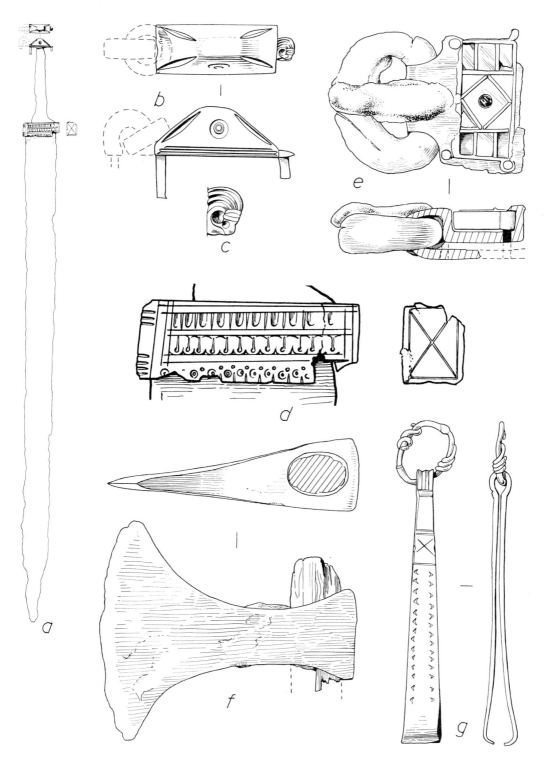

Fig. 18. Petersfinger, Wilts., grave XXI.
Scale: *a*, approx. 1/6; *b, d, e, g*, 1/1; *c*, 2/1; *f*, 1/2.

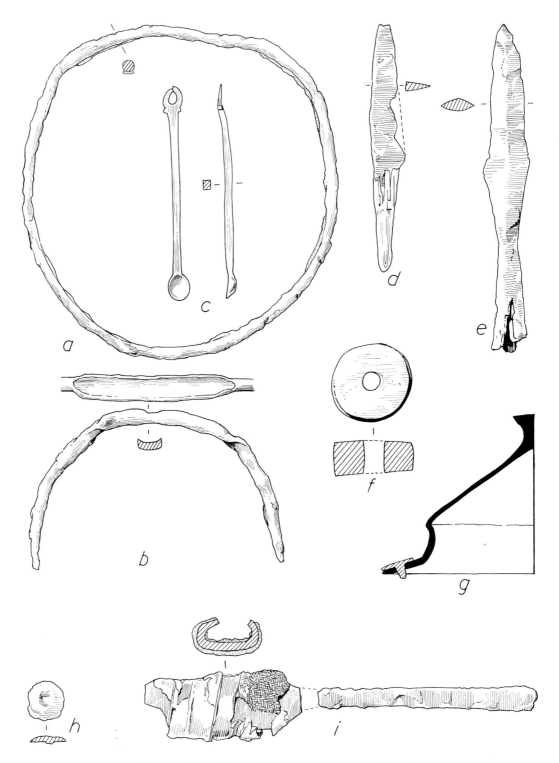

FIG. 19. Petersfinger, Wilts., grave XXI continued.
Scale: all 1/2, except *c, f*, 1/1.

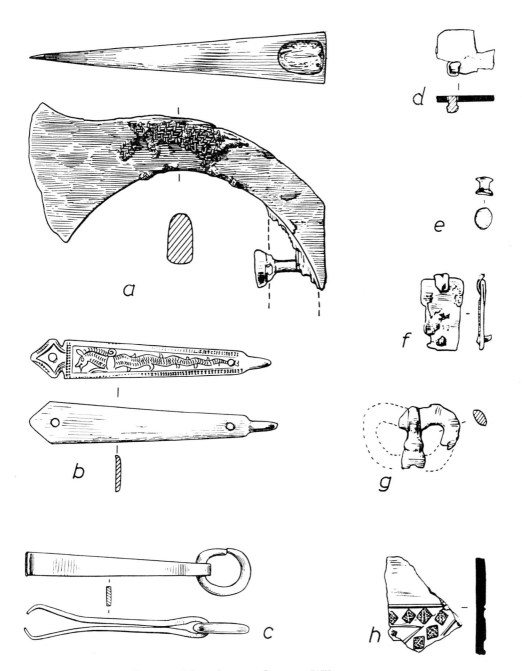

FIG. 20. Winterbourne Gunner, Wilts., grave VI.
Scale: all 1/2 except a, 1/4; b, c, 1/1.

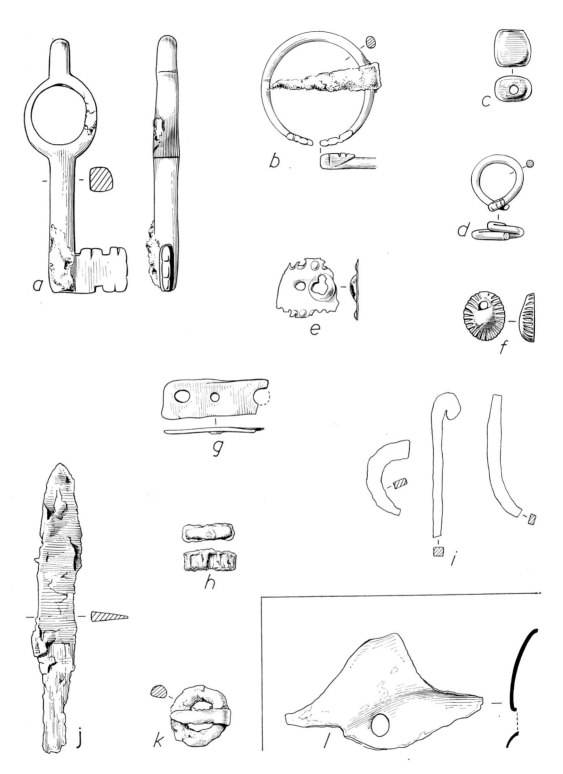

Fig. 21. W. Overton, Wilts. *a–k*, Skeleton IV; *l*, loose find in same barrow.
Scale: *a–g, l,* 1/1; *h–k,* 1/2.

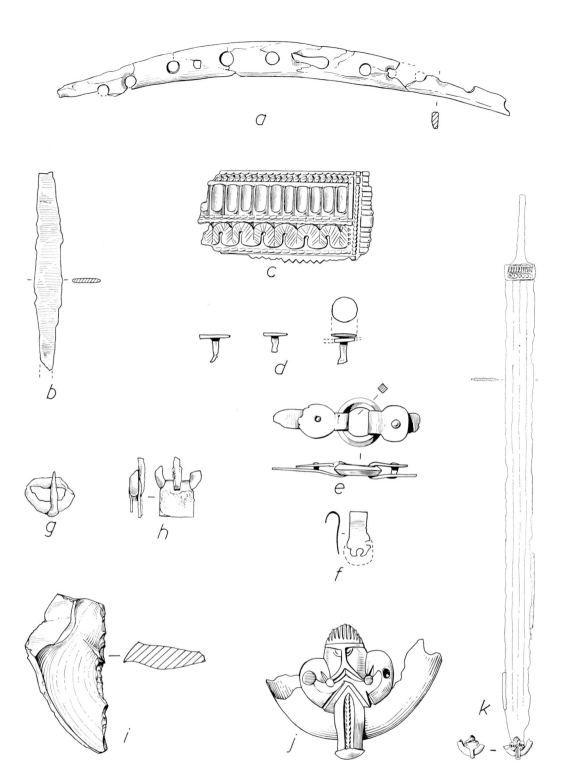

FIG. 22. Abingdon, Berks, grave 42.
Scale: *a, b, g, h*, 1/2; *c–f, i, j*, 1/1; *k*, 1/6.

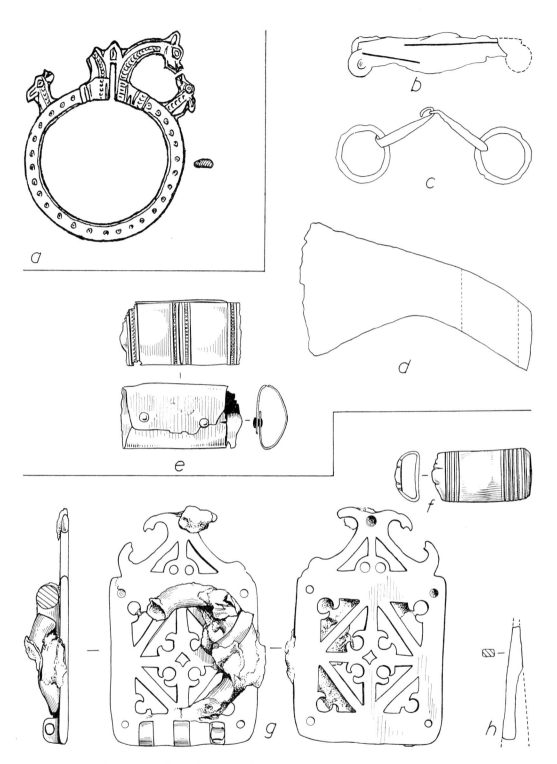

FIG. 23. *a*, Penannular brooch, Laon Museum; *b–e*, Alfriston, Sussex, grave 91; *f–h*, Alfriston, Sussex, grave 103.
Scale: all 1/1, except *b*, *h*, 1/2; *c*, *d*, 1/4.

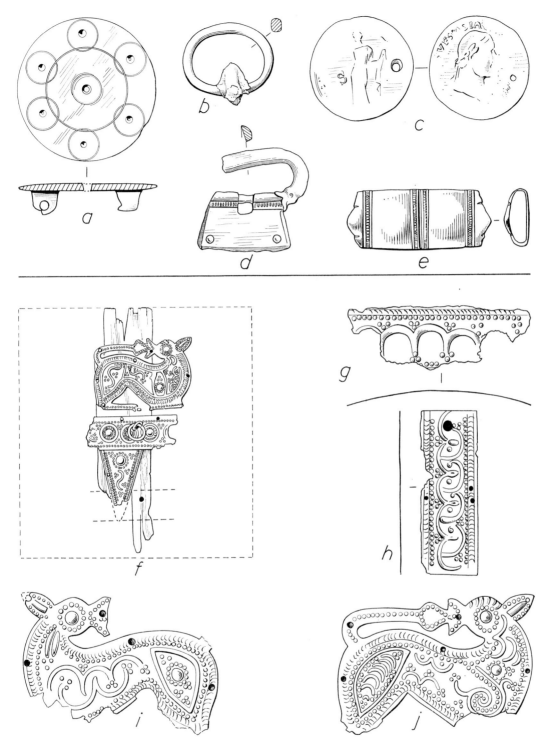

FIG. 24. *a–e*, Alfriston, Sussex, grave 14; *f–j*, Bidford-on-Avon, Warwicks.
Scale: all 1/1 except *f*, 1/2.

Fig. 25. Engraved bronze plate and metal-inlaid pedestal (after Rigollot 1850, pl. xii).

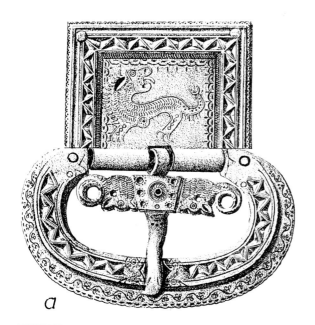

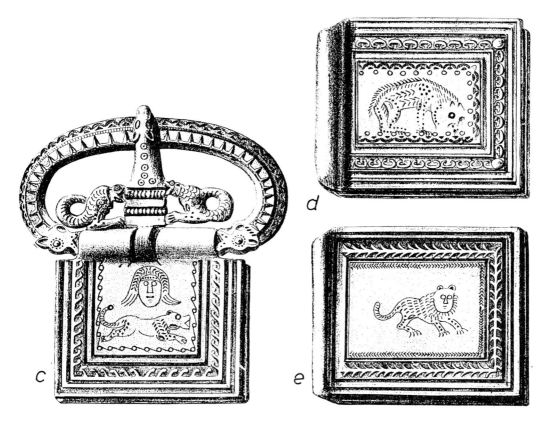

FIG. 26. *a*, *b*, Vermand (Aisne); *c–e*, Vermand (Aisne), grave 321.
Scale: 1/1.

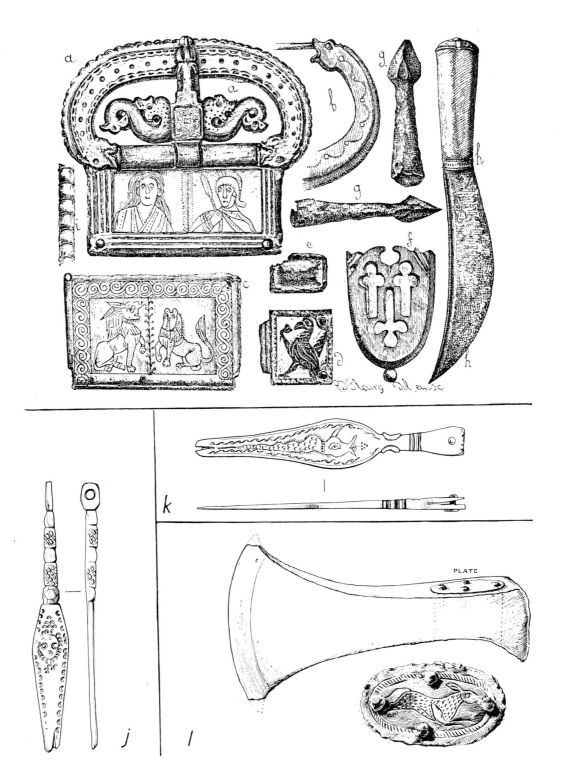

Fig. 27. *a–i*, Landifay, Guise (after Fleury 1877–82); *j*, Wor Barrow, Dorset; *k*, Richborough, Kent; *l*, Howletts, Kent (after *Ant. Journ.* LV, 276).
Scale: all 1/1 except *h*, ?1/2; *l*, ?1/2 and 1/1.

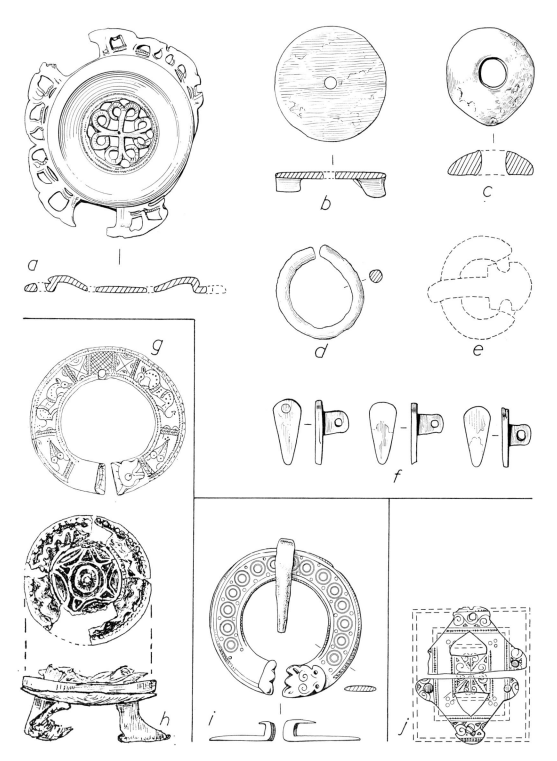

FIG. 28. Quoit Brooch Style. *a–f*, Bowcombe Down, I.o.W., grave 13; *g–h*, Lyminge, Kent, grave 10; *i*, Riseley, Horton Kirby, Kent, grave 22; *j*, Alfriston, Sussex, graves A and 17. Scale: all 1/1, except *d*, 1/2.

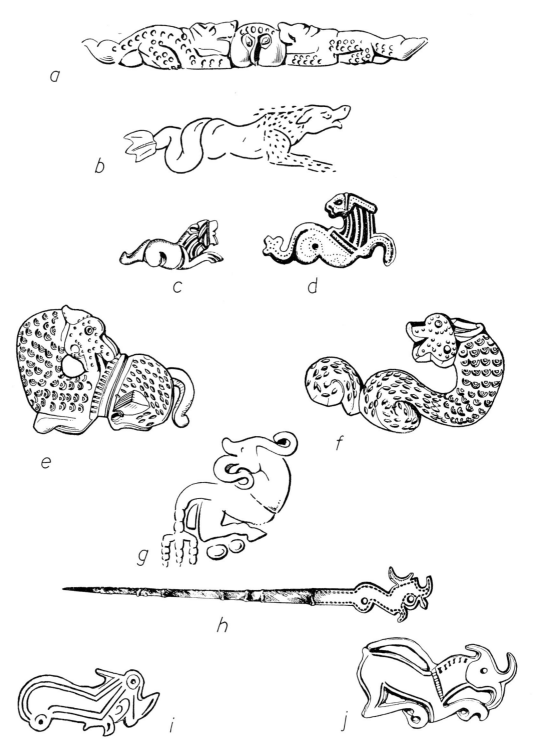

FIG. 29. Continental animals. *a*, Rhenen, Holland, grave 846; *b–d*, development of classical sea-lion (after Werner); *e–f*, Vermand (Aisne); *g*, E. Shefford, Berks., grave 24; *h*, Faversham, Kent (after B.M. Guide); *i*, Alveston, Warwicks., grave 53; *j*, Northfleet, Kent. Scale: *b, d, i, g,* 1/1; *c,* 3/4; *h,* 1/2; *e, f, g,* about 5/2.

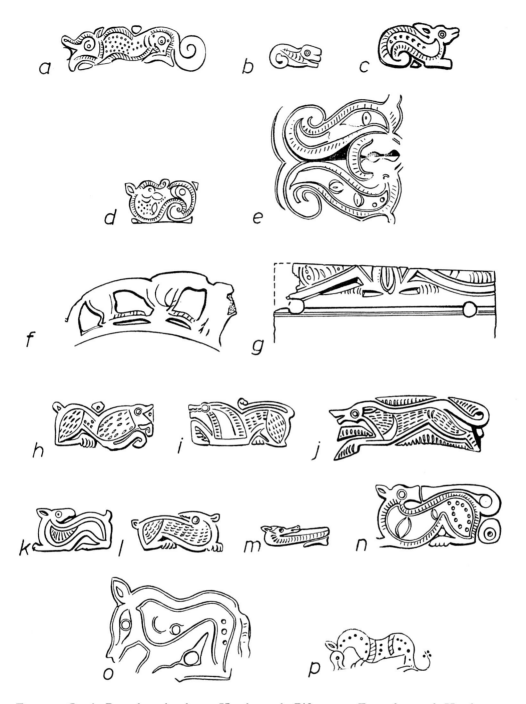

FIG. 30. Quoit Brooch animals. *a*, Howletts; *b*, Bifrons; *c*, Faversham; *d*, Howletts; *e*, Croydon; *f*, Bowcombe; *g*, Howletts; *h*, Bifrons; *i*, Sarre; *j*, Howletts; *k*, Bishopstone; *l*, Sarre; *m*, Howletts; *n*, Alfriston; *o*, Croydon; *p*, Lyminge.
Scale: all 2/1, except *i*, *j*, *l*, *m*, which are slightly larger.

Plates

PLATE I. Vermand (Aisne). Tomb of military leader. *a*, spear-shaft appliqué; *b*, buckle; *c*, *d*, spear shaft ornaments; *e*, shield boss; *f*, shield grip and studs. (Photo: *The Metropolitan Museum of Art. Gift of J. Pierpont Morgan*, 1917.)
Scale: *a–d*, 1/1; *e, f*, 1/3.

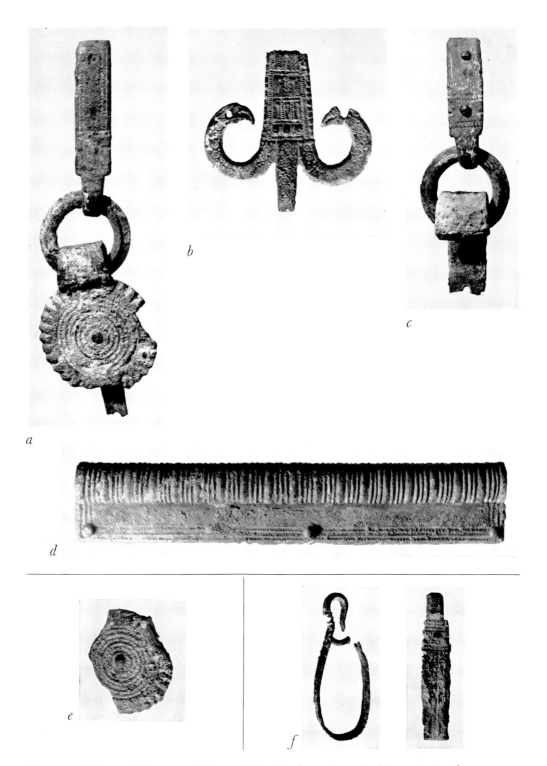

PLATE 2. Belleray, Meuse. *a–d*, bronze belt attachments, probably contents of one grave; *e*, bronze rosette, possible belonging to *c*; *f*, bronze belt attachment, probably part of grave group illustrated in Plate 3.
Scale: 1/1.

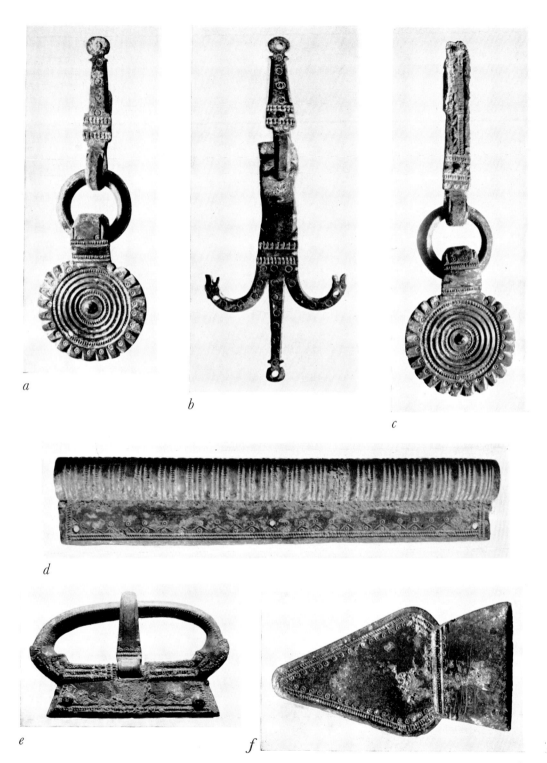

a

b

c

d

e

f

PLATE 3. Belleray, Meuse. Bronze belt attachments, probably contents of one grave with Plate 2, *f*.
Scale: 1/1.

PLATE 4. *a*, *b*, Krefeld-Gellep, grave 43, scabbard mounts (Photo: *Landschaftsmuseum des Niederrheins*); *c*, bronze chip-carved strap slide, Rhenen, Holland, grave 846 (Photo: *Oudheidkundig Bodemonderzoek in Nederland, Amersfoort*); *d*, plaster cast of a bronze ring made from the impression in sealing wax of Childeric's finger ring (Photo: *Ashmolean Museum*). Scale: *a*, *b*, 1/1; *c*, 3/4; *d*, 3/1.

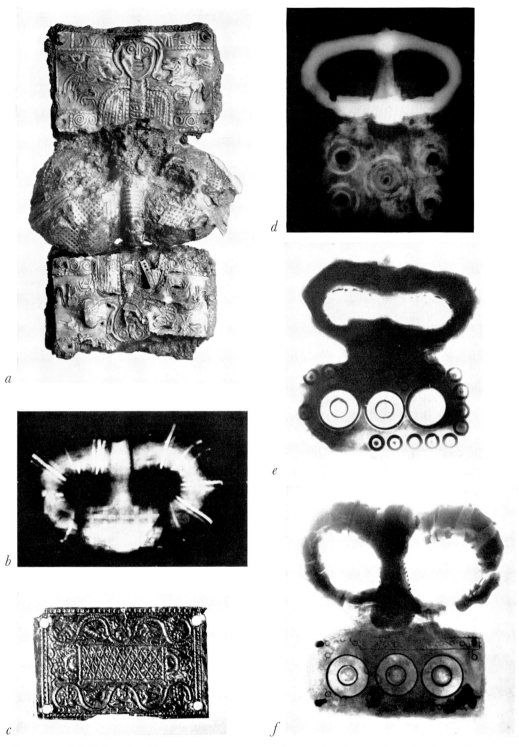

PLATE 5. Inlaid iron buckles. *a*, Bifrons, Kent (Photo: *Maidstone Museum*); *b, c*, Alfriston, Sussex, grave 24; *d*, unknown provenance, Canterbury Museum; *e*, Kempston, Beds.; *f*, Howletts, Kent, grave 28.
b, d, e, f are radiographs. Scale: 1/1.

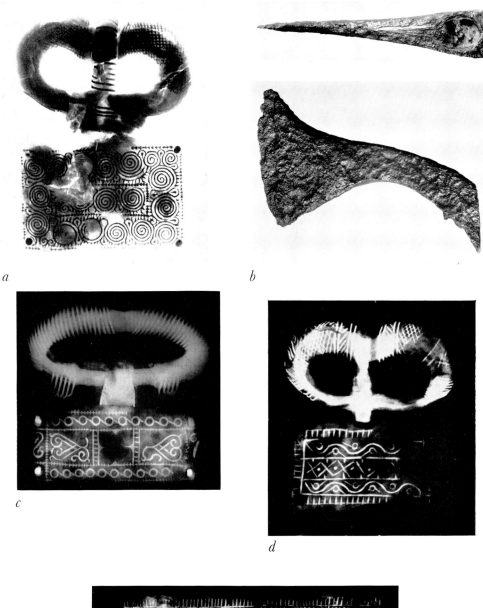

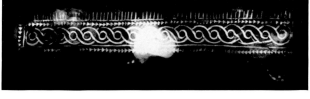

PLATE 6. Inlaid iron objects. *a*, buckle, Howletts, Kent, grave 25; *b*, francisca, Howletts, Kent (Photo: *by courtesy of the Trustees of the British Museum*); *c*, buckle, Droxford, Hants.; *d*, buckle, Alfriston, Sussex, grave 10; *e*, purse mount, Alfriston, Sussex, ? grave B. *a, c–e* are radiographs. Scale: 1/1 except *b*, 1/3.

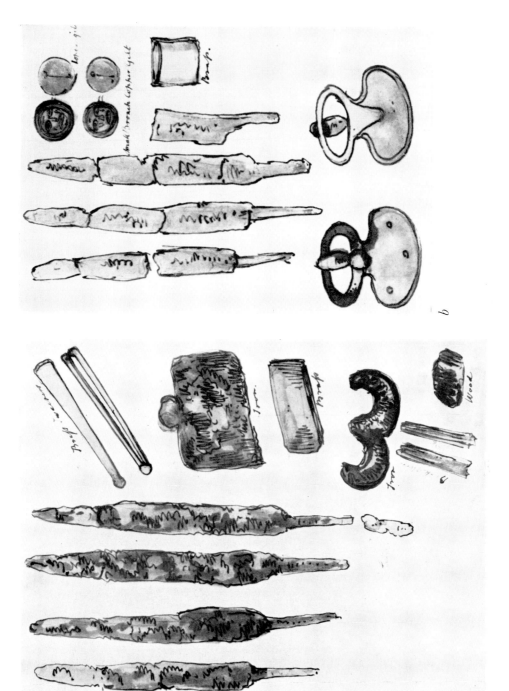

PLATE 7. Chessell Down, I.o.W. *a*, grave 12; *b*, grave 13 (after Dennett MS1).
(Photo: *Carisbrooke Castle Museum, I.o.W.*)
Scale: 2/3.

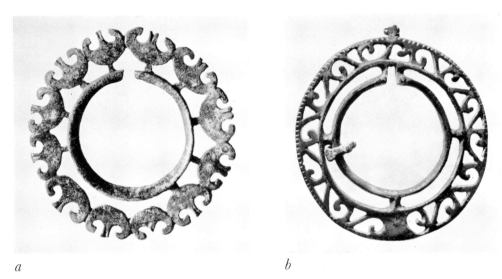

a   *b*

c

PLATE 8. *a*, Late Roman annular brooch, from Enns, Austria; *b*, Late Roman annular brooch, from Linz, Austria (Photos: *Landesmuseum, Linz/Donau, Austria.*); *c*, Bronze plate with hunting scene (Photo: *Louvre, Paris*).
Scale: 3/4.

a

b

c

PLATE 9. *a*, Herbergen, Oldenburg, bronze buckle and plate; *b*, Colombier-sur-Seulles, France, bronze buckle; *c*, Sédan, France, bronze buckle and plate. (Photos: *a*, *Oldenburg Landesmuseum für Kunst- u. Kulturgeschichte*; *b*, *c*, *Musée des Antiquités Nationales, St Germain-en-Laye*.)

Scale: *a*, 3/4; *b*, *c*, 1/1.

a

b

c

PLATE 10. *a*, Faversham, Kent, disc brooch (No 9); *b*, Faversham, Kent, disc brooch, back; *c*, Howletts, Kent, fragmentary quoit brooch (No 11).
Scale: *a*, 2/1; *b*, 1/1; *c*, 3/2.

a

b

PLATE 11. *a*, Bifrons, Kent, strap end (No 8); *b*, Howletts, Kent, quoit brooch (No 10). Scale: 2/1.

a

b

c

PLATE 12. *a*, Bifrons, Kent, silver pendants (No 6) (Photo: *Maidstone Museum*); *b*, Bishopstone, Bucks, bronze plate (No 7); *c*, Sarre, Kent, quoit brooch (No 12).
Scale: 3/2.

PLATE 13. *a*, Croydon, Surrey, strap distributor (No 5); *b*, Howletts, Kent, bronze plate (No 3); *c*, High Down, Sussex, belt slide (No 13).
Scale: *a*, 1/1; *b*, *c*, 2/1.

a

b

c   *d*

PLATE 14. *a*, Chessell Down, I.o.W., strap end (No 14); *b*, Croydon, Surrey, strap end (No 15); *c*, Alfriston, Sussex, buckle and counter plate (No 4); *d*, High Down, Sussex, buckle and plate (No 18).

Scale: *a*, 2/1; *b*, 1/1; *c*, *d*, 3/2.

a

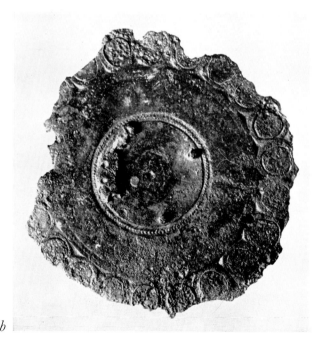

b

PLATE 15. *a*, Alfriston, Sussex, penannular brooch (No 16);
b, Higham, Kent, disc brooch (No 19).
Scale: *a*, 2/1; *b*, 3/2.

a

b

c

PLATE 16. *a*, Howletts, Kent, square brooch (No 20); *b*, High Down, Sussex, square quoit brooch (No 21); *c*, High Down, Sussex, buckle (p. 63).
Scale: *a*, 2/1; *b*, *c*, 3/2.

a

b

c

PLATE 17. *a*, Waben, Pas de Calais, repoussé silver disc; *b*, E. Shefford, Berks, grave 24, gilt bronze applied brooch (Photo: *Newbury Museum*); *c*, Sigy, N. France, gilt bronze applied brooch.
Scale: *a, b,* 3/2; *c,* 2/1.

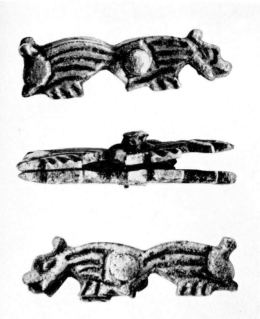

PLATE 18. *a*, Bronze belt mount, unknown provenance (Photo: *Oldenburg Landesmuseum für Kunst- u. Kulturgeschichte*); *b*, Double bronze mount from the Meuse at Heerenwaarde, Holland (Photo: *Museum van Oudheiden, Leiden*); *c*, bronze mount, unknown provenance, Ashmolean Museum; *d*, mount from Staxton, Yorks; *e*, bronze strip from Parfondeval, France.

Scale: *a*, c. 3/2; *b*, 3/1; *c*, 2/1; *d*, 3/2; *e*, 1/1.